DESIGNING AND MANAGING YOUR
RESEARCH PROJECT

Education at SAGE

SAGE is a leading international publisher of journals, books, and electronic media for academic, educational, and professional markets.

Our education publishing includes:

- accessible and comprehensive texts for aspiring education professionals and practitioners looking to further their careers through continuing professional development

- inspirational advice and guidance for the classroom

- authoritative state of the art reference from the leading authors in the field

Find out more at: **www.sagepub.co.uk/education**

DESIGNING AND MANAGING YOUR
RESEARCH PROJECT

CORE SKILLS FOR SOCIAL AND HEALTH RESEARCH

DAVID R. THOMAS AND IAN D. HODGES

Los Angeles | London | New Delhi
Singapore | Washington DC

SAGE Publications Ltd
1 Oliver's Yard
55 City Road
London EC1Y 1SP

SAGE Publications Inc.
2455 Teller Road
Thousand Oaks, California 91320

SAGE Publications India Pvt Ltd
B 1/I 1 Mohan Cooperative Industrial Area
Mathura Road
New Delhi 110 044

SAGE Publications Asia-Pacific Pte Ltd
33 Pekin Street #02-01
Far East Square
Singapore 048763

Library of Congress Control Number: 2009943263

British Library Cataloguing in Publication data

A catalogue record for this book is available from
the British Library

ISBN 978-1-84860-192-5
ISBN 978-1-84860-193-2 (pbk)

Typeset by C&M Digitals (P) Ltd, Chennai, India
Printed and bound in Great Britain by TJ International, Padstow, Cornwall
Printed on paper from sustainable resources

Mixed Sources
Product group from well-managed
forests and other controlled sources
www.fsc.org Cert no. SGS-COC-2482
© 1996 Forest Stewardship Council
FSC

Contents

List of figures and tables

Figures

Tables

1 Designing and Managing Research Projects: An Overview

Topics covered in this chapter

- Origins of the book
- Who the book is aimed at
- Structure of the book
- Overview of chapters
- Source material and literature

For many people, setting out to do a research project for the first time can feel like a voyage into unknown seas. Exciting, perhaps, but also a little bit scary. What dangers might lie lurking just over the horizon? What fate could befall the unwary or ill-prepared? Often this sense of trepidation is compounded by a lack of clear navigational aids for the journey ahead. By this we mean basic, easy-to-follow advice indicating how to design and initiate a new research project, and how to manage the various phases of a research project once it gets going.

This book aims to provide a straight-forward, practical introduction to some of the more crucial knowledge and skills people are likely to need when setting out to do a research project in the social and health sciences. It covers issues such as how to choose a research design for a project, how to write a research proposal, how to apply for research funding and how to think about a project's ethical dimensions. It also looks carefully at how to write up and disseminate research reports, paying particular attention to how to organise and present technical reports, student theses or dissertations, and manuscripts for journal articles. The book also offers a range of tips and suggestions on other important topics such as teamwork and supervision in research, the place of different types of computer software in research and the work options available for people interested in pursuing a career (or at least gainful employment) as a researcher.

A key goal of the book is to try to minimise the amount of trial and error that researchers have to use when learning how to design and do research projects. By considering the ideas and suggestions outlined here, researchers should be able to plan their projects more thoroughly and thoughtfully. This should help reduce the amount of precious time and energy expended on unnecessary tasks or solving unexpected problems, experiences that can be discouraging for the first-time researcher and often lead to projects being significantly disrupted or delayed, or even totally abandoned.

Origins of the book

The idea for this book was conceived over a decade ago when the first author, David Thomas, was operating a research methods advisory service and teaching graduate courses on social and health research at the University of Auckland. Through this work, David encountered many students and staff in the early stages of developing their research skills and pursuing careers as professional researchers. In talking with these people, it became clear that there were certain aspects of the process of designing, conducting and writing up research projects for which people tended to require the most advice or support – aspects that they were most likely to come unstuck on or find challenging. In response, David began developing a variety of course handouts and short webpage articles providing advice on these and other key aspects of the work associated with designing and doing research projects. These handouts and articles included practical tips and examples drawn from David's own research experiences and reading. Later, the second author, Ian Hodges, also began contributing articles on selected topics based on his experiences of working as a researcher in government agencies and as a self-employed contractor.

After feedback from students and staff suggested the various handouts and articles had generally proved helpful, we decided there might be value in using the material as the starting point for developing a more comprehensive introductory workbook or guide for researchers. The structure and content of the current book has evolved out of this initial basic framework, with most of the original text now having been considerably expanded, updated and revised in the course of preparing the book for publication. This has included adding entirely new material on topics such as how to design a research project, getting ethics approval for research, working with colleagues and supervisors, and strategies for disseminating project findings.

Who is the book aimed at?

The book is aimed mainly at new and emerging researchers in the social and health sciences; these may be people who are just beginning their first significant research project, or making their first attempt to secure sizable funding for a research project, or are in the midst of writing up their first major project report. Many of these up-and-coming researchers will be based in universities or other higher learning institutions. Others will be employed in non-university research settings such as government departments or private sector businesses, or pursuing work as independent research contractors or consultants.

In our experience, most of these researchers are likely still to be coming to grips with many of the core tasks normally associated with designing and carrying out a fairly substantial research project. This includes tasks such as selecting appropriate research designs and research methodologies, preparing research proposals, submitting ethics applications, applying to external agencies for funding, managing project staff and resources, writing detailed research reports, and disseminating research findings to different audiences. This book is intended to help accelerate people's understanding and awareness of these and other key areas of the research process. In particular, the book is intended to serve as an accompaniment to more experiential or 'hands on' ways of learning how to design and carry out a research project, such as by working directly alongside a team of more experienced researchers or in collaboration with an academic supervisor.

As readers will appreciate, the boundaries of social and health research are wide, covering such diverse disciplines as social anthropology, sociology, social geography, economics and community psychology, as well as the many health science disciplines such as medicine, nursing, physiotherapy, midwifery, epidemiology and public health. However, what generally unites all these different fields is a broad concern with better understanding the enormous array of conditions and factors influencing human behaviour, social interaction and well-being. Designing and undertaking research projects is central to this work, with the ultimate goal being to try to reveal new insights on these many different conditions and factors through the application of systematic, focused observation and inquiry.

Although new or emerging researchers in these various social and health research disciplines are often interested in very different research questions or problems, there are, in our experience, certain common principles related to designing and carrying out research projects that have general applicability across virtually all the disciplines. It is these common principles that we aim to focus on here, laying out some basic introductory guidelines and advice for up-and-coming researchers to think about and perhaps use as a foundation for their own work in the years ahead.

To make the book as accessible as possible, we have tried to write each chapter in fairly simple language, using only a minimum of jargon or specialist technical terms. In addition, for many of the core topics covered, such as designing a new research project, doing a literature review or organising and writing a research report, much of the information given is pitched at the level of the inexperienced beginner. Very little previous knowledge is assumed and quite a lot of text is devoted in places to spelling out basic principles and giving detailed examples of what we mean. We consider this approach to be appropriate in an introductory guidebook such as this, since in our experience new and emerging researchers are often looking for considerable detail and structure in the advice they get from others. In time they will almost certainly develop their own distinctive approaches for handling different research tasks, but in the beginning they tend to want very specific and unambiguous advice on how to do things.

Of course, we would like to think the book will have some value for more experienced researchers, too, especially researchers looking to refresh their knowledge or reflect on aspects of the research process in which they are particularly interested. Although much of the information presented in the book is quite pared down and simplified, and therefore may not always appeal to the more seasoned investigator, nonetheless many of the points we make could help some experienced researchers to see aspects of their current practice in a new light.

Structure of the book

Perceptive readers studying the contents list will have noticed that the chapters in the book are laid out in a sequence that roughly follows the steps involved in carrying out a research project. Planning and doing a research project often involves a fairly standard set of steps or stages (although not always). These include designing the project, preparing a research proposal, obtaining resources for carrying out the research, conducting and managing the project, writing a research report and communicating research findings.

Table 1.1 outlines in more detail the steps or stages that we believe most experienced social and health researchers tend to follow when designing and running research projects. The table also lists the main activities usually done in each stage. The right-hand column of Table 1.1 indicates which chapters in the book cover skills and knowledge relevant to each research step or stage. For example, information on how to prepare and write a research proposal is in Chapter 4 and information on how to get funding for research projects is in Chapters 5 and 14.

TABLE 1.1   STAGES IN PLANNING AND CONDUCTING A RESEARCH PROJECT

Research stage	Accompanying activities	Chapters in this book
Designing a new research project	Selecting a research topic	Chapters 2, 3
	Choosing research objectives or questions	Chapters 2, 3
	Identifying the rationale for the project	Chapter 2
	Choosing a research methodology	Chapters 2, 3
	Searching existing literature for ideas	Chapter 7
	Thinking about resources (money, people)	Chapters 5, 10
	Discussing ideas with colleagues and/or supervisors	Chapter 10
Preparing a written research proposal	Writing down and finalising details of the project's research design	Chapters 4, 12
	Writing down research objectives and questions	Chapter 3
	Incorporating ideas from previous research	Chapter 7
	Doing a literature review	Chapter 7
Applying for project funding	Identifying possible funding sources	Chapter 5
	Writing and submitting funding applications	Chapter 5
Applying for ethics approval	Thinking about ethical responsibilities	Chapter 6
	Preparing and submitting an application for ethics approval	Chapter 6
Project start (beginning of data collection)	Organising resources and people	Chapters 8, 10
	Managing project tasks, timetables and budgets	Chapter 8
	Working with colleagues and/or supervisors	Chapter 10
Data analysis	Arranging software needed for data analyses	Chapter 9
	Organising data entry and data cleaning	Chapter 9
	Conducting data analysis	
Communicating project findings	Identifying strategies for communicating findings	Chapter 11
	Planning and writing an end-of-project report	Chapters 12, 13
	Preparing manuscripts for journal publication	Chapters 12, 13
	Preparing a conference presentation	Chapter 9
Assessing options for further research	Exploring options for a career in research and possible sources of funding	Chapter 14
		Chapter 5

If you are a largely a newcomer to research and have never designed or undertaken a research project before, it is probably wise to start the book at the beginning and work through each of the chapters systematically. This should provide a fairly good general introduction to the main aspects of doing a research project. However, each of the chapters in the book can also be read as separate, stand-alone pieces. This might be especially handy for people already in the midst of doing a research project who are looking for specific tips on how to do certain things, such as how to structure a research proposal or lay out a technical report.

Overview of chapters

This section provides more detail on the content of each the chapters in the book.

The next two chapters (Chapters 2 and 3) provide some guidance on how to identify and develop new ideas for research. Chapter 2 provides a framework for thinking about how to design a new research project, highlighting some of the key issues to consider. This includes looking at some of the different kinds of research questions, data collection procedures and data analysis techniques commonly used in social and health research. The chapter also introduces some basic research concepts and terms that will be used throughout the book.

Chapter 3 expands on some of the points touched on in Chapter 2, looking in particular at how to logically and succinctly define and write down a research project's aims and objectives. In our experience, newcomers to research often do not pay sufficient attention to ensuring their research aims and objectives are well thought out and clearly expressed. This chapter offers suggestions on how to effectively conceptualise and frame statements describing a project's research aims, objectives, questions and/or hypotheses.

The next four chapters, Chapters 4 to 7, focus on key tasks often vital to getting a new research project up and running. These include preparing a project proposal, submitting a funding application, preparing for an ethics review, and developing and writing a literature review.

A research proposal indicates the aims of a research project, why the project is important and how the project will be organised. Writing a research proposal is an opportunity for researchers to carefully plan a research project before it starts. Draft or completed research proposals can be given to other people for feedback or to raise interest in a project amongst colleagues, supervisors or potential project sponsors. Chapter 4 provides advice on how to organise and write a general research proposal. This type of general proposal could be written as part of planning for a PhD or Masters thesis, or for a similar research-based student project (including those submitted for ethical review). An example of a research proposal is shown in Appendix 1.

Some research projects will only be viable if adequate financial support is obtained from funding organisations. Chapter 5 provides advice on how to identify possible research project funding sources and strategies. It indicates the type of organisations that fund health and social research, how to select suitable funding sources and how to prepare and submit written applications for project funding. Strategies for getting funding for researcher-initiated projects are covered, as well as strategies for identifying and bidding for client-initiated or commercial research project contracts.

All research should be conducted ethically and with sensitivity to the needs of research participants. Chapter 6 sets out the key ethical principles and standards that health and social researchers should know about. It describes examples of the types of ethical requirements stipulated by organisations overseeing the conduct of research. The chapter also provides advice on how to prepare research proposals for scrutiny by ethics committees.

Preparing a literature review is often one of the first things a researcher will do in the early stages of a project. Literature reviews can be useful for detailing the findings of previous studies, identifying gaps in current knowledge and deciding which research methods are the best to use in new projects. Chapter 7 provides advice on how to research and write a literature review. It indicates how to find and critically assess relevant literature. It also outlines a model format for structuring the information presented in a literature review.

The next three chapters, Chapters 8, 9 and 10, are concerned with aspects of the day-to-day running of research projects. Chapter 8 outlines key skills and strategies for managing the ongoing work of a research project. This includes planning the timing and sequencing of tasks, monitoring the use of project resources, and managing the work of project team members. We highlight problems that can arise in these areas, as well as possible ways to prevent or resolve them.

Nowadays almost all researchers use personal computers for writing project-related documents, and storing and analysing project data. Chapter 9 describes the range of computer software programs likely to be required during a research project and the different functions they perform. It also provides tips on how and when to use these programs.

Chapter 10 focuses on the people-side of research. It offers suggestions on how researchers can work more effectively in team-based research situations or, in the case of student researchers, with the people supervising their thesis or dissertation. When two or more people are working closely together on a project, there is always the potential for relationships to get a bit frayed. The tips provided here should hopefully help to reduce the chances of this happening.

Chapters 11, 12 and 13 are concerned with writing and communicating research information. Chapter 11 looks at the different methods of disseminating research findings, from progress reports and conference presentations through to full-scale peer-reviewed journal articles. It indicates which communication methods are likely to be the most suitable for specific audiences and how to maximise their effectiveness. It also emphasises the importance of developing a well-thought-out strategy or plan for communicating a project's research findings.

Chapter 12 offers general tips on how to handle the potentially challenging process of writing research-related documents such as proposals and project reports. It describes important elements of effective research-related writing and suggests a range of strategies that could be used to help make the task of writing research-related documents less fretful and more enjoyable.

Chapter 13 provides specific guidelines and advice on how to organise, write and present three common types of research report used in social and health research:

- technical reports
- manuscripts for journal articles
- theses and dissertations.

Technical reports describe a research project and its findings in detail. Usually they are intended for readers interested in carefully scrutinising all aspects of a research project's design and execution, as well as its findings. Manuscripts for journal articles are usually submitted for publication in an academic or scientific journal. Normally they are shorter than technical reports and are generally read by a larger and more diverse audience. Theses or dissertations are typically written by students as part of qualifying for higher, postgraduate degrees. Usually they include a comprehensive review of previous studies and other literature, as well as reporting in detail on the student's own original research project.

The final chapter, Chapter 14, is concerned with career opportunities for working as a researcher either in a university, another kind of specialised research environment (e.g. a government or private sector research agency), or as a self-employed independent or freelance researcher. Some guiding principles and advice are outlined for those who may be thinking about pursuing a career as a researcher in these different settings.

Source material and literature

While the book aims to be broadly relevant to all research in social science and health, examples given in the text are mainly drawn from research on human services. In our experience, many researchers in social science and health are working on topics related to human services. Human services are services that provide assistance or support for individuals, groups or communities with particular needs. These range from large-scale services provided by government agencies (e.g., education, health, social welfare, police and justice) through to medium-scale services often provided by relatively large non-governmental organisations (e.g., services to reduce alcohol and drug abuse); to small-scale services provided by local organisations such as counselling services.

Given that readers are likely to come from a range of countries, we have tried to be eclectic in the choice of literature cited in the text. Many sources come from North America – probably the largest producer of social science and health research literature – but we also include material from the United Kingdom and Europe, and from our own part of the world, Australia and New Zealand.

A small number of illustrative case studies are also included in some chapters to highlight particular dimensions of being a researcher or doing research. Most of these case studies are fictional in that they do not refer to real people or events, although they have been inspired by our own experience of being researchers and our dealings with students and colleagues over the years. The case studies are mainly intended to provide food for thought and encourage readers to think a little bit more deeply about certain topics or issues.

To assist readers using the book for the active learning of research skills, we have included a number of exercises at the end of each chapter. These can be used for self-assessment, or simply as a way to try out some of the ideas covered in the chapter. Each chapter also includes a final section listing references and further reading relating to the chapter topic. In some cases we have added Internet webpage addresses where these may be helpful.

Readers who wish to comment on any aspect of the book, including making suggestions for revisions or additional topics to include in the book, are welcome to contact the authors via their email address.

2 Designing a New Research Project: Issues to Think About

Topics covered in this chapter

- Designing a new research project
  - Thinking about your research topic
  - Thinking about your research objectives or questions
  - Thinking about the limits of research and research knowledge
  - Thinking about the rationale for your research project
  - Thinking about your research methodology
  - Thinking about your data collection
  - Thinking about your data analysis
- Constraints on your design choices
- Types of research designs used in social and health research
  - Survey research
  - Field research
  - Experimental research
  - Content analysis
  - Existing data research
  - Historical research
  - Evaluation research

A core principle of this book is that good planning is central to doing successful research. In our experience, the more effort put into visualising the dimensions of a research project before it starts, the more likely it is that the project will run smoothly and withstand critical scrutiny by others. For this reason, the thinking that goes on during the initial design of a research project, when the project is first being developed, is enormously important.

In this chapter we present an introductory guide to the process of designing a new research project, highlighting some of the main issues and options we believe it is important to think about. Designing a new research project is all about making well-informed and well-judged choices. A feature of social and health research is its huge diversity of possible research topics and research approaches. The field spans a multitude of different areas of study and an array of potential data sources, data collection techniques, forms of analysis and theoretical concepts. As we will see, there is no one correct or best research design to use for studying social and health topics; rather there is a palate of possibilities that people can choose from and mix together in various ways to create their own unique approach.

The material in this chapter is primarily for people who have never designed a research project before and are looking for a quick introduction to some of the core principles of research design. It is likely to have most relevance for people who are about to embark on their first research assignment or doing their first course in research methods. Ideally this chapter should be read in conjunction with Chapter 3, which provides more detail on how to develop and write a project's research objectives, and Chapter 4 on preparing a research proposal, which looks at how to describe and present a finished research design.

Box 2.1   What is a research project?

A research project can be defined as a systematic effort to learn more about a selected topic, problem or issue. In contrast to general study, which tends to involve reading widely on a topic without necessarily having any particular objective in mind, a research project is a more focused, time-limited exercise with an identifiable purpose and a largely pre-planned set of research procedures. Usually it includes preparing some kind of written report describing the results of the research.

Designing a new research project: The core elements

In our experience there are four key elements (decision areas) that it is important to think about when first setting out to design a new research project:

- the *topic* of the research
- the project's main *research questions* or *research objectives*
- the *rationale* or *justification* for doing the research (why the project will be important or significant)
- the project's *research methodology* (the procedures, techniques and tools that will be used to collect, analyse and generate research information or evidence).

Over the following pages we discuss each of these elements in more detail. However, before starting we should emphasise that the process of designing a new research project should not be treated as a simple step-by-step, linear process where you begin by selecting your research topic, then you select your research questions and define the rationale for the project, and then after that you select your research methodology. In actual practice the process of designing a new research project is almost always much more fluid and unstructured than this, especially in the early stages. The goal is to try to knit together the four elements so that they are properly matched and consistent with each other. Inevitably this requires thinking about all four elements together, in an integrated way, rather than separately. Decisions regarding one element will almost always have implications for one or more of the other elements.

Box 2.2   Why do research?

Two different reasons for doing social and health research are often highlighted in the literature:

- to contribute to basic knowledge or theorising (sometimes referred to as 'pure' or 'fundamental' research).
- to develop knowledge leading to action, new services, new policies or social change (sometimes referred to as 'applied research').

(Continued)

(Continued)

In practice, many social and health research projects do both these things, adding to basic knowledge (exploring what is) as well as investigating options for action or change (exploring what ought to be).

Five general purposes for research are identified by Denscombe (2002, pp. 26–28):

- Describing something (what is it like?)
- Criticising or evaluating something (how well does something work?)
- Forecasting an outcome (what will happen in the future?)
- Developing good practice (how can something be improved?)
- Empowerment (how can research help those who are being researched?)

Thinking about your research topic

A key step when designing any new research project is selecting the topic it will cover, that is to say, the main area of knowledge it will focus on. Box 2.3 gives some examples (the list of potential social and health research topics is of course virtually limitless).

Box 2.3   Some miscellaneous research topics

- Homeless people
- Medical misadventure
- Boy-racer culture
- Racial discrimination
- Pictorial art in Ancient Rome
- Cigarette smoking in the home
- People and their pets
- Humour at funerals
- Text-bullying in the playground
- Sexual relationships on cruise ships
- Home schooling in rural France
- Astronaut retirement hobbies
- Poverty in the South Pacific
- A history of cholera
- Nutrition labelling on food
- Health effects of cell phones
- Women fire-fighters
- Concepts of happiness

For some people, choosing their topic will be the easiest part of designing a new research project. They will already have a clear idea of the topic they are interested in and be ready to move straight on to thinking about other elements of their research design. For other people, selecting a research topic may be less straightforward more fraught with difficulty and indecision. This can happen if someone is interested in several different topics and cannot decide which one to use as the basis for a project. In our experience, it is important in a situation like this not to make any hasty decisions. If you are finding it hard to choose between various possible research topics, try to give yourself as much time as possible to weigh up your options (see Box 2.4). Continue gathering information about the different topics by reviewing previous studies and talking with others. In time, some topics are likely to start to lose their appeal. Eventually it should become clear which topic you ultimately prefer above the rest. Remember, the topic you finally choose should have the potential to sustain your interest right through to the end of the project (and, ideally, well beyond that).

In some cases people may find they cannot get excited by any research topic. Every option seems dull or boring. Where to start, they might ask? What can I do? If you ever find yourself in this situation, remember that the inspiration for a new research project can come from virtually any source at any time. It doesn't necessarily have to be from other people's studies or talking with colleagues or teachers. It can come from experiences in your personal life, or what you read in the newspaper or see on TV. Think about the things you do in your life that you find exciting or regard as significant or important to you. Can any of these be potential topics for research?

Box 2.4   Note to self: 'Designing a new research project requires – research!'

Designing a research project should be treated as a kind of research exercise in its own right. Essentially, you are investigating the best way to do your project. Whatever topic you choose for your project, it can be almost guaranteed that somebody, somewhere will have studied it before. Finding and reading previous studies on your topic is therefore a crucial part of designing any new project. For larger projects this could include doing a formal literature review. This is a systematic effort to track down and read a good amount of previous research reports and other information relevant to your topic. How other researchers have framed their research objectives or questions, and the types of research methods they have used to investigate them, can be a vital source of inspiration and guidance for your own research design. Chapter 7 of this book provides a guide on how to do a literature review.

In some cases, especially if very little previous research literature is available on your topic, you might decide to do a small exploratory project first, to help work out the best way to design a larger study. Usually this will involve doing some preliminary fieldwork or interviews, just to see what information comes up. Ideally, designing a new project should be a reasonably integrated, multi-layered process where choices about the core elements of the project are progressively refined in response to information from previous studies, initial exploratory fieldwork and other relevant sources.

Of course, if you are a researcher working in a commercial environment (such as a research business) then the topics for the research projects you do are likely to be prescribed in most cases by your research clients rather than you. In this situation, the challenge is more likely to be working out the specific research objectives for the project and the most suitable research procedures to use, as discussed below.

Thinking about your research objectives or questions

In parallel with selecting a research topic, you should also start thinking about which dimensions of the topic you are most interested in exploring. To illustrate the diversity of possible research objectives Box 2.5 shows a range of examples. For your project, you need to decide what aspects of the topic you want to focus on. This involves pinning down fairly precisely the specific *objectives* of your research, or the specific *research questions* you intend to try to answer.

Box 2.5   Examples of research objectives

- To survey the attitudes of homeless people to the lack of availability of municipal night-shelter accommodation in an inner-city neighbourhood
- To identify the frequency and types of medical misadventure incidents reported over 12 months in a metropolitan general hospital
- To examine the response of boy-racer group participants to new state laws prohibiting night-time driving by people less than 18 years of age
- To study incidents of racial prejudice reported by Hispanic elementary school children
- To examine representations of the afterworld depicted in pre AD 100 early Roman mosaics
- To evaluate whether a TV and radio anti-tobacco social marketing campaign contributes to reductions in the frequency of cigarette smoking in homes occupied by pre-school-aged children
- To explore explanations for the common perception that pet owners look like their pets
- To investigate the use of humour and joking at funeral ceremonies
- To survey the impact of playground text-bullying on the psychosocial well-being of junior high-school students
- To examine the meanings ascribed to 'one-night stand' sexual encounters on cruise ships
- To measure the contributions made by male- and female-partners to the home schooling of 6–12-year-olds in rural France
- To explore the positive and negative health effects of the retirement pursuits of ex-NASA astronauts
- To compile statistics from existing studies and databases to examine levels of poverty and socio-economic disadvantage in south-western Pacific nations
- To prepare a social history of cholera, detailing its impact on people, economies and politics in different eras
- To survey the attitudes and preferences of main household shoppers regarding the introduction of compulsory country-of-origin labelling for raw fruit and vegetables
- To survey consumer perceptions of the cancer risk associated with regular, sustained cell phone use
- To evaluate levels of job-satisfaction and stress amongst women fire-fighters
- To examine concepts of happiness and life-satisfaction portrayed in TV advertising targeted at children and teenagers

---

To show what we mean, take the example of the topic of 'school free-food schemes'. School free-food schemes generally provide food free-of-charge to school students during school time (e.g., breakfasts, morning teas, lunches). Usually this is with the goal of improving children's nutrition and their ability to learn.

Now, it should be possible to see that there are potentially many different dimensions or aspects of this topic that could be singled out and made the main focus of a research project. Here are just a few examples to show what we mean, phrased in this case as research objectives:

- To identify how many schools are currently providing free-food schemes for their students
- To survey the attitudes of parents of school-age children about the value of school free-food schemes

- To determine whether school free-food schemes are being used by all the students who need them
- To measure the nutritional value of the foods provided in school free-food schemes
- To trace the history of the development and use of school free-food schemes from 1945 to 2005
- To forecast the future financial cost of providing school free-food schemes.

Here are some other examples of statements singling out different aspects of the topic, this time phrased as research *questions* (research intentions or goals can be expressed either as questions or objectives, there is no hard and fast rule on this):

- What type of foods are most commonly provided in school free-food schemes?
- How many schools currently offer free-food schemes?
- Which children use free-food schemes most often?
- Who is responsible for managing the delivery of free-food schemes in schools?
- What are the nutritional benefits for children who use free-food schemes?
- Why do some schools offer free-food schemes and not others?
- Why do only certain children from disadvantaged neighbourhoods use the free-food scheme at their school?

The key message to take away from looking at these examples is that for any given research topic, there is likely to be an almost infinite number of different research objectives or questions that potentially could be singled out. The trick when developing a new research project is to be able to focus down and clearly define which ones out of this huge array of potential research objectives or questions you intend to use as the core organising framework for your project.

For some people, clarifying objectives will not be hard to do at all, as often it will be a very clear question on a topic that first inspires them to start designing a research project. For example, say you have read or observed that some school staff are concerned that certain school children are not accessing school free-food schemes, despite the children coming from disadvantaged neighbourhoods and not bringing any lunches of their own to school. In this way, your research questions or objectives may be fairly well defined from the beginning.

For other people, it may be a struggle initially to pin down their project's core research objectives or questions. This can happen if they have not done enough preliminary thinking or background research on their topic. (For more ideas on how to develop and write a project's research objectives or questions see the next chapter.)

Thinking about the limits of research and research knowledge

In conjunction with defining your project's research objectives or questions, it will be important to consider where you stand in relation to the long-standing debate in social science over what kinds of knowledge it is possible for social and health research (and researchers) to generate about human social life and behaviour (Blaikie, 2007; Crotty, 1998). In particular, it will be important to consider how much you are inclined to support a 'positivist' as opposed to 'interpretivist' position regarding the possibilities and limits of social and health research. As discussed by Denscombe (2002, p. 18), 'positivist' researchers tend to adhere to the following perspectives or assumptions about the practice of research and the place of the researcher in the research process:

- that the human social world and behaviour can be observed or measured objectively using similar scientific techniques and approaches to those used to study the natural world
- that fixed patterns or regularities can be discovered in the human social world or behaviour, including specific cause-and-effect relationships, and that these patterns or regularities have general validity
- that these fixed patterns or regularities are able to be observed or measured without influencing or disturbing them, and they exist or operate irrespective of whether people, including researchers, recognise them or know about them.

By contrast, 'interpretivist' researchers tend to adhere to rather different principles and assumptions about the nature of social phenomena and the types of knowledge social and health research can produce. These include:

- that the 'reality' of the human social world and behaviour does not exist 'out there' available for detached, objective investigation. Rather, it is constructed by people. Different people having different ideas about what constitutes social reality and the meaning of human action or behaviour
- that the researcher studying aspects of the human social world and behaviour can never be truly objective or completely stand apart from the phenomenon he or she is studying. The researcher brings certain values, expectations and assumptions about people and the world to the research process. These colour the types of research topics and questions he or she pursues, as well as the interpretations or meanings they attach to research data or findings
- that people react to being the subject of research, and therefore may alter what they say or do compared to when they are not being studied. People also react to the data or findings produced by researchers, which can result in social phenomena changing as a result of being researched
- that the complexities and contradictions inherent in studying human social life and behaviour mean that it is largely impossible for research to posit general, universal or enduring laws or theories about human social or health phenomena that have validity in all circumstances or for all people.

The position you take in relation to these two broad philosophical 'paradigms', whether you regard yourself as more of a positivist or more of an interpretivist researcher, is likely to play a big hand in shaping (consciously or otherwise) the types of research objectives or questions on which you elect to focus. This includes how you might express or frame these objectives or questions on paper or in discussions with others.

For example, for the topic of school free-food schemes, a largely positivist-oriented researcher is likely to feel comfortable pursuing the following research question:

- Is the food provided in free-food schemes nutritionally adequate?

In addressing this question the researcher is likely to start with the assumption that there is a single, objective, value-free way of defining what is or is not nutritionally adequate food. The researcher is also likely to assume that it is possible to directly measure the nutritional intake of a group of children who use the free-food schemes, and to use the resulting data to determine what proportion of the children are getting a nutritionally adequate diet. These findings are likely to be considered to be fairly generalisable to all children using free-food schemes.

By contrast, an interpretivist researcher is likely to resist organising a research project around this type of research question. He or she may dispute whether there truly exists 'out there' a completely value-free, objective measure of nutritional adequacy. Instead they may be more inclined to view the concept of 'nutritional adequacy' as having a socially constructed or socially negotiated meaning, with ideas about what is a nutritionally adequate diet varying from person to person, group to group and place to place. This would include orthodox scientific or expert knowledge regarding what constitutes a nutritionally adequate diet. Examples of the types of research questions that might be posed by an interpretivist researcher include:

- How do the sponsors and providers of school free-food schemes conceptualise what is a nutritionally adequate diet, and how do these notions influence the types of foods made available in school free-food schemes?
- How do the children who use free-food schemes conceptualise what is a nutritionally adequate diet? How are these ideas about nutrition and diet constructed, negotiated and modified in the course of the children's everyday lives and social interaction?

When investigating these questions, an interpretivist researcher is likely to freely accept that his or her research conclusions will be essentially subjective and coloured by choices they make about how data for the study will be gathered, analysed and interpreted. They are also likely to caution that their research findings may not necessarily be generalisable to all sponsors and providers of school free-food schemes, or all children who use free-food schemes.

While it is beyond the scope of this chapter to discuss in detail the distinction between positivist and interpretivist approaches to social and health research, newcomers to research should aim to familiarise themselves with the issues and debates surrounding this distinction and be in a position to take them into account when designing a new research project.

Thinking about the rationale for your research project

As part of nailing down a project's research objectives or questions, it is also important to think about the rationale or justification for these choices. Essentially this means defining why the research objectives or questions you have chosen are important or worth investigating. The clearer you can be in your own mind about the context and motivations underlying your choice of research objectives or questions, the better it will be in the long run for setting your research project off on the right foot.

For example, consider the research objective:

- To survey the attitudes of parents of school-age children in [specified neighbourhood/city/ district/province] to school free-food schemes.

It might be observed that previous studies and other information (e.g. media reports, personal observation) have indicated that many school free-food schemes are being under-used by students, including students likely to benefit from them, and that not all parents or caregivers of school-age children support the idea of free food being provided in schools. There may also be indications that school boards are debating the cost-effectiveness of continuing to run free-food schemes, with the possibility that schemes may be discontinued in some schools as a result. In this context, surveying parents' attitudes to school free-food schemes could be argued to be important because it will help pinpoint how many parents want or value the schemes, along with the reasons why certain parents like or dislike them. This information could be used by school boards as part of their decision making about whether to continue to provide the free-food schemes, or how the schemes could be improved so that parents like them better and encourage their children to use them.

Note how this rationale for the research objective tends to have a rather positivist flavour. There is an emphasis on objectively measuring parents' attitudes and regarding these measurements as having sufficient reliability and generalisability for them to be able to be used by other people in a practical way to plan services or develop new policy.

By contrast, rationales given for largely interpretivist research objectives or questions tend to focus on other themes. To illustrate, let us look again at two of the interpretivist-styled research questions referred to earlier:

- How do children who use free-food schemes conceptualise what is a nutritionally adequate diet?
- How are these ideas about nutrition and diet constructed, negotiated and modified in the course of the children's everyday lives and social interaction?

These questions point to an intention to look closely at the meanings children associate with food and the different ways children conceptualise what other people might refer to as a nutritionally adequate diet. The questions also point to an intention to try to figure out how these meanings children associate with food are developed, maintained and transformed. In justifying the significance or importance of these questions, a researcher might contend that developing a better understanding of the different ways in which children conceptualise food and nutrition-related issues, and the manner in which these ideas or meanings are maintained or negotiated in social settings, will have value by adding to the sum total of existing knowledge about the ways people in different cultures, places or settings conceptualise food and nutrition. On top of this, it might also be argued that the research will contribute to existing theoretical debates or arguments concerning the social processes or mechanisms involved in constructing the meanings people attach to food and nutrition.

In general, rationales for interpretivist-styled research objectives or questions tend to emphasise developing richer or more sophisticated understandings of the ideas or meanings that people hold in their heads; or of developing a better appreciation of the social processes involved in maintaining or transforming these ideas or meanings. These rationales do not usually focus on the potential for a project's research findings to be used in a practical way, such as improving services or developing policy (although they can).

If, during the initial stages of designing a new research project, you find you are struggling to justify why the research objectives or questions you have chosen are significant or important, it might pay to reassess whether you have selected the right objectives or questions. As emphasised previously, designing a new research project is often a very fluid and dynamic process (Figure 2.1). You can start off with an idea about the topic you want to pursue, or the research questions you are interested in, or the kinds of problems you want to address. However, as time goes by and you think more about what you are ultimately aiming to achieve, and how the research may be potentially significant or important, there is always a possibility you will decide to alter your research objectives or questions, or even completely change your research topic.

Thinking about your research methodology

After reaching some conclusions (albeit provisional) about the types of research objectives or questions you want to pursue, and why these are important, it is time to start

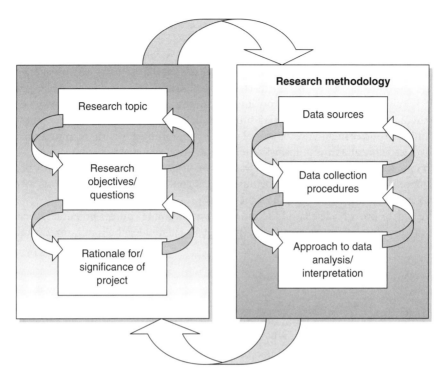

FIGURE 2.1 HOW DECISIONS ABOUT KEY ELEMENTS OF A RESEARCH DESIGN INFLUENCE EACH OTHER

thinking about the research methodology you plan to use in your project. Your research methodology is the set of procedures and techniques you will use to collect or create your project's research information or evidence. For example, if one of your research objectives is to investigate the attitudes of parents of school-age children towards school free-food schemes, then your research methodology is the set of procedures you plan to use to gather information about parents' attitudes to school free-food schemes and to analyse or interpret this information to produce meaningful findings.

Defining the dimensions of your research methodology will usually require thinking about three key areas:

Data sources: who or what will be your project's main source (or sources) of research data or evidence?

Data collection: what will be the specific procedures or approaches your project will use to collect information or evidence from this source (or sources)?

Data analysis: how will the information or evidence collected during your project be processed, analysed or interpreted to produce useful findings?

Thinking about your data sources

A data source is a definable element or part of the human or natural worlds from which information relevant to a research topic is obtained or collected. In principle, for any research topic you decide to investigate, there are likely to be numerous potential data sources. Taking again our example of school free-food schemes, potential data sources for this topic could include school staff, school children and their parents or caregivers, specialists in educational research and nutrition experts. It could also include 'real world' settings or situations involving the actual delivery or use of school free-food schemes, or settings where the effects of school free-food schemes might be expected to be observed. Examples include places where children collect and eat their free school lunches, meetings where officials plan how to deliver free school lunch schemes and teaching situations in the school classroom. Other potentially relevant data sources might include school records or government statistics showing children's levels of academic attainment, historical texts or archival material referring to early school health initiatives, and film, video, TV, newspaper or magazine content referring to aspects of contemporary free-food schemes. Obviously, too, it could include research reports by other researchers who have investigated the topic.

One way to broadly classify all the different types of data sources potentially available to researchers has been suggested by Blaikie (2000). He divides them into three groups:

- people
- events
- items.

People are individuals, or groups of individuals, from whom information about a topic can be gathered, usually either orally or in writing. In the case of the topic of school free-food schemes this would include people like school staff, or the children who use the free-food scheme.

Events are observable episodes of social action: situations and places where people do things and express things (talk, sing, dance, laugh, etc). An example is a situation where school children collect and eat their free food.

Items are essentially things that can be touched or held in some way such as archival records, personal diaries, art works, items of clothing, furniture, jewellery, tools, photographs, CDs and DVDs, books, journals, magazines, research reports and computer databases. For the topic of school free-food schemes, examples might include the printed lunch menu that schools hand out to children, samples of the actual food provided, computerised financial records tracking the costs of providing school free-food schemes, old film footage showing the opening ceremony for the first free-food scheme in the district, or published research studies examining the appropriateness of free-food schemes.

While not everyone will agree with this way of classifying research data sources, it does help to show just how many different types of sources may be available for any given research topic. A key part of the process of designing a new research project is selecting which data sources to use out of the many options available. In many instances, these choices will be shaped by decisions already made (or about to be made) regarding the project's main research objectives or questions. For example, imagine you have already decided that your research objective will be to survey adults and children about their attitudes to school free-food schemes. This obviously suggests you will be using sources in the 'people' category rather than in the 'events' or 'items' categories.

After deciding to use 'people' as your research data source, you will then need to think about which particular categories or groups of people you intend to work with. This will guide the selection of the sample for your project. Will it be just school children, just parents or caregivers of school children, or just representatives of agencies funding or delivering free-food in school schemes? Or do you want to survey people from all three of these groups? Again, decisions on these questions will need to be made in combination with careful reflection on your research objectives or questions and a good understanding of what you are ultimately hoping to achieve with your project. Box 2.6 provides some ideas for thinking about what type of sample you might select.

Box 2.6   Thinking about sampling

In conjunction with choosing your data sources and methods of data collection, you will almost certainly at some stage need to think about how widely or narrowly you intend casting your data gathering net. Say, for example, you intend to survey the attitudes of parents or caregivers of school-age children to school free-food schemes. Will you be aiming to try to survey every parent or caregiver of school-aged children living in your region or district? Or will you be aiming to survey only a selected number out of all these parents or caregivers? In most cases, to save time and resources, researchers will choose the latter option. In social and health research, this selected group is commonly referred to as a 'sample'.

Now, there are many different ways of selecting or creating a sample of people, events or data items. Which approach you take will to some extent be shaped by the specific research objectives or questions you are trying to address.

If, say, your research objective is to try to measure the percentage of parents and caregivers who support the concept of school free-food schemes, then this would suggest that you are wanting your sample of parents and caregivers to be a *representative* sample, meaning that you can rely on the sample group to exhibit pretty much the same range of attitudes to the concept of school free-food schemes as the total population of parents and caregivers in your region or district. One of the most common ways researchers try to obtain a representative sample is by 'random sampling'. This is when a research project is conducted in such a way that every parent or caregiver in the district or region has an equal chance of being invited to take part in the project. For example, if a researcher has an up-to-date list of the names and addresses of every parent or caregiver in a district or region, then a computer program or set of random number tables could be used to randomly choose a certain number of these parents and caregivers for further follow-up.

Of course in real life there are seldom such up-to-date lists of potential research participants available. When no good data exist to create a random sample, researchers might try to develop a suitable sample in other ways. 'Purposive sampling' is one approach. This is when certain people (or events or items) are deliberately selected for inclusion in a research project based on a presumed idea of what mix of people (or events or items) it will be important to cover in order to make the research sample credible in relation to the research objectives. For example, say your objective is to find out from all the different kinds of people involved with the school free-food scheme in your district what they like or dislike about the scheme. Instead of trying to conduct separate district-wide random surveys of parent/caregivers, children, school teaching staff, scheme sponsors and the food-handling staff who work on the scheme, you could select, say, six schools from the district. These schools might be chosen primarily on the basis of socio-economic disadvantage, with three of the schools being located in very disadvantaged neighbourhoods and the other three schools in only moderately disadvantaged neighbourhoods. Then, in each school you might plan to select 10 individuals from each of the following groups: parents/caregivers, children, school teaching staff, scheme sponsors and food-handling staff. In selecting these people you would try to get a good spread of ages and genders, as well as any other characteristics that you consider important, such as having a good mix of senior and junior teachers and so on.

(Continued)

(Continued)

In some projects, if there is no realistic way to create a random sample or another type of sample that can be fairly claimed to be approximately representative, then a researcher may elect to largely ignore the goal of trying to make his or her data sources representative. In fact, this may be the only feasible option if the people (or events or items) intended to be the main data source for the project are hard to find or difficult to recruit. For example, say a researcher on a project studying school free-food schemes wants to interview parents who regularly steal food from supermarkets and grocery stores to help feed their family. One technique sometimes used by researchers in these situations is what is called *snowball sampling*. This is when one research participant (in this case a parent who has shoplifted) is asked to identify other people they know who could also qualify for inclusion in the study. Gradually over time (and with a bit of luck) this approach may eventually lead to the recruitment of a sufficient number of current or former shoplifting parents to make the project viable, although whether or not the group is representative of all shoplifting parents in the district will be hard to know.

The main point to remember in relation to sampling is that for virtually any type of data source – a group of people, a social event, or items such as birth records, published research studies, or magazine articles – you will need to make some decisions (tentative as they may be) about which parts of the total potential set of sources available will actually be used in your study.

If you decide that you will be using 'events' as your main source of research data then you will need to work out what kind of events are likely to be the most meaningful or useful to focus on. Say, for example, your research objective is to observe social occasions and public gatherings in your local community in order to better understand how people view or use school free-food schemes. What events will you choose to concentrate on? Will it be the times and places in the school term when school children collect and eat their free food? Will it be the meetings of the school board where they school's policy on free food is discussed? Will it be in the everyday discussions that go on between children and their parents or caregivers about food and nutrition at home? Or will it be all three of these types of events, plus perhaps other types of events you can think of?

Similarly, if your research objectives or questions imply you should be using 'items' as your data source, rather than (or as well as) 'people' or 'events', then you will need to determine as precisely as you can what kinds of items you are most interested in. If, for example, your research objective is to study the underlying assumptions and meanings about food and nutrition evident in items that refer to or have connections with school free-food schemes, then which items out of all the possible options will you choose to concentrate on? Publicity material (posters, newsletters, pamphlets, etc.) circulated by the sponsors of free-food schemes? Newspaper articles, letters to the editor, or blog sites where people express their opinions about the suitability of school free-food schemes? Books, journal articles and research reports presenting and evaluating evidence on the value of school free-food schemes? Or all three of these different types of sources?

When a research project is based mainly on original source material collected specifically for the project by surveying or interviewing people, or by observing events, or by searching out items such as old diaries or newspaper articles, then the project is often described as being based on *primary sources*. When a research project uses only other research studies as its source material, or data already compiled and/or analysed by other researchers, then the project is often described as being based on *secondary sources*. Examples of the latter include research projects where the main objective is to compile a literature review addressing a particular topic or question, or to combine or re-analyse statistical data from several previous studies in order to confirm or test existing findings.

Thinking about your data collection

In conjunction with deciding who or what will be your project's main source or sources of data, you will also need to decide what techniques you will use to actually gather or collect data or evidence from these sources. These will be your data collection processes or methods.

A wide range of different methods are used in social and health research to obtain or gather data or evidence from sources. It is beyond the scope of this chapter to describe them all in detail. Here are just a few general examples to give you an idea of the possibilities:

For gathering information from people:

- survey questionnaires (e.g. in person, postal, telephone, Internet)
- in-depth, one-to-one discussions or semi-structured interviews
- diary keeping
- focus groups.

For gathering information about events:

- personal observation and/or direct participation (using memory and/or note taking)
- filming or video taping of events in either natural settings or a laboratory or clinic setting.

For gathering information from or about items:

- photographing, video taping or drawing the item
- obtaining copies of paper-based records or digital files, government statistics, previous research literature, etc.
- obtaining copies of archival material (e.g. diaries, letters, old newspaper articles).

Which type of data collection method (or methods) you eventually decide to use to gather information from or about your sources will obviously be determined partly by the nature of the source. You cannot get a newspaper article to fill out a survey questionnaire but you can ask a person to do this. You cannot interview a social gathering, but you can take photographs of it, or film it, or make notes about what you see and hear as you participate in it.

It is probably fair to say that most social and health research projects tend to focus on people as their primary data source. More positivist-oriented studies tend to favour collecting information from people using carefully designed, structured questionnaires. These have the advantage of tightly focusing people's thinking on specific topics or issues selected earlier by the researcher. As well, questionnaires (especially if they are short) are usually a good way to collect information quickly from a large number of people in a relatively cost-effective, straight-forward manner, such as through telephone or Internet surveys.

In other research projects where people are the primary data source, researchers may prefer to use data collection methods that provide more scope for research participants to talk in detail and at length about their personal experiences in a relatively open-ended and unguided manner. An example is the life history interview, where an individual retraces aspects of their life or biography in conversation with a researcher. Another example is the focus group discussion, where several people talk together about their views and experiences connected to a topic, with the researcher often only lightly guiding the direction of the discussion. These comparatively flexible, less structured methods of gathering information from people are typically favoured by more interpretivist-oriented researchers, especially if they are wanting to study in detail how people conceptualise a topic or thoroughly explore the different meanings or ideas people associate with an issue or problem. Often these kinds of interviews or discussions are recorded so that the researcher can go back later and look carefully at what people say, and how they say it.

Once you have selected the kind of data collection method (or methods) you intend to use in your project, you will then need to think about the actual steps you will take to implement this approach. For instance, taking again our example of school free-food schemes, let's say that in order to investigate parents' attitudes to these schemes you decide to carry out a questionnaire-based survey of a sample of parents of school-age children. Specific practical implementation issues you will then need to think about related to this data collection method include:

- How many parents in total do you think would need to participate in the survey to make the survey results meaningful?
- How will you contact parents and invite them to take part in the survey?
- How will you deliver the survey to parents, i.e., how will parents complete your survey? By telephone, in person (self-completion or face-to-face with an interviewer), by mail, by computer via email or through a webpage?
- What specific questions will you ask the parents?
- Will the answers parents give to the survey be entered onto a paper questionnaire or directly into a computer?
- How will all the survey data be stored and kept protected?

As another example, say you decide you want to use first-hand observation as your main data collection method, in particular observing what people do and say in a selection of school dining halls and kitchens where free food is distributed to children. Some of the practical research design issues you will need to consider here include:

- How many sessions of observation do you intend to carry out in each dining hall/kitchen; how long will each session last?
- What days of the week and times of the day do you intend to carry out your observations?
- What techniques will you use to record the things you see or hear during your observations (e.g. making notes during or after observations; dictating notes into an audio-recorder during observations)?
- Will your observation sessions also include the use of video or photography to record certain events; if so, how will this equipment be set up or used?

Or, as a third example, say you decide you want to study the underlying assumptions and meanings regarding food and nutrition expressed in different media materials associated with the public promotion of school free-food schemes, and that to do this you plan to obtain copies of these media materials. Practical research design issues you might need to consider here include:

- How will you physically search for and retrieve copies of relevant textual and media materials – where will you go and how will you look for what you want?
- What will qualify as 'relevant' materials – for example, will it include unpublished material or material that was developed but never released?

- Will you aim to collect physical hard copies of all unique textual and media materials, or will you aim to photocopy or scan all the materials on to a computer?

As you can see, these questions are very much concerned with sorting out the practical steps you intend to take during the data collection phase of your project. Even in the early stages of designing a new research project, it will be useful to begin thinking about these practical issues. It is no good developing a research design that identifies plenty of worthwhile research objectives or questions, but fails to identify a realistic method of collecting data to address them.

Thinking about your data analysis

When designing any new research project, along with defining the data sources and data collection techniques you favour, it will also pay to think about the processes you intend to use to analyse your research data or evidence. In particular, it will be important to make sure that the data you intend to collect will be able to be analysed in the way you intend.

In broad terms, data analysis is the process of drawing meaning from or making sense of the information or evidence collected for a project. For example, say you are conducting a questionnaire-based telephone survey of parents whose children use school free-food schemes. Once all the parents have completed the telephone survey and you have all their responses to the questionnaire recorded on paper or stored in computer, then there is scope to begin looking in detail at this data in order to work out what it means.

Similarly, if you have been doing a series of observations of 'real world' events, such as video-taping school students interacting with each other while picking up and eating their free school lunches, then once you have recorded all the video evidence you think you need, the next step will be to begin to scrutinise your collection of video footage to see what it shows.

Even in a situation where the data collection for your project has simply involved finding and retrieving copies of previous research reports, or copying information from existing datasets, there will still be a need to sit down and carefully examine this material in some way to develop ideas about its meaning.

It is outside the scope of this chapter to summarise all the different data analysis techniques that social and health researchers can use to try to draw meaning from research data. This information is available in other, more lengthy textbooks. In broad terms, however, these techniques can be categorised according to the degree to which they use either *quantitative* or *qualitative* forms of analysis.

As the name suggests, *quantitative* analysis focuses on numbers and counting. Research information that may have been collected using a questionnaire or some other method is converted into numbers. These numbers are then ordered and re-ordered in different ways to look for patterns or relationships in the data. A common example of this is when a survey of the general public is used to identify what percentage of the population agrees with certain ideas about a controversial issue, such as the legal purchasing age for alcohol. A quantitative analysis counts up how many people agree or disagree with a particular idea about the legal purchasing age. The analysis might also be used to show whether certain groups in the population (e.g., males, young people, people on higher incomes) are more or less likely than other groups to agree with the idea.

Qualitative analysis is essentially any form of analysis that uses non-numerical approaches to derive meaning from research data. In most cases this involves working with data in the form of words or images, such as newspaper articles or movies, or textual material that the researcher has created in the course of his or her work such as notes from field observations or transcripts of tape-recorded discussions with research partici- pants. Usually qualitative analysis will involve some form of intensive engagement by the researcher with this textual or visual material in a search for patterns or generalities that have meaning or significance for the project's research objectives or questions. A common example of this is when a researcher spends time reading though the transcripts of inter- views conducted with research participants, identifying recurring themes or ideas in the material, and selecting illustrative quotations. This work may be assisted by using qualitative analysis software for labelling and sorting segments of text into categories.

In general, researchers who veer towards a more positivist position on the limits and possibilities of social and health research often regard quantitative forms of data analysis as the most meaningful or reliable. When designing new research projects, they therefore tend to frame their research objectives or questions, and choose their data sources and data collection techniques, with a view to ensuring the data produced can be effectively analysed quantitatively.

Researchers more inclined to take an interpretivist position on the limits and pos- sibilities of social and health research tend to favour qualitative forms of data analysis. On the whole, these approaches are seen to offer more scope to look in detail at how research participants conceptualise and understand different aspects of their lives. They are also argued to promote deeper reflection by the researcher about his or her role in the research process and in the creation of research results.

Other things to think about – constraints on your design choices

So far this chapter has mainly concentrated on describing how designing a new research project requires thinking carefully about the connections between the project's research objectives or questions and the different data sources, data collection techniques and data analysis approaches that could be used. In particular, we have emphasised the need to ensure that your project's research methodology follows logically from and dovetails closely with the research objectives or questions you have chosen.

However, in conjunction with these elements, there are several other important issues that will also need to be considered when thinking about your overall research design. These issues relate less to the internal logic and consistency of your overall research design and more to what might be termed 'real world' pragmatic aspects of implementing your project. These issues can be grouped under three headings:

- research ethics
- research setting and environment
- project resources.

Research ethics

While in principle there could be a range of different ways that data for your research project could be collected, in practice some of these ways may need to be ruled out because they are considered unethical. For example, say a researcher was interested in studying the nutritional impact of free school lunches compared to lunches entirely composed of junk food. He designs a study where one group of school children is requested to eat food items usually provided in free school lunches every day for a month, while a second group of children is requested to eat various types of junk food for lunch every day for that same month.

Can you see any ethical problems with this research design? Well, one of the central ethical requirements of research is that research participants should not be unnecessarily exposed to the risk of harm. By requesting children to eat junk food every lunch time for a month, this would seem likely to promote ill health and weight gain amongst the children in the group. Given that there are potentially several other ways to evaluate the nutritional impact of a free school lunch diet compared to a junk food lunch diet, there is likely to be very little justification from an ethical standpoint for using the compulsory-month-of-junk-food-eating research approach.

A rundown on the various ethical principles and standards that social and health researchers are normally expected to respect and abide by is given in Chapter 6. It is important to be familiar with these when designing any new research project as they are likely to have major implications for the choices you make about the types of people, events or items you use as sources for your research and the procedures you will use to collect information about or from them. For example, ethical issues are likely to limit your options when it comes to using research methods involving:

- the collection of data about or from people without their knowledge or consent
- the collection of data from people who may be considered vulnerable or unable to give informed consent (e.g. children, hospital patients, people with certain disabilities)
- deception or trickery where research participants are deliberately misled about the real purpose of a study
- fieldwork in non-public settings
- use of hidden recording equipment
- the taking of blood, tissue and other body samples
- concealment of a project's final research results from the research participants.

Research setting and environment

When developing your research methodology, remember to consider the nature of the general environment or setting in which you plan to do your research. For example, say you are thinking about conducting a telephone survey of disadvantaged parents in a particular city neighbourhood to identify their attitudes to school free-food schemes. But what if you find out from the national census that less than 70 per cent of homes in that neighbourhood have a home telephone? What implications could this have for your research design, especially if you are intending your survey to be as representative as possible of all parents in the neighbourhood? Will you need to think about a different method of contacting parents in the neighbourhood who don't have home phones?

Building up some practical knowledge about the likely environment or setting for your research should be a key part of the preliminary research you do when developing your research design. Some of the more important factors you might need to consider include:

- Geography and terrain; population distribution; transport and telecommunication systems – how easy will it be to physically get around your research setting and meet with people or observe events?

- Language, access to translation services; levels of literacy and education – how easy will it be for you or others to exchange information verbally or in writing with potential research participants?
- Local cultural beliefs, assumptions and practices – how accepting are your research participants likely to be of certain research approaches or techniques? Do the research methods you are thinking of using fit with the general cultural ethos and outlook of your research participants?
- Legal and commercial constraints – what is or is not permitted by the laws or rules set down by the people you are intending to study? What legal or commercial barriers limit access to key statistical databases (e.g., data from a national census) or archived texts or other research material (e.g., books, manuscripts, letters, diaries)?

Project resources

When thinking about your research design, it will also be a good idea to try to anticipate the general level of resourcing – money, time and research people – you are likely to have available to do your project.

Budget

Virtually all research projects cost something to run. If you expect (or are hoping) your project will have a substantial budget, then this may make it possible to plan a relatively large project that uses a combination of different data sources (people, events, archival or official records, existing databases) and data collection procedures. However, if you expect realistically to have only modest funding for your project, it is probably a good idea to develop a research design that will be achievable within this budget.

Time

How much time do you have to do the study? Are you limited by deadlines or timetables already set or agreed? For example, say you are planning your Masters research project and you want to have the whole project done and written up in 12 months. This timeframe may well constrain the types of research objectives you set and the types of research methodologies you choose. Similarly, if you are designing a research project to answer a question for a commercial client who needs the research findings delivered within a month, this will also probably limit your methodological options. It may, for instance, rule out doing any extensive survey research or fieldwork. You may instead be limited to basing your project design around an analysis of existing datasets or a review of results from previous studies.

Research people

How many researchers and other people are likely to be available to do the project and what kinds of training, skills and experience do they have (or need to acquire)? Given the wide range of research approaches used in social and health research, individual researchers tend to develop a specialised knowledge and experience of only certain kinds of approaches. When designing a new research project, it could be risky to opt to use a research approach that you or your colleagues have little or no previous experience of using.

Types of research designs used in social and health research

In this last section we outline some of the different types of research approaches commonly used in social and health research. In thinking about your evolving project design, it will be useful to consider how similar or different it is from these various approaches or 'styles' of research. This should help point you in the direction of suitable books and other information giving advice on how to further refine the design of your project.

Categorising the many different types of research approaches that social and health researchers use is difficult. There is no single, widely agreed framework for naming or classifying these. However, one good starting point is the categories developed by Babbie (2007, p. 108). He lists seven different methods of social research:

- survey research
- field research
- experiments
- content analysis
- existing data research
- historical (comparative) research
- evaluation research.

As we will see, some of these approaches (e.g., survey research) focus on obtaining data directly from living people by talking with them or writing to them and asking questions. Other approaches (e.g., field research) are more concerned with observing carefully what people do or say in 'real world' situations, with the researcher trying to minimise the extent to which his or her presence alters what people do. Yet another set of approaches (experiments) aims to manipulate aspects of the 'real world' or create artificial scenarios or environments to see how research participants react in these situations. Certain research approaches are distinguished by their chief reliance on the use of 'indirect' data sources, rather than collecting information directly from people. This includes approaches centred mainly on the study of physical objects or items such as media materials or art works (content analysis), archival records, old texts or other historical materials (historical research) and the review or re-analysis of statistical and/or non-numerical data published in previous studies or held in existing databases (existing data research).

More broadly, some of these approaches also tend to differ from each other in terms of the stance they take to questions concerning the scope and limits of social and health research – whether objective research and knowledge is possible, the extent to which research findings are (or should be) widely generalisable or universally applicable, and the extent to which the practice of research is (or should be) a largely neutral, detached activity providing 'value-free' truths, or whether it is (or should be) essentially a political process or form of advocacy for particular causes, ideas or people.

Survey research

Survey research essentially involves 'collecting data by asking people questions' (Babbie, 2007, p. 218). In many survey projects, especially those based around the use of questionnaires, the questions put to people are usually carefully thought out beforehand. Often this involves doing preliminary interviews (a pilot study) or other forms of background research to work out the best questions to ask. For other survey type research techniques, such as focus groups or in-depth face-to-face interviews, questions are more likely to be developed on the spot by the researcher or interviewer. Surveys or interviews may be conducted in a range of formats including in person ('face-to-face') or by telephone, mail, email or the Internet. In the classic large-scale survey design, survey participants are likely to be a randomly selected sample from a population. Data analysis is usually based on numerical (quantitative) summarising of people's answers, with core findings presented mainly in the form of tables or graphs. Results may be used to forecast or predict future events or behaviours, such as the outcomes of elections or use of human services (see example in Table 2.1). Survey research, especially that using structured questions, is sometimes criticised for being too formal, artificial and detached. It is often hard for a survey, says Babbie (2007, p. 276) to develop a feel for an individual's 'total life situation'.

TABLE 2.1   A SURVEY RESEARCH PROJECT

Topic	Disability in New Zealand
Research objectives or questions	1. To identify the prevalence and severity of disability in the New Zealand population. 2. To identify disabled people's experiences related to: • home life and environment • help received from family and others • use of disability-related equipment and technology • participation in education • employment and income • travel patterns and use of transport
Rationale and justification	Reliable baseline statistics on New Zealand's disabled population are necessary to support the development of new policies, services and research to improve the lives of disabled people and their families and create a less-disabling society
Research methods	
Data sources	A representative sample of over 7000 adults and children with disabilities living in private households and over 900 adults with disabilities living in institutions
Data collection	A structured survey questionnaire administered by face-to-face or telephone interview
Data analysis	Numerical (quantitative) analysis of questionnaire data, with results weighted to provide estimates for the total New Zealand population

Source: Ministry of Health/Intersectoral Advisory Group (2005). *Living with Disability in New Zealand: Summary: Key Results from the 2001 Household Disability Survey and the 2001 Disability Survey of Residential Facilities.* Wellington: Ministry of Health

Field research

Field research involves directly observing human activity or events in natural ('real world') settings. Specific research traditions in this category include ethnomethodology, grounded theory, case studies (including the extended case study method) and ethnography.

Ethnography is a research approach initially developed in anthropology. It involves direct engagement by the researcher in the everyday lives of the group or community being studied, with the researcher aiming to join in with and become a recognised member of the group or community, at least to a degree. The method usually includes a major focus on observation in natural settings, although it also includes scope for gathering information on how people interpret their social and natural worlds by conversing with them or by getting people to tell their life stories (see example in Table 2.2). These different ways of collecting data may also be supplemented by photographs and audio or video recordings, or by examining aspects of the people's material culture (e.g., technology, clothing, art). Sometimes the researcher becomes a strong advocate for the group or community being studied. One version of advocacy research is participatory action research (see Box 2.7), or 'action research', where the researcher works collaboratively with research participants through collective action that is intended to lead to project outcomes that benefit the people involved (e.g., McIntyre, 2008).

TABLE 2.2   A FIELD RESEARCH PROJECT

Topic	Call centre workers in India
Research objectives or questions	How do call centre workers negotiate the call centre space as a place physically inside but temporally outside of India (i.e. working 'American time')?
Rationale and justification	Advocates of globalisation often identify transnational call centres as exemplars of progress in cross-national cultural integration and economic equality. But what is the experience of working in call centres really like for white-collared, third world employees?
Research methods Data sources	People and events in two Bangalore and New Delhi call centres that provide back-office services for various North American businesses
Data collection	Participant observation and informal interviews
Data analysis	Contemplation and interpretation of field observations and interviews

Source: Varma, M. (2007). India wiring out: ethnographic reflections from two transnational call centres in India. Anthropology Matters Journal, 9(2), 1–7

Box 2.7   Participatory Action Research

As already noted, there are many different ways of doing social and health research. One of the more interesting approaches to emerge in recent years is participatory action research (sometimes also called action research, emancipatory research or empowerment research).

Unlike more orthodox research approaches, such as survey research or experiments, participatory action research generally aims to create a situation where the research participants themselves decide what kinds of questions or objectives the research project will pursue, and the kinds of research methods that will be used to do this. The researcher then works closely with the research participants to put the planned research into practice.

Participatory action research is in many ways a reaction to more traditional styles of research where research is seen to be done 'on' rather than 'with' people. In particular, people from disadvantaged or marginalised groups or communities often contend that conventional research treats them largely as passive research objects placed under the microscope,

(Continued)

(Continued)

with little ability to control the way the research involving them is framed or carried out. They may disagree with the conclusions studies make about them or resent the way studies are used to justify policies or programmes that they regard as unhelpful or oppressive.

Participatory action research and other similar research approaches aim to counter this by placing control of the research process directly in the hands of the people in these disadvantaged or marginalised groups and communities. The researcher uses his or her research skills to facilitate the development of new research projects that the people themselves regard as important or useful.

Experimental research

Experimental research is a type of research approach where the researcher deliberately does something to alter, re-arrange or modify outcomes for an individual or group in an effort to try to better understand how or why certain things happen, or how certain people or things affect other people or things. Experiments tend to have very specific, highly defined research objectives, questions or hypotheses. Because such tight control usually needs to be maintained over aspects of the behaviour of the people being studied, or the environment where people are interacting, experiments are often conducted in a laboratory or clinical setting. An example is a psychological experiment that aims to try to identify whether people behave differently in social situations where alcoholic drinks are available, compared to social situations where only non-alcoholic drinks are available. To perform the experiment, research participants are asked to socialise with each other in a simulated bar room setting in a university research laboratory. For some sessions only non-alcoholic drinks are available from the bar, for other sessions both non-alcoholic and alcoholic drinks are available. The sessions are video taped, with the tapes analysed to track similarities and differences in group dynamics across the different sessions.

Similarly, in clinical research, quite tightly controlled experiments are frequently used to try to isolate the health effects of a particular therapy or drug. One common strategy is to recruit a number of patients and divide them into three groups. Group one receives the particular therapy or drug being investigated, group two receives an alternative therapy or placebo drug (e.g., a sugar pill) and group three receives no treatment or drug at all. The research participants in all three groups are assessed on relevant health outcomes and perhaps questionnaires or diaries to complete at intervals throughout the study. The information from these is then used to try to trace any positive or negative health-related changes that may have occurred over the period of the experiment, to see if the outcomes for the group receiving the therapy or drug are better than for the other two groups.

A particular type of experiment especially favoured in health research is what is known as a 'randomised, double-blind, placebo-controlled trial'. This is a type of experiment where all the patients receiving the therapy and all the members of the research team evaluating the effects of the therapy are 'blinded' to which patients are actually receiving the therapy and which the non-therapy or placebo (see Table 2.3). This research design is intended to limit the scope for the researchers and patients to knowingly or unknowingly influence the results of the experiment.

As a form of research approach, experiments are sometimes criticised for not necessarily have 'real world' applicability. How people respond to situations, therapies, drugs or other types of interventions in the relatively contrived and artificial setting of a laboratory or clinic may be quite different from how they respond in normal everyday life.

TABLE 2.3   AN EXPERIMENTAL RESEARCH PROJECT

Topic	Acupuncture for sports injuries
Research objectives or questions	To establish the effect on straight leg raise, hip internal rotation and muscle pain of dry needling (acupuncture) treatment to the gluteal muscles in athletes with posterior thigh pain referred from gluteal trigger points
Rationale and justification	Posterior thigh pain is a common problem identified in Australian Rules football players and participants in other running sports presenting at sports medicine clinics. Often these patients continue to participate in these sports despite reporting subjective performance limitations
Research methods	
Data sources	59 Australian male runners with hamstring pain
Data collection	Randomised, double-blind, placebo-controlled trial – observation (recorded by digital handycam) before and after treatment of participants' range of motion during passive straight leg raise and hip internal rotation; collection before and after treatment of visual analogue scale questionnaire data rating participants' hamstring and gluteal pain and tightness at rest
Data analysis	Numerical (quantitative) analysis where the effects of the intervention were compared in each group using a repeated measures analysis of variance

Source: Huguenin, L., Brukner, P.D., McCrory, P., Smith, P., Wajswelner, H. & Bennell, K. (2005). Effect of dry needling of gluteal muscles on straight leg raise: a randomised, placebo controlled, double blind trial. *British Journal of Sports Medicine*, *39*: 84–90

Content analysis

Content analysis refers to the general set of research approaches that aim to reveal or interpret the messages or meanings available in 'real world' objects or items made or produced by people. This includes objects or items of human communication such as novels, diaries, emails, blogs, scientific books, photographs, films, music, songs, dance, TV advertisements or posters. Content analysis research projects often seek to look behind the obvious messages conveyed in texts or images to try reveal largely hidden, secret or not-so-obvious meanings, beliefs or assumptions about aspects of the world or people that are being expressed, whether consciously or not (see Table 2.4). In related approaches, such as discourse analysis, conversational analysis or thematic analysis, recordings of discussions, interviews or everyday conversations with research participants are sometimes used as the raw data for analysis.

Existing data research

This is a type of general research approach where the data sources used are mainly *secondary* data, i.e. data other people have already collected and processed ready for researchers to use, such as official statistics or transcripts kept in oral-history archives.

A literature review is a good example of a research approach based on the analysis of existing data (for more details see Chapter 7, Doing a Literature Review). Normally a literature review will involve looking closely at the findings of previous published studies in an effort to summarise or critique them. This approach can often have value in situations where the collection of entirely new research data from *primary* sources is not possible because of time or resource constraints.

TABLE 2.4   A CONTENT ANALYSIS PROJECT

Topic	Alcohol messages on radio
Research objectives or questions	1. To examine the quantity and type of alcohol-related messages, including advertisements, broadcast on commercial music radio stations 2. To identify factors that radio station staff say influence the quantity and type of alcohol-related messages broadcast by their station
Rationale and justification	Alcohol advertising has been permitted on New Zealand radio since 1992. The broadcasting of alcohol-related messages is governed by various codes of practice, including codes specifying how alcohol should be portrayed. In order to evaluate the effectiveness of these codes, it is necessary to have detailed information about the actual alcohol-related messages broadcast on radio
Research methods *Data sources* *Data collection* *Data analysis*	 Radio station broadcasts. Radio station staff Audio tape recording of 714 hours of broadcasts from a sample of 17 commercial radio stations located. Face-to-face interviews with senior radio station staff Numerical (quantitative) and non-numerical (qualitative) analysis of all tape-recorded broadcasts to identify the frequency and types of alcohol-related messages. Messages coded into categories including: alcohol industry advertisements and sponsorship messages; health promotion advertisements and sponsorship messages; other alcohol-related messages. Non-numerical (qualitative) content analysis of taped interviews with radio station staff.

Source: Maskill, C. & Hodges, I. (1997). *Alcohol Messages on New Zealand Radio 1995/96*. Wellington: Alcohol Advisory Council of New Zealand

Systematic reviews and meta-analyses are two are other distinct types of existing data research. Both approaches mainly involve reviewing statistical data presented in previous studies. Systematic reviews usually aim to weigh up the strength of the total available research evidence relating to a particular research question or issue, e.g. the effectiveness of acupuncture for treatment of low back pain. Strict criteria are normally used to judge the quality of the statistical evidence presented in individual studies. Meta-analysis is a slightly different approach that mainly aims to *combine* the statistical results from several existing studies in an effort to provide more robust or reliable findings regarding whether or not a particular intervention, therapy or service is effective (see Table 2.5).

Historical research

As the name suggests, this research approach aims to reconstruct or analyse events that occurred in the past. Some of the main primary data sources used in this type of research include historical records such as old letters, diaries, public records, newspapers, magazines and other texts (see Table 2.6). The analysis performed on this information is usually qualitative or interpretive rather than quantitative, although the use of statistics is not uncommon in historical research.

Evaluation research

What makes evaluation research distinctive is not so much its choice of research methods as the types of topics or research questions on which it concentrates. Evaluation research

TABLE 2.5   AN EXISTING DATA RESEARCH PROJECT

Topic	School food programmes
Research objectives or questions	Do school food programmes improve the physical and psycho-social health of disadvantaged children?
Rationale and justification	Socio-economic differences in nutrition may be one of the most important factors causing socio-economic differences in health and mortality. Early malnutrition and/or micronutrient deficiencies can adversely affect children's physical and psycho-social health. Programmes providing food for students at school are designed to improve children's attendance, achievement, growth and other health outcomes. Considerable money is spent on these programmes, but are they effective?
Research methods	
Data sources	Previous research studies reporting results of trials (experiments) measuring the effects of school food programmes on socio-economically disadvantaged children
Data collection	Electronic and hand-searching of research journal articles, email communication with selected experts
Data analysis	Synthesis of statistical results from all relevant research reports (meta-analysis)

Source: Kristjansson, B., Petticrew, M., MacDonald, B., Krasevec, J., Janzen, L., Greenhalgh, T., et al. (2007). School feeding for improving the physical and psychosocial health of disadvantaged students. *Cochrane Database of Systematic Reviews*, January 24 (Issue 1). Art. No. CD004676

TABLE 2.6   AN HISTORICAL RESEARCH PROJECT

Topic	Origins of research ethics committees
Research objectives or questions	What were the interests and forces that underpinned the rapid expansion of research ethics committees in the United Kingdom in the late 1960s and early 1970s?
Rationale and justification	To date there has been very little historical research on how the UK's research ethics committees were originally set up and evolved
Research methods	
Data sources	Letters, memos, manuscripts, and other documents; previous research reports
Data collection	Retrieval of archived letters, memos, manuscripts from UK Royal College of Physicians Archive, Wellcome Library Archives, National Archives. Search and review of published research literature
Data analysis	Qualitative analysis and interpretation of textual material

Source: Hedgecoe, A. (2009). 'A form of practical machinery': The origins of research ethics committees in the UK, 1967–1972. *Medical History, 53,* 331–350

is concerned with investigating the conduct and impact of human services and social interventions. For this reason it has a very applied focus, aiming to determine what does and does not work in real world settings, and why. Questions addressed by evaluation research tend be along the lines of 'is the programme working?', 'how can we improve the service?' or 'how can this organisation be more effective?'.

Evaluation researchers often use a mixture of data collection methods in their projects (see Table 2.7). This can include surveys, focus groups, interviews, observation in natural settings and analysis of existing data. In some projects, certain kinds of experimental (or quasi-experimental) research techniques are also used. For example, to study the effects of introducing a free-food scheme into schools, some schools in a disadvantaged neighbour-hood may be given the scheme, while other similar schools in the neighbourhood are not (at least temporarily). Data collected in various ways from all the schools is then analysed to see if the schools with the free-food schemes changed in any way compared to the schools not receiving the scheme.

TABLE 2.7   AN EVALUATION PROJECT

Topic	Arts programmes in mental health care settings
Research objectives or questions	1. Is it feasible to run an eight-week multi-module creative arts programme in a secure inpatient psychiatric care unit? 2. Can barriers to creative expression by unit residents be overcome? 3. What are the benefits of the arts programme for unit residents' self-esteem, interactions with others, and perspectives on the world? 4. Does the presence of artists, art activities and completed art works in the unit enrich the life and work of unit residents and staff?
Rationale and justification	Research identifying the feasibility and impact of providing large-scale arts access programmes in mental health care settings is important for underpinning decisions on future support and funding
Research methods	
Data sources	Unit residents, unit staff, programme artists, events occurring in and around the unit, art works and other items produced during the programme
Data collection	Participant observation in events; semi-structured interviews with unit residents, unit staff and programme artists; questionnaire-based survey of unit staff
Data analysis	Non-numerical (qualitative) analysis of fieldwork and interview notes; numerical (quantitative) analysis of staff surveys

Source: Hodges, I. & Norton, V. (1991). *Artists at Stewart Villa: The Evaluation Report*. Wellington: Health Research Services, Department of Health

Other branches of evaluation research include *needs assessment* (sometimes called *needs analysis*) and *social impact assessment*. Needs assessments aim to identify gaps in services and ways of improving existing services in a neighbourhood, district or region. Community consultation is often a core element of this work. This typically involves conducting inter-views or focus groups with selected representatives of local community groups, service providers, political leaders, business people, and so on. In addition, relevant statistical data and other information might be compiled to help to better understand the nature and size of the issues under investigation.

Social impact assessment is a form of evaluation research mainly concerned with pre-dicting the likely future impact of major economic or business developments or policies on people living in a region or district. In this sense, it is a kind of social forecasting. However, social impact researchers sometimes also study what actually happens *after* the introduction of a new industry or service to a region or district.

Many forms of economic analysis, such as cost–benefit studies, can also be considered a type of evaluation research. These studies often aim to estimate the likely future costs and/or benefits of certain events or actions, such as the dollar costs of the health effects of cigarette use to the national economy. The data for these kinds of projects tend to come mainly from other studies, although the researcher may also consult directly with specialists or experts in certain fields to help determine the economic assumptions and cost estimates to be used in the research.

Conclusion: Designing a new research project

This chapter has provided a flavour of the diversity of research approaches or research 'styles' available in social and health research as a whole (see Table 2.8). Are any of these research methodologies similar to the approach you plan to take with your project?

TABLE 2.8 FEATURES OF DIFFERENT RESEARCH APPROACHES

	Research approaches						
	Survey research	Field research	Experiments	Content analysis	Existing data research	Historical research	Evaluation research
Data sources							
People	●	◖	●			◖	●
Events		●	◖				●
Items/objects		◖		●	●	●	●
Data collection methods							
Questionnaires	●		◖			○	●
Focus groups	◖	○					●
Interviews	◖	◖				◖	●
Observation in natural settings		●	◖				◖
Observation in laboratory or clinic settings			●				
Obtaining numerical secondary data sources					●	●	●
Obtaining non-numerical secondary data sources				●	●	●	●
Data analysis methods							
Numerical (quantitative)	●	◖	●	◖	●	◖	●
Non-numerical (qualitative)	◖	●	○	●	●	●	●

Key: ● Often used
    ◖ Sometimes used
    ○ Rarely used

The ability to design good, original research projects is a core skill that most researchers aspire to master as early as possible in their careers. This chapter has introduced some important basic principles of research design and provides a guide to some of the main issues we believe it is useful to think about when first developing a new project.

It must be emphasised that the chapter does not in any way set out to completely 'solve' the problem of how to design a new research project. Far from it. All it really aims to do is provide a roadmap to the process, as well as indicating some of the more important questions to ask along the way (Table 2.9). We do not provide any hard-and-fast answers to these questions. In fact we cannot. Finding them is up to you, based on your own reading, exploratory research and discussions with colleagues and advisers.

TABLE 2.9   CHECKLIST FOR DESIGNING A NEW RESEARCH PROJECT

Have you thought about:

- ☑   The topic of your research?
- ☑   Your project's main research objectives or research questions?
- ☑   Why you think these objectives or questions are important?
- ☑   Your underlying assumptions about the practice of social and health research? How much do your research objectives or questions reflect a positivist or an interpretivist stance?
- ☑   The people, events or items that will form the main data source/s for your project?
- ☑   How you are going to collect or gather data from these sources?
- ☑   Whether you are going to collect data from only a sample of your data sources? If you are, how you are going to select or create this sample?
- ☑   How you are going to analyse your data?
- ☑   Research ethics? What implications do these have for your research design decisions?
- ☑   Features of the setting, place or community where you plan to do your research. How could these constrain your research design decisions?
- ☑   Resourcing constraints (time, budget and staffing). What implications could these have for your research design decisions?
- ☑   How similar (or different) is your research design to the common research approaches used in social and health research?

Exercises for designing a new research project

1. Imagine you have won a $50,000 scholarship enabling you do research on any topic you like for the next 6 months. What topic would you choose? Why does this topic appeal to you? What specific research questions would you like to investigate?

2. Look around you right now. How many different types of potential data sources for social and health research can you identify? What kind of 'events' are happening? What kind of physical objects or items can you see that could be used as data sources?

3. Next time you are reading a research report or journal article on a topic that interests you, look carefully at what the author says about how data for the report was obtained. How would you describe the type of research design used for the study? Would you classify it as survey research, field research, an experiment, an evaluation, or some other type of research approach? Is the project mainly based on an analysis of primary or secondary data, or is it a mixture of both? Would you describe the study as 'positivist' or 'interpretivist'?

References and further reading

Babbie, E. (2007). *The Practice of Social Research.* Belmont, CA: Thomson Wadsworth.

Blaikie, N. (2000). *Designing Social Research: The Logic of Anticipation.* Cambridge: Polity Press.

Blaikie, N. (2007). *Approaches to Social Enquiry: Advancing Knowledge.* Cambridge: Polity Press.

Crotty, M. (1998). *The Foundations of Social Research: Meaning and Perspective in the Research Process.* St Leonards: Allen & Unwin.

Denscombe, M. (2002). *Ground Rules for Good Research: A 10-Point Guide for Social Research.* Buckingham: Open University Press.

McIntyre, A. (2008). *Participatory Action Research.* Thousand Oaks, CA: Sage.

3   Developing Research Aims and Objectives

Topics covered in this chapter

- Why defining your research objectives is important
- How to develop and write good research objectives and questions
- Common errors when writing research objectives
- Linking research objectives to research methods
- Developing research objectives for exploratory studies

A crucial task in any research project is defining its core objectives or questions. What is the central goal or purpose of the research? What research topics, questions or problems does the project intend to address, and why? Many projects get into difficulty because not enough time and thought is devoted at the start to properly defining the project's research goals. As a result, precious time and resources can be wasted collecting irrelevant or unnecessary research data.

This chapter looks at the process of defining a project's research objectives and questions. It offers tips on how to ensure your research objectives and questions are well thought out and clearly expressed. It also provides examples of well-written and not-so-well-written research aims and objectives, as a guide for people who might be struggling to get their aims and objectives down on paper.

What are research aims, objectives, questions and hypotheses?

In a research context, the terms 'research aim', 'research objectives', 'research questions' and 'research hypotheses' tend to have specific meanings. Table 3.1 defines these commonly used research terms. Study these definitions so you can apply them appropriately in your work.

Research aim

The term research aim usually refers to the main goal or overarching purpose of a research project. Sentences stating the aim of a project are usually quite brief and to the point. An example is:

Aim: To investigate factors associated with partner violence.

Because of their generality, research aims are almost always positioned at the very beginning of a statement of research aims and objectives (or questions). They are broad and introductory rather than specific and focused.

TABLE 3.1   COMMONLY USED TERMS RELATED TO RESEARCH AIMS

Term	Definition
Research aim	A statement indicating the general aim or purpose of a research project. Usually a research project will have only one broad aim
Research objectives	Specific statements indicating the key issues to be focused on in a research project. Usually a research project will have several specific research objectives
Research questions	An alternative to research objectives, where the key issues to be focused on in a research project are stated in the form of questions
Research hypotheses	A prediction of a relationship between two or more variables, usually predicting the effect of an *independent variable* on a *dependent variable*. The independent variable is the variable assumed to have causal influence on the outcome of interest, which is the dependent variable

Research objectives

A research aim will usually be followed by a series of statements describing a project's research objectives. Research objectives indicate in more detail the specific research topics or issues the project plans to investigate, building on the main theme stated in the research aim. Normally at least two or three research objectives will be stated. It is good practice to put these in a numbered list so they can be clearly identified later in a proposal or report. Here is an example of a set of research objectives:

> Objective 1: To examine whether alcohol consumption is associated with increased partner violence.
> Objective 2: To examine whether labour force status (employment, unemployment, not in the labour force) is associated with variations in the incidence of partner violence.
> Objective 3: To explore differences between couples with an extended history of partner violence and couples with only a brief, recent history of partner violence.

Research questions

In some situations, rather than stating research objectives, researchers will prefer to use research questions. In the example below, the objectives stated in the previous example are reframed as research questions:

> Question 1: Is alcohol consumption associated with increased partner violence?
> Question 2: Is labour force status (employment, unemployment, not in the labour force) associated with variations in the incidence of partner violence?
> Question 3: Are there differences between couples with an extended history of partner violence and couples with only a brief, recent history of partner violence?

Research hypotheses

Research hypotheses are predictions of a relationship between two or more variables. For example, a research project might hypothesise that higher consumption of alcohol (an independent variable) is associated with more incidents of partner violence (the dependent variable). Data would then be gathered and analysed statistically to see whether the results support the hypothesis or not.

> Hypothesis 1: Higher consumption of alcohol will be associated with more incidents of partner violence.

It is important to note that even if a research hypothesis is supported by the statistical analysis, it does not necessarily confirm that the independent variable (e.g., higher alcohol consumption) *causes* the differences observed in the dependent variable (e.g. partner violence). Establishing causation requires rigorous research designs (such as experimental designs) and more than one study.

In general, hypotheses are used only in quantitative research, not qualitative research, and normally only when previous research, or a literature review, indicates a specific prediction is warranted. Some studies present hypotheses instead of research objectives, while others present a combination of research objectives and hypotheses.

How to develop and write good research aims and objectives

Good, clear statements indicating a project's research aims, objectives or questions do not normally spring forth fully formed in a sudden eureka moment. They tend to emerge slowly, after considerable thought, and take time to develop and finalise.

When first designing a project, try to give yourself plenty of time to think through your aims and objectives. Ideally, this thinking should not be done in a hurry or under pressure. Read around your subject. Analyse previous studies in the area. Look at how other researchers frame their aims and objectives. What key technical terms or concepts do they employ? The better you understand the published literature on your topic, the more likely you are to be able to effectively conceptualise your own research aims and objectives.

If you are doing a formal literature review as part of your study, try to link your research objectives directly to the main conclusions of your review. This can strengthen the case for your study by showing how your research objectives build on the current state of knowledge. (For guidance on how to do a literature review, see Chapter 7.) When reviewing published articles on research topics similar to the one you are planning, look at how the authors have phrased their research objectives. Taking objectives or questions from an existing study (e.g., Box 3.1) and reviewing how clear they are, can help you think about how to frame your own research objectives.

Box 3.1   Example of research questions

1. Does students' fruit/vegetable intake vary between schools and does this between-school variation remain after adjusting for the student composition of schools?
2. Are school-level effects consistent across different measures of fruit/vegetable intake?
3. Does school availability influence intake of fruit/vegetables among boys and girls differently?

> 4. Do students from homes with low availability consume more fruit/vegetables if enrolled in schools with high availability of fruit/vegetables versus schools with low availability?
>
> *Source*: Krølner, Due, Rasmussen, Damsgaard, Holstein, Klepp, et al., 2009, p. 1417

Another important way to help clarify your research aims and objectives is to write them down and ask other people to comment on them. Draft up an initial statement of your aims and objectives. Revise it until you are satisfied with it as an opening or provisional attempt to describe your goals. Show it to colleagues, supervisors, friends and family. Ask them what they think. Do they understand what you mean? Do they agree with the particular objectives you have chosen? Do they regard them as feasible?

Use all the feedback you get from other people as a basis for critically assessing the clarity, relevance, logical consistency and practicality of your research aims and objectives. This should help ensure your project starts off on the right foot and minimise the scope for you (or other people) to later become dissatisfied with your stated research goals.

Common errors when writing research aims and objectives

The clarity and precision of a statement of research aims and objectives can be reduced in a number of ways. Examples of some of the more common errors are shown in the boxes below. Reflect on these and try to avoid them in your own work.

One quite frequent error is collapsing all the information on a project's research aim and research objectives into a single paragraph (see Box 3.2). This makes it hard for readers to absorb the information and distinguish the project's overall research aim from its more specific research objectives. A project's general research aim and specific research objectives should be clearly distinguished. Present them in separate sentences or paragraphs. Each research objective should be numbered.

Box 3.2   Single statement combining aim and objectives

This project aims to investigate factors associated with partner violence and in particular whether alcohol consumption and labour force status (employment, unemployment, not in the labour force) is associated with increased partner violence, and whether there are differences between couples with an extended history of partner violence and couples with only a brief, recent history of partner violence.

Another common error is phrasing research aims or objectives in such a way that their meaning is vague or ambiguous (see Box 3.3). It is important that a final statement of research aims and objectives minimises the potential for misunderstanding or misinterpretation by readers.

Box 3.3   Ambiguous aims

This project aims to investigate partner violence and:

1. Alcohol consumption in couples with a history of partner violence
2. The labour force status of couples engaged in partner violence
3. Couples with an extended history of partner violence and couples with only a brief, recent history of partner violence

---

Occasionally, a mix of research objectives and research questions will be presented as a single list (Box 3.4). This can be quite confusing and difficult to follow. A better approach is to list only a series of research objectives or only a series of research questions.

Box 3.4   Mixing objectives and questions

This project aims to investigate factors associated with partner violence. More specifically, it aims to:

1. Examine whether alcohol consumption is associated with increased partner violence.
2. Is labour force status (employment, unemployment, not in the labour force) associated with variations in the incidence of partner violence?
3. Are there differences between couples with an extended history of partner violence and couples with only a brief, recent history of partner violence?

Another reasonably common error is confusing 'research objectives' with 'project objectives'. As indicated above, research objectives refer to the areas of knowledge the project is aiming to build on or advance. Project objectives are something quite different. They are the practical steps involved in getting the day-to-day work of the project completed. Examples of project objectives include completing fieldwork or interviews within a scheduled timeframe, writing a project report, or communicating project results to different audiences.

Occasionally, researchers incorrectly include project objectives in their statement of research objectives. In the example shown in Box 3.5, the first objective is a research objective, the second and third objectives are project objectives. Combining research and project objectives in a single list is not appropriate as the focus of the statement should be the project's research goals, not processes associated with the management of the project or the dissemination of findings. Project objectives should be listed separately in the project management section of a research proposal and linked to a project timeline.

Box 3.5   Mixing research and project objectives

This project aims to investigate factors associated with partner violence.

Objective 1: To examine whether alcohol consumption is associated with increased partner violence.

(Continued)

(Continued)

Objective 2: To complete face-to-face interviews with a purposive sample of 10 couples with a history of partner violence by 20 September 2010.
Objective 3: To present the final results of the study to a meeting of representatives of key stakeholder groups in December 2010.

Linking research objectives to research methods

Having a clear understanding of a project's research objectives or questions paves the way for other important decisions about the design and running of the project. This includes decisions about which populations or demographic groups to include in the study and what data collection methods to use.

In some poorly designed studies the research methods chosen for the study do not properly match the research objectives. As a result, the data obtained often does not directly address the research objectives. Think carefully about the relationship between your research objectives or questions and your choice of research methods. Aim to describe as clearly as possible how the sampling, data gathering and analysis methods you intend to use will help meet each of the research objectives or questions.

An example of a description of the links between research objectives and research methods is shown below in Table 3.2. It refers to a project interested in identifying factors that may encourage people living in urban environments to go walking more often than they normally do. In the table, each research objective is linked to the specific samples of people from whom information will be gathered. Also shown are the data gathering methods that will be used (interviews), plus some examples of topics or questions that

TABLE 3.2   RESEARCH OBJECTIVES AND DATA COLLECTION METHODS FOR A STUDY OF WALKABILITY IN URBAN ENVIRONMENTS

Research objectives	Data sources (samples)	Methods	Examples of questions
1. To examine the specific factors that influence people to walk in urban environments	Pedestrians and drivers of motor vehicles	Interviews	What makes it more likely for you to walk? What places or routes are you most likely to walk? Why do you walk in these places? What places would you not walk? Why?
2. To identify what physical features contribute to the walkability of urban environments	Pedestrians Urban planners	Interviews Key informant interviews	What aspects of the physical environment make it easier for you to walk? what places do you most often see people walking?
3. To identify what physical features relating to walkability can be enhanced by urban planners	Urban planners	Key informant interviews	What are some examples of physical changes which have increased the number of people walking?

could be covered in the interviews. This helps show the logical connection between the research methods chosen and the project's research objectives.

Developing a table such as this is recommended for researchers starting out on their first project, to check that the proposed data gathering methods will clearly produce data that addresses the stated research objectives.

Another example of how to link specific research objectives to data gathering methods is shown in Table 3.3. In this example, the project topic is an evaluation of the effectiveness of a training programme. The table indicates the links between each of the project's seven research questions and the different data sources and data gathering methods to be used during the evaluation.

TABLE 3.3   RESEARCH QUESTIONS AND DATA COLLECTION METHODS FOR EVALUATION OF A TRAINING PROGRAMME

Research questions	Data sources	Methods
1. To what extent is the training delivered as planned?	Trainers and training sessions	Key informant interviews Training documents Observation of training sessions
2. What innovations or adaptations not in the original plan are used by trainers when delivering the training programme?	Trainers and training sessions	Key informant interviews Observation of training sessions
3. What resource and implementation issues arise during the training programmes	Training manager and trainers	Key informant interviews
4. What do programme participants report as their most important learning outcomes?	Programme participants	End of workshop and 6-month follow-up surveys
5. Do programme participants identify any limitations or gaps in the training programme?	Programme participants	End of workshop and 6-month follow-up surveys
6. To what extent do participants report using their learning in practice?	Programme participants	6-month follow-up surveys
7. To what extent will the training programme be suitable for use by other practitioner groups?	Training manager and trainers	Key informant interviews

Developing research objectives for exploratory studies

In exploratory studies, research aims and objectives may need to be framed in a relatively open-ended way. In these studies, researchers are usually investigating a topic about which very little is known. For this reason they may want to keep their initial research aims and objectives reasonably non-specific or general, or perhaps include an option to alter their original research objectives if the project reveals unexpected information. This way of doing things is particularly common in qualitative, open-ended research studies, especially those conducted as a preliminary to designing larger, more structured or intensive studies on new or emerging issues. Some examples of objectives from qualitative exploratory studies are shown in Box 3.6.

Box 3.6   Examples of research objectives from exploratory studies

… we set out to explore how evidence of serious adverse effects from SSRIs [selective serotonin reuptake inhibitors] is managed by those who have a professional stake in using or promoting the drugs. Specifically, we were interested in identifying and unpacking the rhetorical strategies available in response to the dilemma that this evidence presented to their support of SSRIs. (Liebert and Gavey, 2009)

This paper … [explores] how ritualised practices in primary care clinics may embody and entrench power relations, being potentially functional for some constituencies while being dysfunctional for others. (Lewin and Green, 2009)

… we conducted an ethnographic study of technology transfer offices (TTOs) in Canada in 2007, to consider the place of health and health system imperatives in judgments of value in early-stage health innovation. (Miller, Sanders and Lehoux, 2009)

By contrast, it is more feasible to adopt a very specific, tightly defined set of research objectives at the start of a study and apply them consistently throughout if a lot is already known about the study topic from previous studies.

If you are doing a project where the research objectives evolve or change over the course of the project, aim to keep a record of the different objectives applying at each stage of the project so you can refer to these later in research reports (see Box 3.7).

Box 3.7   How objectives evolved during a project literature review

In a project involving a literature review looking at public knowledge about the risk factors for cardiovascular disease (CVD), with which one of the authors (DRT) worked on, the initial review objectives, as set out in the research proposal, were to focus on:

1. Specific risk factors for CVD
2. Public awareness of risk factors
3. Questionnaires and specific questions used to measure public awareness of risk factors

Part-way through the process of carrying out the literature review the review objectives were revised. The focus changed to:

1. Sample and survey methods used to study public knowledge of CVD risk factors
2. Types of questions included in CVD surveys
3. Differences in knowledge among population groups
4. Interventions to improve knowledge about CVD and reduce the risk of CVD

The team made these revisions to the objectives as it became clearer what the important priorities for the review were, after reading the literature.

Before committing to projects likely to involve considerable research time and resources, aim to do some exploratory information gathering to get a feel for the practicality or feasibility of the project's research objectives. Sometimes an initial field exploration may lead to major changes in a project's research objectives (see Box 3.8).

Box 3.8   Changing research objectives

Even though a project's research objectives are finalised and written down, they can still be modified later, or even completely changed.

Leroy is a postgraduate student with an interest in youth car culture – boy-racers. He does not consider himself to be a boy-racer – he only rides a small scooter – but he is intrigued by how so many other young men his age seem to be obsessed with powerful cars, speed and big noisy stereos. After discussions with his supervisor, Leroy decides he would like to do an ethnographic study of some of the local boy-racer groups in his city. This would involve hanging out and getting to know some boy-racers and riding with them in their cars at night.

As a first step towards developing the project, Leroy does some initial reading on the topic. He finds there are already several studies of boy-racers published in the academic literature. However, none of these studies looked specifically at boy-racers in Leroy's city or region.

Leroy spends two months putting together a detailed project proposal for his supervisor outlining his research plans and how he would do the fieldwork. The proposal includes a list of Leroy's research objectives. These all relate to trying to better understand the motivations and experiences that encourage young men to become boy-racers.

After obtaining approval from his university's ethics committee to proceed with the study, Leroy starts out on his first week of fieldwork. Eventually, after several hours hanging about nervously in backstreet neighbourhoods after dark, he gets to talk to some boy-racers parked up at the kerb. After telling them about his study plans, the boy-racers eventually agree to take Leroy for a ride to give him a first-hand introduction to the boy-racing culture.

Within moments, Leroy is in the back seat of the car of his newly found research participants roaring along the inner city streets. In the hours that follow Leroy and his fellow passengers participate in burnouts, donuts, quarter mile drag races, drifting and numerous other competitive car stunts that leave Leroy's mind reeling and his heart thumping. On at least three occasions Leroy is sure he is about to die or be seriously injured in a car crash.

Meeting with his supervisor the next day, Leroy announces that he is intending to modify his research plans as he no longer regards his current research objectives to be feasible or safe. He indicates he plans to develop a new research project looking at the culture of multi-player Internet computer car racing games and why young men find these games so compelling.

In later chapters, we will refer to research aims and objectives again. As will be seen, the work put into developing clear and feasible objectives will pay off in subsequent stages of your research project by providing a core organising framework that assists with preparing literature reviews and research proposals, managing your project's data collection and analysis, and writing research reports.

Exercises for developing research objectives

1. Develop a suitable research aim and three specific objectives for a research topic in which you have an interest.
2. Change the research objectives you developed above into research questions.
3. Using personal contacts or an Internet search, find some examples of completed research proposals on a topic in which you are interested. Note the style used to write the research aims and objectives.

(Continued)

(Continued)

4. Locate three recent journal articles covering a topic in which you are interested. Look at the introduction section of each article. How well do you think the authors describe their research aims or objectives? In what ways could their aims or objectives be written more clearly?

References and further reading

Creswell, J. W. (2009). *Research Design: Qualitative, Quantitative, and Mixed Method Approaches* (3rd edn). Thousand Oaks, CA: Sage. (See Chapter 7)

Krølner, R., Due, P., Rasmussen, M., Damsgaard, M. T., Holstein, B. E., Klepp, K.-I., et al. (2009). Does school environment affect 11-year-olds' fruit and vegetable intake in Denmark? *Social Science & Medicine, 68* (8), 1416–1424.

Lewin, S. & Green, J. (2009). Ritual and the organisation of care in primary care clinics in Cape Town, South Africa. *Social Science & Medicine, 68* (8), 1464–1471.

Liebert, R., & Gavey, N. (2009). 'There are always two sides to these things': managing the dilemma of serious adverse effects from SSRIs. *Social Science & Medicine, 68* (10), 1882–1891.

Miller, F. A., Sanders, C. B., & Lehoux, P. (2009). Imagining value, imagining users: academic technology transfer for health innovation. *Social Science & Medicine, 68* (8), 1481–1488.

Punch, K. F. (2005). *Introduction to Social Research: Quantitative and Qualitative Approaches* (2nd edn). London: Sage. (See Chapter 3)

4   Preparing and Writing a Research Proposal

Topics covered in this chapter

- Why prepare a research proposal?
- Planning a proposal
- Drafting a proposal
- A model structure for a proposal
- Reviewing and finalising a proposal

A research proposal is a detailed written plan for a research project. It describes the aims of the project, why the research project is important and how the project will be carried out. It also indicates the timeframes and resources needed for the project. Knowing how to write good research proposals is central to getting support, both professional and financial, for your research ideas and projects.

Why prepare a research proposal?

Writing a research proposal can be useful in a number of ways. Table 4.1 summarises some common reasons for writing proposals.

When designing a new research project, writing a research proposal can help structure and focus the thinking you do about the project's research objectives and research methodology. If you commit your project plans to paper they are more likely to be well thought through, logical and realistic.

Once you have prepared an initial draft of your research proposal, this can be circulated to other people for comment. Colleagues, supervisors, community representatives, potential research participants and others can look at the details of what you are planning to do and provide feedback. This can be useful for refining your research aims or objectives, checking the feasibility of your intended research methodology, encouraging other researchers to join the project, identifying potential funding or other resources, and arranging initial approvals to access key people or data.

Once you have prepared a final version of your research proposal, this can be used to obtain official approval to commence your project from supervisors, managers, host institutions or ethics committees. Many research projects will not be able to start until their feasibility, risks and benefits have been formally assessed. Submitting a written research plan is usually a vital part of this process.

Writing a research proposal will also be useful if you are aiming to get financial support for your project from research funding agencies or sponsors. Most potential funders will need to see a detailed written project plan before agreeing to support a project.

Once a project begins, a research proposal can be used as a framework for organising and managing the day-to-day work of a project. For example, a timeline in a research

TABLE 4.1 REASONS FOR WRITING A RESEARCH PROPOSAL

Reason	Rationale
To focus thinking	Preparing a research proposal can assist with the process of designing a new research project. Writing research plans down on paper encourages deeper thinking about their appropriateness or feasibility
To get feedback	A written proposal can be circulated to colleagues, supervisors and others to get feedback about the suitability of a project design. Comments people give can result in the design being significantly improved
To obtain formal approval	Before a project can officially start, a finished proposal may need to be approved by supervisors, managers, host institutions or ethics committees
To apply for funding	If a project requires external funding to be viable, a research proposal can form the basis of funding applications to potential sponsors
To assist project planning and management	Once a project starts, parts of a proposal (e.g., the timeline) can provide a framework for organising and managing the day-to-day work of the project
To document how a project was carried out	After a project is finished, a written proposal can form part of the records used to indicate how the project was carried out. It can also be used to check a project was done in the way it was originally intended for audit, funding or ethical reasons

proposal can be adapted to create a detailed task list showing how and when different project tasks will actually be carried out.

Another good reason for preparing a research proposal is to provide a written record of how it was expected a project would be conducted. Sometimes, after a project is finished, there may be queries about how aspects of the project were carried out. A written proposal can form part of the evidence used to trace back when and how certain things were done. Similarly, a written proposal can also be used as a basis for verifying that a project has been conducted as it was originally intended, for audit, funding or ethical reasons.

Planning a proposal

Before starting work on your proposal, do some background reading on the research topic. Conduct at least a preliminary literature search and review some key readings (see Chapter 7, Doing a Literature Review). Find out what other work has already been done on the topic.

Consult with people with specialist knowledge of the topic. Ask them what they think about your research plans. The more feedback you can get from knowledgeable people about your research intentions, the more likely you are to end up with a good study design.

Make sure you are clear about your study's research objectives and the main research methods you intend to use (see Chapters 2 and 3 for guidance on this). The better your project objectives and methods are conceptualised before starting to write your proposal, the easier it should be to write your proposal. Poorly thought-through project plans will hinder the writing of a research proposal. Aim to start with a coherent framework already in mind. Ideally, this should be sketched out on paper and used as a basis for preparing the first draft of your proposal.

If you are hoping to get other people to work closely with you on the project – whether in an advisory capacity (e.g., statistical analysis, analysis of qualitative interviews) or as a part of a research team – involve these people as soon as possible in the proposal development process. Discuss with them what you are hoping to do, and why. Find out how willing they are to support your project and how much time they could potentially commit to assisting you with it. If necessary, determine how your project plans may need to be modified so potential collaborators feel more comfortable with them.

If your project is likely to involve research participants from specific interest groups or cultures, it will be important at an early stage to discuss the proposed research with representatives from these groups or communities. These people may end up having an advisory role throughout the project or even become part of the project team.

Many research institutions and agencies now require all research proposals they support, regardless of the topic, to address how the project might affect or assist indigenous or minority peoples. If this is the case for you, get suggestions and advice from other researchers who have experience on these issues about how to incorporate this information into your proposal.

If a team of people is working on the preparation of a research proposal, ideally nominate one team member to coordinate the process and draft the project proposal. Their responsibilities could include:

- arranging regular team meetings to review aspects of the research design
- revising draft proposals and circulating them for comment
- compiling literature
- liaising with ethical committees
- arranging consultations with stakeholder and community representatives
- investigating funding sources and funding application processes
- preparing budget details
- obtaining and refining team members' CVs.

Drafting a proposal

It is a good idea to start writing a proposal by first mapping out its main headings and sub-headings. The next section presents a suggested structure for this. It also indicates the type of information to include under each heading and sub-heading.

A research proposal should be written as clearly and concisely as possible. Try to use plain language. Only use specialised technical terms when absolutely necessary. Aim to maintain a consistent writing style, especially if there's more than one person involved in the writing process.

Be prepared to write several drafts of a project proposal. Feedback on drafts from interested colleagues and stakeholders will normally produce a range of new information and ideas. Sections of a proposal may have to be revised, sometimes quite heavily, to incorporate this fresh material. For more tips on general writing techniques see Chapter 12 on writing for research.

A model structure for a research proposal

Table 4.2 provides an overview of a generic structure for organising a research proposal. The structure shown can be used as a general guide for preparing your own proposals. It

TABLE 4.2   STRUCTURE FOR A PROPOSAL

Proposal section	Description of content
Cover page	Title of proposal, authors name(s) and contact details, date proposal prepared
Summary	For proposals longer than about six pages, provide a 300–400 summary of the main features, including the objectives and proposed research design
Introduction	Provides the context for the research, including: the goals and objectives of the proposed project, the 'problem' addressed, why the problem is important and key literature sources
Research design	Describes the research design and methods to be used in the project, including: the sampling plan and data gathering procedures, methods of data analysis, the rationale for the choice of methods and the ethical review plan
Dissemination of research findings	A summary of the ways in which the project results will be communicated to others and the primary audiences for the research findings
Timeline	The research timeline (or timetable) lists the major phases of the research project in time sequence, along with the key tasks to be completed in each phase
Resources required	Summarises the resources needed to do the research, including people, services and equipment. May include a detailed budget
Management of the project	Describes the people who will be responsible for conducting the research project and their relevant experience
References	A list of all publications and other source material referred to in the proposal

could also be modified or extended to include other information if required. Good proposal writing often requires artful adaptation of a proposal to suit the different purposes for which it might be used. More detail is given below about the types of information to cover in the sections listed in Table 4.2.

Cover page

The cover page is positioned at the very front of the research proposal. Normally it presents the following key information:

- *Title of proposal,* indicating briefly and clearly (maximum 12 words) what the research project intends to study or investigate. It is good practice to include the word 'proposal' in the title.
- *Author(s) name,* affiliation, postal address, email address and contact phone number.
- *Date* this version of the proposal was completed.
- The *name(s)* and contact details for the main client organisation, group or service involved (if relevant).

Box 4.1 gives an example of how to set out a cover page.

Box 4.1   Example of cover page

PROPOSAL TO EVALUATE THE FAMILY COUNSELLING PROGRAMME AT
BROWNS BAY FAMILY SERVICES

Jill S. Researcher

Department of Applied Social Science

University of Auckland

Private Bag 98765, Auckland

Phone: Day (909) 3737599 Ext 1234

Mobile 022-234-5678

Email: j.researcher@research.org

27 May 2010

Prepared for:

Jocelin Caregiver

Director, Browns Bay Family Services

P.O. Box 1234, Auckland

Phone (909) 862-1439

Summary

If your proposal is longer than about six pages (whether single or double spaced), at the beginning provide a summary describing the main elements of your research project, including:

- the purposes or objectives of the project
- the main research procedures to be used
- the project's expected start and finish dates
- the total estimated cost of the project (if the proposal includes a budget)
- the people or organisations providing funding or other resources for the project.

Do not include unnecessary or trivial information in the summary. Ideally, it should be only about 300–400 words long and formatted so it fits on a single page. Position the summary on a separate page immediately following the cover page. Alternatively, a very short summary (e.g. 6–8 lines) could be placed near the bottom of the cover page if there is room.

The best time to write a summary is after finalising all other sections of the proposal. This avoids having to continually update the summary as you make changes to other parts of the proposal.

Introduction

A proposal's Introduction should outline the goals of the research project, the central 'problem' it intends to address, and why the problem is important. Key literature sources should be referred to where relevant. Ideally the Introduction should also indicate:

- how the proposed research will make a contribution to knowledge relating to the problem
- how generalisable the research findings might be
- the possible contribution of the research to theory
- the potential practical applications of the research (where relevant).

Information presented in the Introduction can be arranged under the following sub-headings:

- Aims and objectives
- Need or problem statement
- Background
- Significance of the research

Below is a description of what to include in each of these sub-sections.

Aim and objectives

This summarises the overall aim and/or specific objectives of the research project. Objectives can be numbered and listed if appropriate. If using a list, it should be introduced with suitable text. Specific, achievable research objectives provide clear criteria against which the proposed research methods can be assessed. In quantitative research, research objectives may be stated as hypotheses or specific models to be tested. If existing theory or knowledge permits, an explicit hypothesis that predicts research outcomes can be written. Do not use *null hypotheses* (e.g., statements that there will be no significant relationships between variables or differences between groups), as these are usually inappropriate in a proposal. (For more detail on defining and writing research objectives, see Chapters 2 and 3.)

Be careful in this section not to promise more for your project than can be delivered. A broad and complex problem is unlikely to be solvable or manageable in a single research project.

Need or problem statement

This describes the problem or issue the research addresses. Points to discuss here include:

- key features of the problem or issue
- why the research is needed
- causes of the problem or circumstances creating the need
- approaches or solutions that have been tried so far.

Background

This should outline the context and history surrounding the development of your research proposal. In particular, it should include information on:

- the proposed setting or location of the research (e.g., service, organisation). What organisations, programmes or services are involved? Are any approvals required for the research or has approval been given?
- characteristics of the communities, organisations, clients or consumers who might have an interest in the research (often referred to as 'stakeholders')
- features of the people who have helped define the project's objectives and scope
- who will benefit from the research
- who might use the project's findings
- your connection to the research problem and/or key people or groups (stakeholders) with an interest in the study.

In this sub-section it could also be useful to include a brief review (1–2 pages) of relevant research literature addressing points such as:

- the extent of the problem or issue in your country or internationally
- key findings from previous research on the topic
- gaps in existing research.

Significance of the research

This should describe how the project will make a contribution to knowledge. If relevant, indicate the extent to which the project's findings might be generalised to other settings, contribute to theory building, or have practical applications (e.g., to policy development or service delivery).

Research design

This section (sometimes called the Research Methods section) should describe, as fully as possible, the research techniques to be used in the project. Specific information to cover here includes:

- sampling plan and data gathering procedures
- methods of data analysis
- the rationale behind the choice of methods (why the research methods chosen are appropriate to the research questions being investigated; advantages they offer over other methods)
- potential methodological problems that could arise and strategies that will be used to handle them.

Where appropriate, findings from the literature can be cited briefly here (e.g., to indicate the reliability of an existing survey questionnaire or other research instrument to be used in the project).

When setting out the research design section, the following structure is recommended:

- Overview of research design
- Sample
- Data gathering methods (sometimes labelled –'measures,''tools' or 'instruments')
- Procedures
- Data analysis
- Ethical review.

Overview of research design

Begin by briefly summarising the main features of the research methodology. This can be especially important if the research design is complex. Outline the general type of research design to be used (see Box 4.2 for examples).

Box 4.2   Common research designs

Quantitative designs

- a single sample
- a case–control prospective observational design (e.g., with intervention and comparison groups)

(Continued)

(Continued)

- an experimental design with two or more groups where the researcher allocates participants into each group.

Qualitative designs

- a single sample
- a stratified sample design where potential participants are sampled across one or more variables to ensure sufficient numbers in each sub-group (e.g., gender, ethnicity, experience of specific services).

Sample

This sub-section should indicate the project's expected overall sample size or anticipated total number of research participants. If sub-samples are planned, also indicate the size for each of the sub-samples. If the project intends to use focus groups, the sample size for the project is the number of focus groups, not the number of participants in the groups.

The characteristics of the population group or groups from which the project's research participants or sample/s will be selected should also be indicated (e.g., men and women between 20 and 50 years of age living in a specific city or location).

Data gathering methods (measures, instruments, tools)

This sub-section should outline the data gathering instruments or tools to be used in the project. Common examples include:

- key informant interviews
- focus group interviews
- surveys (e.g., using telephone interviews or self-completion questionnaires)
- selection and examination of documents and records
- observation of participants.

When choosing the data gathering methods to use in a project, make sure they are consistent with the project's central research objectives. Try to avoid including questions or topics that are unlikely to yield information relevant to your objectives.

If new survey instruments are to be designed especially for the project, sufficient time must be allocated early in the project to develop and pilot test these. A new questionnaire or interview schedule may need to be tested and redrafted several times before it is ready to administer to a large sample.

Procedures

Describe here how the project's data collection measures, tools or instruments will be administered. Cover key information such as:

- how, when, where and by whom participants will be contacted, given information about the project and asked to participate
- how consent will be obtained
- how, when, where and by whom the project's data collection measures, tools or instruments will be administered or applied

- any special precautions or procedures that will be needed because of the nature of the research or the characteristics of the participants (e.g., how consent to participate will be obtained from people who have a first language other than English)
- how the research data will be recorded (e.g., for interviews, will written notes or an audio tape recorder be used).

If you intend to return interview transcripts or other project data to participants for comment or checking, state specifically how this will be done.

If a research project will include a number of data collection stages or phases (e.g., if your project is a multi-methods study), aim to describe the procedures to be used in each stage or phase in separate sub-sections or paragraphs. This should make it clearer to readers what data collection procedures are to be used, when and in what order.

Data analysis

This section should outline how the data will be collated and analysed. Data cleaning and checking procedures should also be briefly discussed.

Qualitative data (e.g., interview transcripts, notes from focus groups) are usually stored in a computer using word-processing software. Analysis of this material normally involves developing a set of categories, topic areas or themes. Any data storage system used should allow for easy identification and retrieval of case study material and quotations. There are several commercial database software packages available that can assist with the analysis of qualitative data, including the calculation of frequencies and percentages if required. Examples include Lotus Approach, Paradox, QSR NVivo and Ethnograph. Chapter 9 provides more information about qualitative analysis software.

Quantitative data are normally entered into a computer file using software such as a spreadsheet, a database or a specialist statistical software package. Data are usually first checked for completeness, then coded in preparation for analysis. Quantitative data are normally analysed using a statistical package. Examples of these are SPSS, SAS, and Minitab. Other software is also available for creating graphs and figures directly from data.

If you have no prior experience with either the quantitative or qualitative data analysis software you plan to use, allow time (e.g., several days or weeks) to learn how to use the software. Aim to carry out a small trial analysis on the project data before starting the main data analysis.

Ethical review

This sub-section should discuss ethical issues relevant to the proposed research. If the project intends collecting new information from individuals or groups, or accessing existing confidential or unpublished information or data, the research proposal will probably need to be assessed by an appropriate ethical review committee (for more detail on this see Chapter 6, Research Ethics and Ethics Reviews). If this is the case, describe the procedures to be used to ensure the project is conducted ethically: for example, how research participants will be recruited on the basis of informed consent; steps to be taken to minimise the risk of harm or injury to research participants or research team members; procedures for protecting confidential information.

If researchers on the project are bound by the code of ethics or guidelines of a professional body or association (e.g., psychological society, sociological association, evaluation society), the implications of this may also need to be discussed in this section.

Dissemination of research findings

This section should indicate the ways the project results will be communicated to others. It should identify the expected main audience for the project findings and the specific procedures to be used to distribute the results to these people. These could include oral or written briefings, technical reports, seminars, conference presentations, non-technical reports, talks at public meetings, journal articles and so on (for more detail see Chapter 11, Communicating Research Findings).

If it is intended to prepare a final report of the project, describe how this will be prepared and who will review initial and final drafts. Where appropriate, identify people who will be given an oral briefing on the research findings when the project is finished and who will receive copies of the final project report (include approximate dates). Good practice for dissemination is to send a summary (e.g., 2–4 pages) to all interested parties and a copy of the full research report to key project stakeholders. The distribution list for the full report should be made clear in the proposal. If relevant, describe procedures that will be used to communicate the findings to other potential users of the research besides the primary stakeholders or clients (e.g, a media release, production of a general non-technical report).

Remember to allow for at least one copy of the final report to be provided to each of the researchers working on the project. One researcher should be designated as the contact person for the project and be responsible for holding electronic copies of all datasets and reports after the project is finished.

Timeline

A research timeline (or timetable) should chronologically list the major phases of the research project, along with the key tasks to be completed in each phase. Typically, start and finish dates for the overall project are indicated, as well as perhaps start and finish dates for each main phase. The timetable can either be set out as a list of main headings and subheadings (Box 4.3 shows an example of this) or as a table. If a table is used, summarise the start and finish dates for major sections of the project in the accompanying text.

Box 4.3   Example of a timeline

Month 1 **(Planned start date: March 2010)**
Initial proposal prepared
Project proposal submitted for ethical review
Literature search started
Initial development of items for interview schedule
Contact organisations for approval to recruit clients as participants
Purchase and learn how to use qualitative data analysis software

Months 2–3
Initial literature review completed
Interview schedule finalised
Pilot testing of interview schedule with four interviewees
Revision of interview questions
Initial data entry and start of qualitative data analysis
Main interviewing started

(Continued)

(Continued)

Month 4
30 interviews completed
Data analysis partly completed …(etc.)

When devising a timeline, one approach is to work backwards from the planned completion date for the project (where known). This involves estimating the amount of time likely to be required to complete the last task on the list, then counting backwards (e.g., in days or weeks) to the required starting time for that task. This process is then repeated for each task further up the list, until the start and finish times for all tasks are calculated.

After completing this exercise, many researchers are surprised to find they should have started their project several months earlier! Normally there are only two possible solutions to this predicament: either reduce the size of the project to a realistic level so that it can be done in the time available, or significantly extend the finishing date for the project.

Resources required

This section should summarise the resources needed to do the research. This includes people, services and equipment. Typical examples are:

- researcher(s) time
- travel and accommodation
- access to computers for data entry, data analysis and report writing
- data entry services and equipment
- data analysis services and equipment
- transcription and word processing services
- photocopying and printing
- electronic communications, equipment (e.g., tape recorder, batteries), stationery, postage.

Usual practice is to list the resources required under separate headings such as 'personnel', 'equipment' and 'advisory services'.

It should be indicated if professional or technical assistance for project planning, monitoring or data analysis is required. This could include supervision by experienced researchers, advice on statistical analysis, or advice on qualitative data analysis.

If it is not obvious why certain resources are required, the reasons should be explained when listing the resource. For example, under travel it will be important to explain the destinations of trips and their purpose.

In some research proposals, especially those used to apply for funding, it may be necessary to provide an estimate of the total number of hours (or days) of work that will be required to complete the project. To work this out, first estimate how many person hours or days it will take to do each project task. Then add these up to get the estimated total number of hours or days of work needed for the entire project.

Bear in mind it can be very difficult at the start of a project to accurately predict how much time it will involve. Experience suggests some projects will take at least double the time initially predicted.

Budget

In some proposals, especially those intended to be reviewed by funding agencies, it may be necessary to include a budget showing a project's estimated monetary costs. Normally a

TABLE 4.3 EXAMPLE OF A RESEARCH BUDGET

Type of cost	Cost calculations	Amount
Researcher time	100 hours × $50	$5,000
Focus group facilitation	3 groups @ $1000	$3,000
Interviewers	30 interviews @ $40	$1,200
Travel for interviews	800 km @ 0.62c	$496
Transcription of audio tapes	400 hours @ $16	$3,200
Data entry	50 hours @ $20	$1,000
Photocopying and stationery		$300
Telephone costs		$200
Literature search fees		$200
Preparation of final report	100 copies @ $10	$1,000
Gifts for participants	60 × $20 per participant	$1,200
Total costs		**$16,796**

budget should be presented in the form of an itemised list. This should include all services or items for which it is expected there will be an actual dollar cost involved in acquiring or using them. Examples include researcher salaries or contract payments, travel, accommodation, computer and data processing, photocopying, report printing and distribution, and so on. Costs of individual items should be grouped into categories of expenses such as salary/wages/fees, equipment, travel, etc. (see example in Table 4.3). Small, relatively inexpensive items such as pens, notebooks and clipboards should not be itemised separately but grouped together and costed as a single category (e.g., stationery).

Make clear in the budget how all major costs have been estimated. Calculate the cost of each researcher's time at an appropriate hourly rate (e.g., 100 hours @ $50/hour). In the text accompanying the budget, indicate who will be paying for the budgeted costs, where known. If the researcher(s) time is not being charged to any funding agency, note this in the text or in a footnote.

Schedule of payments

If a research project is being paid for, or expenses reimbursed, by a funding agency or research client, then it may be useful to include a proposed schedule of payments. This suggests what proportion of the total project funding or expenses should be paid at different stages of the project. Box 4.4 shows an example of a payment schedule. Note that the final details of the payment schedule will probably still need to be negotiated in discussions with the funding agency or research client.

Box 4.4 Example of schedule of payments

Schedule of Payments

It is proposed the payment be made as follows:

Agreement to proceed with the proposal	30%
Completion of data collection	30%
Completion of final report	40%

Payment will be made to the researcher within four weeks of an invoice being received from the researcher.

Ownership of data and final report

If the research project is being funded by another agency, or if it is planned to get project data from a third party such as a health service, government department or private business, then it may be necessary to include an appropriate ownership statement in the research proposal. This statement makes it clear who will own the project's research data and final report, and which people will have continuing access to, or retain copies of the original data. It may also be important to state where the raw data will be stored, which person or organisation will control access to the data, and any conditions or restrictions that will apply should either party wish to use the project data in subsequent studies or publications (e.g., acknowledgement of support or authorship). A sample ownership statement for a client-funded research project is shown in Box 4.5.

Box 4.5   Sample ownership statement

All research data collected for the project will be jointly owned by researchers and (*name of client organisation*), except for specific identifying information, which may be held solely by the researchers or destroyed to protect the confidentiality of research participants. The researcher (*and university supervisors – if applicable*) retains the right to hold copies of the research data and to publish research papers arising from the research. Research papers will not be published before the client organisation has received the final report. Research papers prepared for publication will be shown to the client organisation for comment before they are published.

Management of the project

This section describes the people who will be responsible for conducting the research project. If only one researcher will be working on the project, indicate:

- his or her research background and experience
- the host agency where the researcher will be based (e.g., university department, government agency, private research firm)
- where appropriate, who will be supervising or managing the work of the researcher (e.g., university supervisor, senior research manager, project advisory group).

If the research is to be carried out by a team, indicate:

- who the team members are likely to be (ideally include a biographical paragraph, e.g., 5–10 lines for each researcher describing that person's research background and previous experience)
- the host agency or agencies where the team will be based (e.g., university department, government agency, private research firm)
- each team member's expected tasks and responsibilities
- how the work of the team will be structured and managed.

References

Provide a list of all publications and other source material referred to in the proposal. Use a standard referencing format for social science, health or medical publications. See Chapter 7, Doing a Literature Review, for more details.

Reviewing and finalising a proposal

Before submitting a research proposal for formal assessment by a host institution, senior manager, funding agency or ethics committee, make sure it is reviewed by an experienced person who can advise on the appropriateness of the research design. The proposal should also be thoroughly checked for typographical, formatting and other presentational errors. Often it can be quite difficult to find someone willing to spend time reviewing your proposal. Some possibilities include: supervisors (if it is a thesis proposal), co-investigators (if a group project), colleagues at your workplace and fellow students (you could agree to review each other's proposals). Another possibility is to arrange to present a seminar on your proposal and ask those attending to provide feedback on the strengths and weaknesses of the proposal.

TABLE 4.4   CHECKLIST FOR ASSESSING PROPOSALS

General points	• Proposal includes all necessary sections and sub-sections, presented in a logical order • Sequencing of text and other information is appropriate and easy to follow • General layout and formatting (including grammar and spelling) is appropriate • Referencing of literature sources and reference list is in a consistent style and is accurate and complete
Introduction and literature review	• Aims and objectives of the study are precisely defined and feasible • Convincing information is given justifying the need for the study and why it is important • The context or proposed setting for the research is well described • Literature review is relevant to the topic and presents information from other studies appropriately
Research design	• Shows good understanding of research terminology and techniques. • Detailed, well-organised description of sampling approach, data collection methods, procedures and data analysis plans • Research procedures are appropriate to the project objectives, and are feasible and achievable • Ethical requirements for the project are indicated, including how these will be met in practice
Project management and resources	• Details provided on who will manage the project and specific roles of research team members • Project timetable is logical and consistent • Estimation of the resources needed is well-considered, realistic and sufficiently detailed
Formatting	• Cover includes all important contact details • All pages after cover are numbered • Suitable margins such as 3 cm left margins; 2 cm for top, bottom and right margins. • Pages of proposal are stapled or securely fastened • Both an electronic and paper copy of proposal retained by applicant

It can be a useful experience to review other people's proposals to help form a better idea of what a good proposal looks like (see Box 4.6). If you are asked to review someone's proposal, consider how you might write the kinds of comments you would like to see if someone else was reviewing your proposal. Table 4.4 provides a checklist for assessing how well a research proposal conforms to expected standards. The criteria shown in this checklist are commonly used by assessment committees when reviewing proposals submitted for project funding.

Box 4.6   Critiquing other people's research proposals

Jerome is a senior academic in a busy mid-city campus. For over 30 years he has conducted research on health and social topics and he has a lengthy list of publications to show for it. He is often asked to review research proposals submitted by students and colleagues for research grants or ethics approval.

Jerome has come to realise that writing a good review of somebody else's research proposal is something of an art form. He admits that early in his career he was often too quick to condemn other people's research designs, leading to some bruised egos and ill-feeling among colleagues. Nowadays he feels he has mellowed a bit and is able to provide a more even-handed assessment of the merits of a proposal. He aims to be as positive and encouraging as possible with his feedback, while at the same time clearly indicating where he thinks a proposal is weak and needs improving.

Jerome has a few tips on the art of reviewing other people's proposals:

1. Address the person whose proposal is being reviewed as you would like to be addressed yourself.
2. Don't get too bogged down in detail. Keep the big picture in mind and aim to ensure that the fundamental design of a proposal is sound.
3. When criticising aspects of a research design, suggest constructive alternatives.
4. Get your facts right. If you opt to find fault, make sure your claims can be substantiated.
5. Keep a sense of humour. Do not be afraid to tell stories about the times when research went wrong for you.
6. Model good writing in your review. It can help inspire others.

Conclusion: Preparing a research proposal

Preparing a research proposal is arguably the central creative act underpinning the development of new research. Typically it involves taking raw ideas for a project design and fashioning them into a coherent and credible written project plan. In most cases, this project plan will be organised and presented along the lines described above.

Be realistic about the intensity and complexity of the work involved in preparing a good research proposal. Even when the basic idea for a proposal is identified, a lot of work can still be needed to transform it into a viable research design. This can be overlooked at the start of developing a research proposal, when enthusiasm is high.

Remember that research proposals do not need to be written for every research project you do. Small, simple projects that do not take much time or involve many people or resources normally will not have to be described in a full research proposal. However, the more complex and more person- or resource-intensive your project, the more useful it will be to prepare a detailed proposal.

Appendix 1 (at the end of the book) provides an example of a finished research proposal. This uses a generic structure that could be adapted to suit the specific requirements of any research proposal you are writing.

Exercises for preparing proposals

1. Inspiration for a new research project can come from many directions: personal life experiences; suggestions from a teacher or mentor; debates in the academic literature or popular media; or priority topics for research identified by funding agencies. Identify three new ideas for research projects on a topic that interests you. To help organise your thinking, prepare a research proposal title page for each of the projects. What would you put on the title pages? What would you call the projects? What information will it be important to include in the project titles?

2. Select a suitable report or journal article describing a completed research project on a topic that interests you. Imagine you have been transported back through time to when the project was first being designed. Write a draft abstract or summary to be placed at the front of a research proposal for the project. Indicate the project objectives, why the project is important and the intended research design. Try to keep the abstract or summary as short as possible. Remember to write in the correct tense for a proposal (e.g., 'this project will investigate' or 'this project plans to investigate').

3. Take the same research report or journal article used for Exercise 2. Look closely at the description given of how the research was carried out. Create a retrospective timetable or timeline for the different phases, stages or parts of the project. How do the phases, stages or parts connect together? Do any overlap? How long did it take to do each project stage, phase or part? How long did it take to do the whole project? Was this shorter or longer than you expected?

Further reading

Locke, L. F., Spirduso, W. W., & Silverman, S. J. (2007). *Proposals That Work: A Guide for Planning Dissertations and Grant Proposals* (5th edn). Thousand Oaks, CA: Sage.

Polit, D. F. & Hungler, B. P. (2008). *Nursing Research: Principles and Methods* (8th edn). Philadelphia, PA: Lippincott Williams & Wilkins. (Chapter 27: Writing a Research Proposal)

Punch, K. F. (2006). *Developing Effective Research Proposals* (2nd edn). London: Sage.

Shore, A. R. & Carfora, J. M. (2010). The Art of Funding and Implementing Ideas: *A Guide to Proposal Development and Project Management.* Thousand Oaks, CA: Sage.

Silverman, D. (2005). *Doing Qualitative Research: A Practical Handbook* (2nd edn). London: Sage. (Chapter 10: Writing a Research Proposal)

5   Getting Funding for Research

Topics covered in this chapter

- Types of research and agencies that fund research
- Getting funding for researcher-initiated projects
- How funding applications are assessed
- Getting client-initiated project funding
- Responding to client requests for proposals

Funding is central to research. Without money to pay for people, services and equipment, most research projects cannot get started. A career as a researcher is therefore often heavily dependent on finding financial support for projects. This chapter looks at the different sources of funding available for researchers and research projects. In particular, it examines:

- the types of organisations that fund research
- how to find and select suitable funding sources
- how to prepare applications for project funding.

In discussing the funding of research, it is common to classify research projects into one of two categories:

- researcher-initiated projects
- client- or sponsor-initiated projects.

A researcher-initiated project is a project where a researcher develops an idea or design for a research project and gets other people or organisations to fund the project. Normally the aims and methods of the project are decided by the researcher, not the people or organisations providing funding for the project.

In a client- or sponsor-initiated project, an organisation or person has an idea or design for a research project, then employs or contracts a researcher to do the project. In this situation, the research topic and aims, and possibly the choice of research methods, are usually decided by the funding or sponsoring organisation, not the researchers doing the project.

Box 5.1   Examples of researcher-initiated projects

- A university researcher with an interest in sexual health practices gets a grant from a funding agency to undertake a study of young people's attitudes to condom use.
- A medical school researcher develops a new nicotine replacement therapy and gets a grant from a charitable foundation to conduct a clinical trial to test the effectiveness of the therapy.
- An independent researcher, interested in the history of medical training, self-funds an archival study of nineteenth-century medical student exam papers.

Box 5.2   Examples of client- or sponsor-initiated projects

- A government department contracts a research firm to conduct a nationwide telephone survey to measure public reaction to a new health service.
- A community-based asthma support group commissions an independent researcher to evaluate the effectiveness of its community outreach programme.
- A multinational pharmaceutical company commissions a university research team to conduct a randomised controlled trial testing the effectiveness of a new oral pain medication.

When looking for funding as a researcher, it is important to be clear which of these two categories of research is most relevant for you. Are you seeking funding for a project you have developed or designed yourself? Or are you more interested in working on research projects that other people or organisations have devised or need? Your decisions on this will determine:

- where and how you start looking for research funding
- the processes you use to apply for funding.

Getting funding for researcher-initiated projects

If you are looking for funding for a researcher-initiated project, you first need to identify the agencies in your country or region that support this kind of research. Start by doing some detective work. Conduct an Internet search using search terms such as 'research funding', 'research proposal funding' and 'research grants' – limiting the search to your particular country or region. This should produce an initial list of names and organisations to follow up in more detail. The search is also likely to identify websites specifically designed for researchers looking for funding (see Box 5.3 for examples). These websites usually include links to websites of many of the main research funding agencies.

Box 5.3   Websites with links to agencies funding researcher-initiated projects

The chronicle of Philanthropy: Guide to Grants
http://philanthropy.com/grants

Foundation Centre [includes a database of US grant makers]
http://foundationcenter.org

Grants.gov [information on US government-funded grant programmes]
www.grants.gov

InfoEd's SPIN [an academic and research funding opportunities database]
www1.infoed.org/modules/grantsAndContracts.cfm

(Continued)

(Continued)

Social Psychology Network (USA) [Sources of research funding]
www.socialpsychology.org/funding.htm

RDFunding – [UK health-related research funding opportunities]
www.rdfunding.org.uk/default.asp

ResearchResearch [US sources of research funds]
www.researchresearch.com

Note: Information on some of these websites may be subscriber only and require payment
for access.

The types of agencies listed will likely include:

- State-funded research grant making agencies. Typically, these agencies have been set up by government to support research in the public interest. Examples include the United Kingdom's Medical Research Council and Canada's Social Sciences and Humanities Research Council.
- Private, community or special interest foundations and charities that fund research as part of their work, e.g., alcohol and drug foundations, heart foundations.
- Professional associations, societies, institutes, colleges or councils whose activities include funding research, e.g., sociological associations, colleges of general practitioners, asthma societies.
- University and other higher learning institution internal research funds. Most universities offer scholarships, prizes, bursaries, studentships, fellowships, travel grants and other awards to support research by their students and staff.

Checking individual funding agencies

The next step is to go to the websites of individual funding agencies that seem to most closely fit your research topic area or interests. Most funding agencies have websites where you can access information about the agency's funding policies and processes. Often these include downloadable application forms and other important background documents. In some cases you may have to phone or email the agency to get these documents sent to you.

Look carefully through the information each agency supplies indicating who is eligible for funding and how to apply. Scrutinise the details of application forms and other relevant documents. Try to find out as much as you can about the processes and criteria each agency uses for selecting the projects they fund. In particular, work out whether or not the agency specifically funds researcher-initiated projects, as opposed to projects that it requests or commissions itself. It is no good applying to an agency for funding for a researcher-initiated project if the agency does not support this type of research. Box 5.4 lists examples of funding agencies that do support researcher-initiated social science and health projects.

Check if the agency has any guidelines on what research topics or types of research have priority for funding. These guidelines will often be developed to try to encourage researchers to initiate projects in new or neglected areas, or on topics seen to have national or international significance. If your proposed research does not match these priorities, this may lessen your chances of getting funding.

Box 5.4 Examples of agencies funding researcher-initiated projects

Australia and New Zealand
Australian Research Council
www.arc.gov.au

Foundation for Research, Science and Technology Public Good Science Fund
(New Zealand)
www.frst.govt.nz

Health Research Council of New Zealand
www.hrc.govt.nz/index.html

Lottery Community Sector Research Fund (New Zealand)
www.dia.govt.nz/diawebsite.nsf/wpg_URL/Services-Lottery-Grants-Lottery-Community-
Sector-Research-Fund?OpenDocument

National Health and Medical Research Council (Australia)
www.nhmrc.gov.au/index.htm

National Heart Foundation of New Zealand
www.nhf.org.nz

VicHealth (Victoria, Australia)
www.vichealth.vic.gov.au

Canada
Canadian Institutes of Health Research
www.cihr-irsc.gc.ca/e/37788.html

Canadian Health Services Research Foundation
www.chsrf.ca

Canadian Cancer Society Research Institute
cancer.ca/research

Social Sciences and Humanities Research Council (SSHRC)
www.sshrc.ca

United Kingdom and Ireland
British Academy
www.britac.ac.uk

Chief Scientist Office (Scotland)
www.sehd.scot.nhs.uk/cso

Economic and Social Research Council (ESRC)
www.esrcsocietytoday.ac.uk

Irish Research Council for the Humanities and Social Sciences
www.irchss.ie

Leverhulme Trust
www.leverhulme.org.uk

Medical Research Council (UK)
www.mrc.ac.uk/index.htm

Nuffield Foundation
www.nuffieldfoundation.org

(Continued)

(Continued)

United States
Carnegie Corporation of New York
www.carnegie.org

Haynes Foundation
www.haynesfoundation.org

James McDonnell Foundation
www.jsmf.org

National Institutes of Health
grants.nih.gov/grants/guide/index.html

National Science Foundation
www.nsf.gov/funding

National Institute of Nursing Research
www.ninr.nih.gov/ResearchAndFunding

National Endowment for the Humanities
www.neh.gov/grants/index.html

Robert Wood Johnson Foundation
www.rwjf.org

Russell Sage Foundation
www.russellsage.org

William T. Grant Foundation
www.wtgrantfoundation.org

Some funding agencies may also indicate other desirable features for the projects they fund. This could include preferences for:

- programmatic research, rather than one-off projects (programmatic research is when a series of closely related projects are developed to address a single theme or research problem)
- projects where the research findings will have direct applicability or use, e.g. to inform policy or improve practice
- research that develops in a progression from smaller (pilot) studies through medium and then larger project grants, with local institutions providing 'seeding' grants for the initial small studies
- projects where the researchers are supervised by an expert advisory group or technical support group
- projects that involve a team of researchers rather than a sole researcher
- projects that promote interdisciplinary collaboration (e.g. when social researchers work with researchers from the physical sciences)
- project teams that include people with different roles (e.g. researchers, service providers or practitioners, policy makers)
- project teams that include a mix of experienced and less experienced researchers, to provide a mentoring environment for less experienced researchers
- project teams led by members of under-represented groups (e.g. indigenous groups, non-dominant ethnic groups, people with a disability).

Check out the maximum level of funding that agencies are offering. If an agency only supports projects up to a value of $25,000, but you estimate you will need $100,000 to do your project, it is probably not worth applying to this agency for funding unless you substantially modify your research goals.

Find out how long agencies will take to review your funding application and indicate whether you have been successful. If an agency takes six months to review applications, but you need to get your project up and running in the next two months, then you will either have to look elsewhere for funding or reassess your project timetable.

Note that many funding agencies are unlikely to support independent researchers not affiliated with a recognised host institution such as a university, polytechnic or government agency. If you are an independent or freelance researcher looking to get funding for your own projects, it may be best to develop a joint funding application with a colleague from a suitable host institution.

Similarly, if you are a comparatively inexperienced researcher without a track record of completed projects, it may be best to team up with a more established researcher to develop a joint funding application.

Note, too, that many funding agencies offer other types of support for research and researchers apart from straight project funding. This can include funding for research-related travel, purchasing research equipment, assisting with running conferences or seminars, preparing research proposals, or completing the writing up and publication of research findings. As well, many agencies offer fellowships, studentships, training bursaries or other types of awards specifically to support the development of new or emerging researchers (see Box 5.5).

Box 5.5 Research apprenticeships: Funding for new and emerging researchers

Work towards a Masters, PhD or other advanced university degree usually includes a significant research project carried out under the guidance of a supervisor or mentor. The student's host institution normally provides office space, equipment and access to essential services (e.g., library, specialist software, statistical advice).

A range of organisations, including universities, offer grants, scholarships and other awards to assist students doing advanced degrees. Most of these awards are allocated on a competitive basis. Some of the most sought-after provide the equivalent of a salary plus support for research expenses such as equipment, travel and publication. Other awards assist just with travel, equipment, tuition fees, or other incidental training costs.

A range of awards are also available to support researchers after completing their PhD or other final degree work. These include postdoctoral fellowships providing salaries and assistance with research project costs. Competition for these fellowships is usually intense.

The scope and design of most Masters, PhD and other degree-level research projects tend to be governed by the financial assistance available. Usually it is not possible for projects to include highly time-consuming data collection procedures with very large numbers of research participants. However, in some cases a student's project can be part of an existing, larger study, such as work being done by the student's supervisor. In rare instances, a student will secure major funding for their project from a government department, private company or other agency. However, usually the project has to be designed to fit the agency's information needs.

Most university websites include detailed information on the awards available to support postgraduate and post-doctoral study.

Applying for researcher-initiated project funding

If, after thoroughly reviewing a funding agency's application processes and requirements, you decide you have a reasonable chance of getting funding from this agency, then the next step is to write up and submit your funding application.

At this stage it will be crucial to have already developed a presentable plan of your intended research project. Filling in a funding application form is likely to be very difficult if you only have a vague idea of what your project will involve. Ideally, you should already have written a research proposal outlining your project aims and methods (see Chapter 4, Preparing and Writing a Research Proposal). This proposal can then be used as the basis for filling in the funding agency's application forms and preparing any other documentation required.

Some funding agencies now use a two-stage funding application process. First, applicants are required to submit a summary of their proposed research. This may be in the form of a letter, a 4–6 page 'mini-proposal' or some other format. This summary is reviewed by the funding agency. Then, if the research is considered to fit the agency's eligibility criteria and research priorities, the applicant is invited to submit a full research proposal along with other relevant documentation.

This two-stage approach is designed to cut down the amount of work involved in preparing and assessing funding applications. Researchers do not have to go to the trouble of preparing a full funding application if there is little chance of their project being supported. Similarly, the funding agency does not have to spend a lot of time reviewing and responding to detailed project proposals that do not meet its criteria for funding.

Information required in a full funding application

If you do get to the stage of submitting a full funding application, the agency is likely to ask you to provide a range of information. This will include information normally covered in a basic research proposal, such as:

- project title
- summary or project abstract
- statement of project objectives or questions
- rationale or justification for the project
- research methods
- data analysis plan
- timeline
- reference list.

As well, the agency is likely to request the following information, not necessarily covered in a basic research proposal.

- *Detailed cost estimates for the project including a project budget.* Anticipated costs may need to be itemised in considerable detail, especially for projects seeking large amounts of funding. Items to be covered may include staff, services, technology and equipment, office hire, insurances and perhaps overheads to be paid to a host institution. Overheads are when a host institution takes a proportion of a project budget (e.g., between 10 and 40 per cent) to cover the costs involved in providing services and facilities for the project. If some direct financial support for the project has already been promised from other funding agencies, the details of this may also need to be shown.
- *A summary of the research credentials, training and experience* of you and any other people who will be working on the project. You may also be asked to provide details of previous research completed.
- *Names of referees* that the funding agency can approach for confidential feedback on your research skills and experience.

- *Signed guarantees of support* for the project from senior managers or administrators in your host institution, as well as perhaps from representatives of communities, organisations or groups that will be closely involved in your project.
- *An indication of how any formal ethical clearances required for the project will be obtained* from a recognised ethics committee or institutional review board.
- *A description of how results of the project will be communicated to potential users,* e.g., technical reports, journal articles, briefings, presentations to policy makers or practitioners.

Writing and presenting a funding application

Preparing a good funding application takes time. Start preparing your application at least two or three months before the closing date for applications. Try to avoid writing your application in the last days or hours before the submission deadline. Rushing to complete an application usually leads to mistakes. Ideally, aim to finish writing all of your application at least a week before it is due. That way, there will be time left to carefully review your application and proofread it for errors.

Remember that people's ability to do good research is often judged by their ability to write good funding applications. *How* you write your funding application is therefore likely to be just as important as *what* you write in it. Pay attention to every detail of what you put in your application. Make sure your application looks professional, conforms to the funding agency's guidelines and requirements, and is clear and easy to follow. Sloppy, untidy, incomplete, inaccurate or hard-to-follow funding applications usually have a much lower chance of success (for more tips on writing see Chapter 12, Writing for Research).

One of the best ways to learn how to write a good quality funding application is to read examples of other people's successful applications. Opportunities to do this can be limited, though, as many researchers regard their funding applications as professionally sensitive, private documents. This is understandable given the competitive nature of research funding. However, if you are being supervised or mentored by a person with a track record of successful research funding, this person may be prepared to let you read some of their funding applications to assist your development.

Another way to get to see other researchers' funding applications is by being appointed to boards or committees that assess research funding applications. However, usually only experienced researchers get the chance to serve on these bodies. New or emerging researchers are less likely to get these opportunities.

Other potential sources of advice on writing funding applications include research offices, research coordinators or research methods services at your local university or polytechnic, as well as Internet resources (see the list of examples in Box 5.6). There are also a number of books available on how to write funding or grant applications (e.g., Brewer and Achilles, 2007; Miller, 2009). Many of these are written for audiences in specific countries. Some of the information in these books may not be applicable to other countries.

Box 5.6   Internet resources for writing funding applications and getting research grants

Grants Net, United States Department of Health and Human Services
www.hhs.gov/grantsnet

(Continued)

(Continued)

The Scientist [search the database using 'grant writing']
www.the-scientist.com

University of Wisconsin – Madison
http://researchguides.library.wisc.edu/content.php?pid=16143&sid=108666

Science careers
http://sciencecareers.sciencemag.org/funding

Applying to multiple agencies

There may be merit in submitting funding applications for a project to more than one agency at a time, provided you believe each application has a reasonable chance of success – and provided the extra work involved in preparing and submitting multiple applications does not impact on their quality.

When submitting funding applications to several different agencies, a good idea is firstly to prepare an application in a general format on a word processor and then adapt this format to suit the specific requirements of each agency to which you intend applying.

Try to be realistic about your chances of obtaining funding from multiple agencies. Better to focus your efforts on preparing one really good application for an agency likely to support your work, rather than wasting time preparing numerous applications that are unlikely to succeed.

How funding applications are assessed

Most research funding agencies have their own distinct criteria and systems for selecting which research projects to fund. Typically, funding applications will be reviewed by an agency's assessment committee or expert group. They may advise on which applications to fund, but they may not necessarily be the people who finally decide if a project gets funding, or how much. An agency's senior executives, administrators or board may make these decisions.

The criteria on which funding applications may be assessed include:

- importance of the research question, including its fit with the funding agency's priorities or key programme areas
- the research project's theoretical relevance or practical applicability
- adequacy of the research design and methods
- safety of the research for research participants and others
- the availability of appropriate personnel and facilities
- reasonableness of the budget
- the experience and publication record of the research applicants
- how well the application is written and presented in the style and format expected by the agency (see Box 5.7).

Box 5.7   Operation of an assessing committee for research funding applications

One of this book's authors (DRT) was for several years a member of a health-related funding agency's research assessing committee. The committee included researchers from a wide range of disciplines in medicine, public health and social sciences.

Annually the committee received around 30 researcher-initiated applications for research project funding. Each application was sent to at least three external referees for review. At a two-day meeting of the assessment committee, two committee members were assigned to lead the review of each application. One outlined key features of the application's research design and presented an assessment of its strengths and weaknesses. The second committee member reviewed the application's external referee reports. Following discussion, the application was then scored by all the committee members. In total, the committee took about 20–30 minutes to review each application.

In the final part of the assessment process, all the applications were rank ordered by their scores, with the amount of funding sought noted beside each application. Then the committee chairperson added up the accumulated funding sought, starting from the top-scoring application and working downwards. The cut-off point for funding was determined to be the point at which the funding applied for was about the same as the funding available. Then the two applications just above and the two applications just below the cut-off point were re-examined by the committee. Often all four of these re-examined applications were considered worthy of funding.

What factors helped to push an application's score above the funding cut-off point? The overall quality of the application, the research track record of the applicants and the appeal of the proposed research to the committee members in terms of its novelty and potential to add new knowledge were all important at this critical point in the decision making.

There might also be other factors that could influence whether applications get funded. These include:

- feedback from referees
- how many other researchers have submitted applications for funding on similar topics
- how much money the agency has available for a particular funding round.

Responding to success and failure

Applying for research funding is a competitive process – there are winners and losers. Normally, there are more applicants for funding than there is money to go around, so inevitably somebody misses out. Many research funding agencies are only able to support a small proportion of the applications they receive, often less than a quarter.

After submitting a good quality funding application, and perhaps with a bit of luck on your side as well, you may receive the pleasant news that your funding application has been successful. This is something to celebrate. Hopefully, it means your project can now get started.

In some cases, before agreeing to fund your project, a funding agency may come back to you seeking clarification on aspects of your project plans or asking for more information about you or other members of your research team. You could even be asked to modify certain parts of your project plan or research design.

In other cases, agencies may only agree to part-fund your application. This could include a proviso that you find another agency willing to fund the balance of the project budget.

Of course, there is also a reasonable chance that your funding application will be unsuccessful. Outright rejection of a funding application can be a difficult thing to accept. However, it goes with the territory of being a researcher. Remember that you are not alone and that in many countries probably thousands of researcher-initiated funding applications are turned down every year. The key thing is to learn from the experience and identify ways you could do better with your next application.

Getting client-initiated project funding

Client or sponsor-initiated project funding involves doing research on a tightly defined topic specified by the organisation funding the project. If you are:

- a researcher in a commercial research firm or business
- a researcher in a university research centre reliant on external research funding
- an independent or freelance researcher

then a major part of your work is likely to include identifying and securing client or sponsor-initiated project funding. This may include projects commissioned by:

- government agencies, e.g., to support or evaluate new policies or services
- businesses, e.g., to test consumer reactions to products or services
- community organisations or charitable agencies, e.g., to develop knowledge in areas relevant to their interests.

Finding out about client-initiated research projects

When agencies have a research project that needs doing, there are different ways they can arrange for researchers to do the work. Potential strategies agencies might use include:

- *Contacting a researcher directly and asking whether they are interested in doing the work.* The researcher may have a track record of successful work with the agency and therefore be regarded as a 'preferred provider'. This is someone with whom the agency is comfortable working and keen to maintain an ongoing professional relationship. If the researcher is interested, then the terms and conditions of the project work can be negotiated there and then.
- *Advertising the work in a closed tender process.* This involves contacting several different research suppliers in confidence and inviting them all to consider applying to do the work. This introduces an element of competition to the researcher-selection process. If more than one researcher applies, there may be scope to choose the most skilled or experienced applicant, or the applicant proposing the most cost-effective research strategy.
- *Advertising the work in an open tender process.* This involves publicly advertising the research project widely to any research supplier who may be interested.

In some countries if government or public sector agencies want to commission research projects it is compulsory to advertise the work as an open tender so any research supplier can apply. This is seen as important for maintaining fairness and openness in the allocation of government contracts. In some cases, only higher priced contracts (e.g., those worth $50,000 or more) may be required to be advertised. Lower priced contracts may only be required to be circulated on a closed tender basis to a small group of preferred providers. Some very low price contracts may even be able to be offered directly to a single research supplier.

Researchers keen to pick up research contracts should keep an eye out for public notices advertising client-initiated projects. There are now a number of websites in different countries providing central access to publicly advertised project contracts, especially government contracts. Some examples are shown in Box 5.8. Appendix 5.1 lists some of the research contracts offered by New Zealand government agencies in 2008 and 2009. Similar types of projects may be commissioned by government agencies in other countries.

Box 5.8   Examples of websites publicising client-initiated research contracts

Australia and New Zealand
Tenderlink.com
www.tenderlink.com

New Zealand Government Electronic Tenders Service (GETS)
www.gets.govt.nz

Canada
MERX Canadian Public Tenders
www.merx.com

United Kingdom and Ireland
Etenders (Ireland)
www.etenders.gov.ie

Supply2.gov.uk [the only official government lower-value (typically below £100,000) contract opportunity portal]
www.supply2.gov.uk

tendersdirect
www.tendersdirect.co.uk

United States
Community of Science (COS) Funding Opportunities
http://fundingopps.cos.com

Foundation Directory Online
http://fconline.fdncenter.org

FedBizOpps (FBO)
http://www.fbo.gov

GrantSelect
www.grantselect.com
[US sponsored research opportunities]

Note: Information on some of these websites may be subscriber only and require payment for access.

As well, it can be useful to send staff responsible for managing research contracts in relevant agencies a copy of your CV and examples of your work. Ask them to include you on their mailing list when they are publicising future project opportunities.

Project briefs, RFPs and expressions of interest

As part of the research commissioning process, an agency may prepare a written project brief outlining its research needs and formally inviting qualified researchers to apply to do the work. The brief may be circulated in various ways – by email, fax or standard post, by advertising in newspapers or on webpages, or by making it available for download from websites, depending on how extensively the agency wants to publicise the project (i.e., a closed or open tender process).

A project brief will normally ask researchers to submit either:

a fully developed multi-page research proposal; or
a much shorter document (e.g., 2–3 pages) outlining their research experience and credentials and briefly indicating how they would carry out the research.

A project brief asking researchers to submit a fully developed proposal is usually referred to as a *request for proposals* or RFP.

A project brief asking researchers to provide a shorter, more concise indication of their experience and project plans is often referred to as a *call for expressions of interest.*

Agencies will often issue a call for expressions of interest if a project brief is being circulated widely to a large number of research providers. Information provided by researchers in their expressions of interest will then be used as a basis for selecting a small group of researchers. This group will be contacted directly and invited to submit a full research proposal outlining how they intend to carry out the project.

This two-stage process – issuing an expression of interest followed by a second round requesting a short-list of applicants to submit a detailed project proposal – has the advantage of not requiring all applicants to go to the trouble of preparing a detailed research proposal. As well, it reduces the risk of the contracting agency having to spend a lot of time reading through a large number of detailed project proposals.

For large, complex or expensive research projects, agencies may sometimes appoint an internal group or bring in external advisers to oversee the process of selecting researchers to do the project. These people will assess the project proposals and other information provided by the researchers. Short-listed researchers may also be asked to give an oral presentation outlining how they intend to do the research (see Box 5.9).

Box 5.9   On the short-list for a major evaluation contract

Bidding for client-initiated project funding can be a hit-and-miss affair, with no guarantee of success.

Imelda is a senior researcher with SurveyInfo Ltd, a social survey and market research firm. In recent weeks, Imelda has been working on a bid for a substantial government

(Continued)

(Continued)

contract to evaluate a nationwide social marketing campaign promoting healthy food choices. The bid included submitting a 120-page research proposal stating how Imelda and her colleagues would conduct the evaluation and for what price.

Imelda has just received a call indicating that SurveyInfo has been short-listed for the final selection round for the evaluation contract. She and her three colleagues have been invited to make a formal presentation to a group of government officials in a week's time. The presentation is a chance for the officials to meet Imelda and her colleagues and ask questions about SurveyInfo's evaluation design.

A week later, Imelda and her colleagues, dressed in their best business clothes, travel to the central city offices of the government agency managing the evaluation contracting process. Just after 11am, they are ushered into a conference room to meet the team of officials for the first time. The officials, 15 in total, are seated at tables arranged in a semi-circle facing a small lectern and side table. The convenor of the meeting welcomes Imelda and her colleagues and asks everyone seated at the tables to introduce themselves. The convenor then invites Imelda and her colleagues to begin their presentation.

Imelda starts by talking about how pleased she and her colleagues are to have the opportunity to bid for the evaluation contract. She introduces her colleagues and gives a quick rundown on the history of SurveyInfo, listing some of the major evaluation projects the firm has successfully carried out in recent years. She then outlines the evaluation design that SurveyInfo recommends for the project, highlighting its particular strengths for meeting the evaluation's key objectives. After this, Imelda hands over to one of her colleagues to talk in more detail about how SurveyInfo would carry out the project. Imelda then returns and opens up the presentation for questions.

Several people in the audience raise concerns about elements of SurveyInfo's evaluation design. Others praise the design for its thoroughness and attention to detail. Imelda responds to the criticisms of the design as best she can, reassuring people that SurveyInfo can address these concerns and deliver a comprehensive, top-level evaluation. After about 25 minutes of questions and discussion, the convenor indicates it is time to wind up the presentation. He thanks Imelda and her colleagues for their interesting and useful presentation.

Three days later Imelda receives a call from the convenor to say that the meeting had decided to pursue a contract with one of the other short-listed research firms. The convenor notes that SurveyInfo had offered a very credible and worthwhile evaluation design but that a competitor firm had proposed a simpler evaluation approach that was cheaper.

For small projects not involving large amounts of funding, it is often seen as unnecessary (and inefficient) for the researcher to go to the trouble of preparing a detailed project proposal. Instead, the work to be done will be outlined in a short letter of agreement prepared by the project client in discussion with the researcher.

Responding to client requests for proposals

Preparing a project proposal for a client-initiated project has some similarities to preparing a funding application for a researcher-initiated project, but also some differences.

As with funding applications for a researcher-initiated project, it is important to remember that your skills as a researcher will be judged by your ability to design and write a good project proposal – one that meets the project client's requirements and standards. Incomplete, inaccurate or poorly presented proposals are not likely to win you any favours.

Especially for larger projects, it is quite common for the client – or their advisers – to prepare extensive documentation outlining their expectations and requirements for the project. These specifications may in many cases be very finely detailed and prescriptive. There may already be strict timelines and budgets set down for certain components of a study, or a range of non-negotiable conditions or requirements about the type of research methods to be used. You may therefore find that a good deal of how the research should be designed and carried out has already been decided for you.

However, do not let this put you off. Clients should be willing to listen to your suggestions about how the research could be done differently, especially if your ideas are well-argued and reasonable.

Ask around your networks to find out as much as you can about what it could be like working on a project contract for the agency. There may be a history of difficult or unsuccessful contractual relationships. There may be restructurings going on in the agency, or other tensions that could pose difficulties. Knowing about these, and taking them into account during the contract application process, is preferable to finding out about them only after you have signed up to do the project.

Many requests for proposals invite researchers to contact a member of the funding agency if they have questions about the research. Taking up this invitation can be important for learning more about the context in which the research is being developed. It can also be useful for identifying special points to emphasise in your research proposal.

If an agency sends you a request for proposals but you don't think the project suits you, or you are too busy with other work to consider taking it on, then write back to the agency and let them know. You don't want the agency to overlook you when other projects are being developed and you are available for work.

Remember that there may be pressures on some agencies to obtain value for money on every external contract they enter into, research included. Be careful not to get yourself into a situation where you end up agreeing to do a research project for too low a price. If anything, try to negotiate a price at least slightly above what you expect the actual cost of the project will be. This provides at least some buffer for the extra, unanticipated work or costs that often crop up in a research project.

Look for any warning signs in your dealings with project clients suggesting they have already made up their minds about what the research project will find or prove. You will be entering a potentially dangerous situation if the people paying for your services are adamant they already know what the results of your project will (or should) show. It is vital to uphold your independence and professional standards as a researcher in the face of these (sometimes subtle) pressures. If other researchers or research clients come to suspect your professional independence and integrity has been undermined, and that the results of your research have been swayed by the nature of your commercial relationship with a project client, this could seriously jeopardise your reputation and chances of winning future project funding.

Conclusion: Getting funding for research

In most countries, a wide range of agencies offer funding opportunities for researcher or client-initiated research projects. However, usually there is no shortage of skilled and experienced researchers lining up to apply for these funds. The ability to pinpoint realistic opportunities for project funding and to develop high quality funding applications is therefore vital to the ongoing career development of most researchers (see Box 5.10).

In the ideal scenario, well-thought-out, well-presented funding applications lead to the completion of well-resourced, properly conducted research projects. For the researchers involved, this sets up a kind of virtuous circle where the kudos attached to successfully completing a significant, well-funded research project often increases the chances of attracting more research funding in future.

Box 5.10   Research careers and project funding

After gaining a Masters degree, PhD, or other similar qualification, emerging researchers in social science and health are likely to develop their careers in a range of directions. Some of the more common include:

- university appointments
- employment as researchers in government agencies, community organisations or private companies
- work as freelance research consultants or independent researchers.

In all these situations, there is likely to be an emphasis on competing for research project funding.

In university appointments, job prospects are likely to be tied closely to the quantity and quality of research outputs and publications, especially for researchers employed in specialised research centres or programmes. The financial viability of a centre or programme may depend on successfully competing for research funding from sources outside the university.

Similarly, for researchers employed in government, community or private sector research jobs, an important part of their work may include seeking out new research funding opportunities. This could include recouping some or all of their salary and other costs by attracting project funding from other parts of their organisation, or from external agencies.

By definition, the livelihood of a freelance or independent researcher will rely mainly on securing commissioned or client-initiated project contracts (for more information on careers in research, see Chapter 14).

Exercises for getting funding

1. Search through some of the webpages listed in Box 5.6. Find three articles providing advice on writing funding applications. Based on these, make a list of 10–12 tips on how to write a funding application. These tips should be relevant to research topics you are interested in and to agencies in your country or region that potentially could fund your research.
2. Do an Internet search to identify the webpages of up to 10 agencies in your country or region that fund research in your area or discipline. Search each agency's webpages for information on how to apply for funding. Look for details such as: type and size of project funding available; listed priority areas for research; closing dates for applications; contact details for key staff. Copy the key information you find for each funding agency into a database, spreadsheet or text file for future reference.
3. With a colleague or another researcher, hold a brain-storming session to identify research topics you are interested in that might be attractive to funding agencies in your country or region. Develop a list of potential funding agencies to contact. Select two agencies from this list that you regard as priorities for submitting a funding application. Identify key features to include in a funding application that may increase your chances of getting funding from these two agencies.

References and further reading

Bioscience (2009). *Guidelines for Writing Grant Applications*. Retrieved October 22, 2009. from: www.bioscience.org/current/grant.htm.
Brewer, E. W. & Achilles, C. M. (2007). *Finding Funding: Grantwriting from Start to Finish, Including Project Management and Internet Use* (5th edn). Thousand Oaks, CA: Sage.
Burke, M. A. (ed.) (2002). *Simplified Grantwriting*. Thousand Oaks, CA: Corwin Press.
Gerin, W. (2006). *Writing the NIH Grant Proposal: A Step-by-Step Guide*. Thousand Oaks, CA: Sage.
Miller, P. W. (2009). *Grant Writing: Strategies for Developing Winning Government Proposals* (3rd edn). Munster, IN: Patrick Miller & Associates.
National Institutes of Health (2009). *Grant Writing Tips Sheets*. Retrieved October 22, 2009, from: http:// grants1.nih.gov/grants/grant_tips.htm.
National Institute of Neurological Disorders and Stroke (2009). *How to Write a Research Project Grant Application*. Retrieved November 11, 2009, from: www.ninds.nih.gov/funding/write_grant_doc.htm.
Shore, A. R. & Carfora, J. M. (2010). *The Art of Funding and Implementing Ideas: A Guide to Proposal Development and Project Management*. Thousand Oaks, CA: Sage.
Walters, M. W. (2009). *Write an Effective Funding Application: A Guide for Researchers and Scholars*. Baltimore, MD: Johns, Hopkins University Press.
Yuen, F. K. O., Terao, K. L., & Schmidt, A. M. (2009). *Effective Grant Writing and Program Evaluation for Human Service Professionals*. New York: Wiley.

APPENDIX 5.1

Examples of client-initiated research projects from the New Zealand GETS database

New Zealand's Government Electronic Tenders Service (GETS: www.gets.govt.nz/) is a web-based database that list publicly advertised (open tender) government contracts, including research project contracts. The database also lists details of contracts awarded. The following table shows some examples from the database of research project contracts awarded in 2008 and 2009. Items on this list indicate the types of projects that may be commissioned by government agencies in other countries.

Project title/area of research	Commissioning agency	Contract value (range) $NZ	Length of contract
Engagement of youth in literacy, language and numeracy	Department of Labour	100,000–125,000	9 months
Changing roles of grandparents project	Families Commission	0–50,000	3 months
Understanding child neglect: literature review	Ministry of Social Development	0–50,000	5 months
Focus groups and interviews with former quota refugees on issues of long-term settlement integration	Department of Labour	50,000–75,000	4 months
Evaluation of the SPELL programme, an autism spectrum disorder training programme	New Zealand Guidelines Group Inc	50,000–75,000	6 Months
Customer satisfaction survey services	Earthquake Commission	50,000–75,000	3 years
Review the implementation of the New Zealand Coaching Strategy	Sport & Recreation New Zealand	75,000–100,000	6 months
Stock-take and mapping of sport and recreation facilities in New Zealand	Sport & Recreation New Zealand	75,000–100,000	6 months
Levels of charitable giving and sponsorship to cultural organisations	Ministry for Culture & Heritage	0–50,000	4 months
Monitoring and evaluation of Mission-On youth branded website	Sport & Recreation New Zealand	50,000–75,000	3 months
Public transport non-user research project	NZ Transport Agency	200,000–225,000	12 months

(Continued)

(Continued)

Project title/area of research	Commissioning agency	Contract value (range) $NZ	Length of contract
Students Against Driving Drunk (SADD) evaluation	NZ Transport Agency	50,000–75,000	12 months
Evaluation of the Road Sense Ata Haere Strategy	NZ Transport Agency	75,000–100,000	12 months
Research into public attitudes to knowledge of New Zealand citizenship	Department of Internal Affairs	75,000–100,000	7 months
Public perceptions of the National Certificate of Educational Achievement	Ministry of Education/ NZ Qualifications Authority	125,000–150,000	2 years 3 months
Review of population movement in the Pacific	Department of Labour	0–50,000	6 months
A national survey of children and young people's physical activity and nutrition behaviours and awareness of Mission-On and its key messages	Sport & Recreation New Zealand	1,250,000– 1,500,000	15 months
Contract for the purchase and provision of statistical analysis and write-up of 1996, 2001 and 2006 census data on migration/ethnic youth	Department of Labour	0–50,000	6 months
Conducting the Settlement Experiences Feedback Survey (SEFS)	Department of Labour	0–50,000	7 months
Research into Pacific communities and organisations social and economic contribution to Pacific migrant settlement outcomes in New Zealand	Ministry of Pacific Island Affairs	75,000–100,000	8 months
Annual face-to-face survey of public attitudes to road safety	Ministry of Transport	225,000–250,000	2 years
Review of current government policies and practices that impact on labour market transitions by informal carers. Literature review of support and services available to informal carers	Department of Labour	0–50,000	3 months
Feasibility study on the labour market impacts of temporary immigration policy	Department of Labour	0–50,000	2 months

6   Research Ethics and Ethics Reviews

This chapter provides an introduction to the ethical issues that need to be considered when planning a research project. It looks at the types of ethical standards researchers are expected to abide by and the practices researchers typically use to try to ensure they carry out their projects in an ethical manner. The later sections of the chapter outline the steps involved in submitting a research proposal for ethical review.

What are research ethics?

Research ethics are the standards of professional conduct that researchers are expected to maintain in their dealings with colleagues, research participants, sponsors and funders, and the wider community. These include responsibilities to ensure research projects are designed and conducted safely, fairly and with integrity.

Recent decades have seen much attention and controversy focused on the ethics of research, partly in response to a growing recognition of the ways research can be misused or misrepresented. This has resulted in a variety of organisations that fund or administer research, or represent the professional interests of researchers, issuing formal guidelines or codes defining the principles and practices that go to make up ethically sound research (see Box 6.1). Social and health researchers need to keep these principles and practices at the forefront of their thinking throughout the process of designing and carrying out a research project. This includes at the start of a project when selecting the project's research objectives and methods, and when anticipating the project's possible benefits, risks and impact.

Box 6.1   Topics often covered in professional ethics for researchers

- Professional integrity
- Scientific standards
- Technical competence
- Training and supervision
- Responsibilities to research participants
- Informed consent
- Privacy and confidentiality
- Data sharing
- Offering inducements to research participants
- Use of deception in research
- Covert research
- Relations with employers, sponsors or funders
- Safety of research team members
- Conflicts of interest
- Disclosure of funding sources
- Importance of peer review

See Appendix 6.1 for examples of ethical guidelines and professional codes of conduct issued by different research disciplines.

Key ethical principles

Some of the more important ethical principles and practices promulgated by organisations representing social and health research disciplines, or agencies that administer or fund research, are highlighted below.

Honesty and truthfulness

Fundamental to research ethics is the need for openness and honesty when reporting research objectives, methods and results. Researchers should not knowingly misrepresent or distort their research procedures or findings. As well, researchers should not misrepresent their professional qualifications or expertise to prospective employers or project sponsors.

Conflicts of interest

In some cases, researchers may work for or have financial, professional or political dealings with organisations, groups or businesses that have fixed views or policies on certain problems or issues. This opens up the possibility that the work of the researcher may be influenced, consciously or unconsciously, by these links. For example, researchers' choice of research objectives or questions, or how they frame or interpret their research results, may be shaped by these links. From an ethical standpoint, this is defined as a potential conflict of interest situation (Box 6.2). A researcher's ability to carry out a fair and balanced study of a topic may be compromised, or at least may be *seen* by other people to be compromised.

Box 6.2 Defining a conflict of interest

This definition of 'conflict of interest' has been developed for editors of medical journals:

Conflict of interest exists when an author (or the author's institution), reviewer, or editor has financial or personal relationships that inappropriately influence (bias) his or her actions (such relationships are also known as dual commitments, competing interests, or competing loyalties). These relationships vary from negligible to great potential for influencing judgment. (International Committee of Medical Journal Editors, 2008, p. 4)

When designing or conducting a research project, researchers should aim to identify all employment, financial, professional, political or other types of links that might potentially open them to conflict of interest allegations. These links should be openly disclosed in all research-related documents, including research proposals, funding applications, ethical review applications and research reports.

Scientific standards and bias

It is important that researchers adhere to appropriate scientific standards and avoid as much as possible the various forms of bias that can influence the conduct of research and reporting of research findings. While defining bias in research can be challenging and contested (cf. Hammersley & Gomm, 1997), in general it is acknowledged to be when a researcher's personal values or attitudes influence their choice of research topic, research methods or findings in *undesirable* ways. Such biases can include: exaggerating the importance of particular research data, neglecting to consider valid data or evidence reported by other researchers, or not considering alternative explanations for observed findings.

In research projects involving controversial topics, organisations or individuals with specific views on the topic may seek to discredit research findings that are inconsistent with their views. In this situation, researchers should expect to have their research design, data collection procedures and data analysis closely scrutinised. Examples of controversial topics include:

- availability of firearms and firearm violence
- suppressed memories relating to childhood abuse
- exposure to visual and electronic violence and aggressive behaviour
- effectiveness of alternative medicines.

Some academic journals occasionally run special issues or articles to foster debate on themes related to bias in research. For example, in a review of research funded by the pharmaceutical industry, Sismondo (2008) concludes that when pharmaceutical companies fund clinical trials of their drugs, the published results of these trials are more likely to favour the interests of the pharmaceutical companies compared to studies of drugs that are trialled by researchers funded by other agencies (see Box 6.3).

Box 6.3   Biases in pharmaceutical research

Sismondo (2008, pp. 1911–1912) identified the following potential sources of bias in clinical drug trials:

Design bias: this is when trials use research designs that are more likely to produce results favouring the drug being evaluated. This includes designs that use placebos or other poor comparators, inappropriate doses, carefully constructed experimental populations, poor surrogate endpoints, and trial durations unlikely to show side effects.

Interpretive and rhetorical effects: this is when narrative commentaries in reports of drug trials interpret the results of the trial in ways that favour the drug's being evaluated, even though plausible alternative interpretations of the results may be possible. This can include interpretations regarding a drug's therapeutic benefit and side effects.

Publication bias: for industry-funded trials, positive reports (i.e., reports favouring the drug being tested) tend to be over-reported relative to negative reports. In a series of 42 trials of one type of pharmaceutical (five selective serotonin reuptake inhibitors – SSRIs), the 21 positive trials produced 19 stand-alone journal articles, whereas the 21 negative trials produced only six journal articles.

Plagiarism

Plagiarism is when researchers present other people's work as their own. During all research, it is important to clearly identify information or ideas sourced from previous studies or literature. It is also important to acknowledge any assistance provided by other people during a project, such as help with research design or conducting parts of a study.

Protecting the welfare of research participants

When a research project intends collecting information directly from people, there are several ethical principles that will normally need to be adhered to throughout the project's design and execution. The main ones include ensuring:

- the risks of research participants being harmed or upset are minimised
- potential research participants are identified, contacted and/or selected for participation in the project without infringing their rights to privacy
- research participants are properly informed about the objectives and methods of the research project and what they will be expected to do when taking part in the project
- research participants at all times retain the option to freely choose whether or not to continue to take part in the research project, without coercion or pressure
- all personal information supplied by research participants is protected.

These ethical principles and practices related to research participants are discussed in more detail below when outlining ethical procedures to cover in a research proposal.

Maintaining the safety of research assistants and support staff

Another key ethical principle is to minimise any risks that a research project may pose to the welfare of research team members and other project personnel. A research project may involve contact with people with a history of violence, or with communicable health problems. Other projects may require research assistants to visit people in their own homes, or travel to places with hostile climates or living conditions. In all instances, it will be important to implement strategies to try to reduce any risks to the safety of researchers, research assistants or other project staff (see Chapter 8, Managing a Research Project). During research that involves investigating sensitive or stressful topics, it may be necessary to provide formal debriefing and support sessions for research team members.

Ethical review of research plans and proposals

As we have already emphasised, when planning any new research project it is important to give careful thought to the project's ethical dimensions, starting with the broad principles just highlighted. At an early stage in the development of a project plan or research proposal, get people with a good understanding of research ethics to review your intentions. This could be done in a low-key way initially, such as talking with a project supervisor or a colleague. Once your research proposal is close to being finalised, it could be submitted to a specialist group of ethical advisers for a more formal, detailed review.

In many places around the world, formal research ethics authorities have been set up to scrutinise the ethics of research projects (cf., Dixon-Woods, Angell, Ashcroft, & Bryman, 2007). Some of these ethics authorities are linked to national and regional health or hospital services (see Box 6.4 and Appendix 6.2 for information sources and examples). Others are linked to education and training institutions such as universities or technical colleges.

Box 6.4   Examples of information sources for ethical standards and reviews

Australia
- Research conduct and ethics – Australian Research Council
  www.arc.gov.au/about_arc/research_ethics.htm
- Health ethics – National Health and Medical Research Council
  www.nhmrc.gov.au/health_ethics/index.htm

Canada
- Tri-Council Policy Statement: Ethical Conduct for Research Involving Humans – Government of Canada.
  http://pre.ethics.gc.ca/english/policystatement/policy statement.cfm
- Panel on research ethics – Government of Canada
  www.pre.ethics.gc.ca/english/index.cfm
- Ethics – Canadian Institutes of Health Research
  www.cihr-irsc.gc.ca/e/2891.html

(Continued)

(Continued)

International
- Ethics and health – World Health Organization
  www.who.int/ethics/topics/en/
- Research ethics – Applied ethics resources on the WWW (Canada)
  www.ethicsweb.ca/resources/research/index.html

New Zealand
- Ethics reports and guidelines – Health Research Council
  www.hrc.govt.nz/root/Publications/Ethics_Reports_and_Guidelines.html
- New Zealand Health and Disability Ethics Committees
  www.ethicscommittees.health.govt.nz/

United Kingdom
- Developing a Framework for Social Science Research Ethics – University of York [has a Knowledge Base section with ethics resources for UK, Europe and the world]
  www.york.ac.uk/res/ref/kb.htm
- Ethics and research governance – Medical Research Council
  www.mrc.ac.uk/PolicyGuidance/EthicsAndGovernance/index.htm

United States
- Bioethics resources on the Web – National Institutes of Health (NIH)
  http://bioethics.od.nih.gov/

Note: If the URLs shown do not work, do a search on the organisation title.

If you are a university or polytechnic student or staff member, it is likely that some kind of group has been set up in your department or faculty to formally assess ethical standards in research. In some institutions there may be a requirement that all research proposals prepared by students and staff be submitted to an in-house ethics group for assessment and approval. In other institutions the requirements may be less strict, but staff and students will still be strongly encouraged to submit their proposals for comment, in the interests of maintaining ethical standards (Box 6.5).

Box 6.5   Ethical review required?

When writing a research proposal:

- Find out if your research proposal needs to be reviewed by an ethics authority.
- If your proposal does need to be reviewed, find out exactly what the application process involves.
- Follow all instructions carefully.

If your research project is focusing on health issues, it will be vital to work out whether your research plans need to be formally assessed by a recognised hospital or health district ethics authority. Find out which health sector organisation in your area has responsibility for overseeing the ethical conduct of health research. Go to the website of this organisation and check out the expected ethical standards relevant to the research you are planning.

What types of health research projects are required to be submitted to the ethics authority? Does your project fit these criteria?

Ethical requirements vary in different countries and regions and among different research disciplines. In general, if your project intends to collect health-related data from hospital or health clinic patients or staff, then your project plans will probably need to be formally approved by a health sector ethics authority. Formal approval may also be required if your project intends to gather potentially sensitive health information from people in the community. Your project plans will almost certainly need to be approved by a health sector ethics authority if you intend to give research participants medical treatment or do any form of testing involving the taking of body fluids or tissue samples.

If you are not sure whether your proposal needs to be submitted to an ethical authority for approval, seek further guidance directly from the most relevant authority for your discipline or research topic.

Ethical review procedures

Most ethics authorities operate a committee system for vetting and approving research proposals. Ethics committees tend to include a mix of community representatives, researchers and ethics experts. Ethics committees scrutinise a research proposal and decide whether the project's design and methods meet ethical requirements. If the proposal is found to be ethically sound, written approval for the project to start will generally be given by the committee. If the proposal is found to be lacking in some way, then the committee may require the proposal be revised and resubmitted for a further review at a later meeting. Occasionally, some research proposals will not be approved, even after extensive revision.

If your research proposal needs to be submitted to an ethics committee, it will pay to do your homework on the steps involved in the process. Find out as much as you can about the particular application forms, checklists and other paperwork that will need to be completed. Individual ethics committees often have their own distinctive requirements and processes for obtaining ethical approval, reflecting local frameworks and circumstances. (To see examples of these, go to some of the university ethics authority websites listed in Appendix 6.2 at the end of this chapter.)

Find out when the ethics committee will be meeting and the closing dates for submitting proposals to these meetings. If a committee only meets once every two months, it will be important to work towards submitting your proposal in time for the earliest available committee meeting. Missing a submission deadline by just a day or two could mean your proposal is not reviewed or approved for another three or four months. Some ethics authorities include the option for a research proposal to be fast-tracked through the review and approval process. However, sometimes this option is only available if the study is considered low risk from an ethical standpoint.

Aim to complete all required forms and paperwork as accurately and completely as possible. In many cases, ethics committees will require you to provide a detailed research proposal as well as fill in a questionnaire covering aspects of your project. Committees may also require written letters of support to be obtained from representatives of community groups or organisations in the location where you are planning to do your research. These are intended to show you have consulted at an early stage with relevant community representatives and that these people consider your research plans to be appropriate and viable.

Ethics committees may also want to see documentation confirming the qualifications and experience of the researchers who will be working on the project. The main aim of this is to check that research participants will not be exposed to untrained or inappropriate practitioners, and that student researchers will be supervised by qualified people.

Some ethics committees also require researchers to supply a literature review on the topic being investigated. Find out as soon as you can if you will need to provide a literature review as part of your ethics application. Preparing a literature review can be a sizeable task and should not be done in a hurry. Committees use the literature review to help decide if the aims and methods of the research project are justified in terms of the new research information likely to be gained. If a proposed study is merely repeating studies done elsewhere, or not likely to yield any new or important knowledge, an ethics committee may question if it is right to proceed with the study. This is especially likely if research participants will be asked to do time-consuming questionnaires or interviews, or potentially painful or risky treatments and tests. For similar reasons, ethics committees may discourage research projects that are primarily a training exercise for students, without any intention to publish the results.

Ethics committees may also want to know how many research participants you plan to include in your project, and how you worked out these numbers. Again, this is part of trying to ensure that research participants are not researched unnecessarily. Committees may want to be sure that you are recruiting only the minimum number of research participants required to get meaningful results for your study.

If your proposed research involves collecting information from people living in different regions or districts throughout a country, your project may need to be reviewed and approved by ethical authorities in each of these regions or districts. In some countries, special administrative systems have been set up to try to make it easier for researchers to submit proposals to multiple ethical review agencies.

Once a research proposal gains ethical approval, it is usually possible to start recruiting research participants and collecting data. However, contact with the ethical committee is not necessarily ended at this point. Many committees require researchers to submit regular project progress reports. This includes reporting any substantial changes to the project's research procedures.

If your project proposal is queried by an ethical review committee, or declined approval for any reason, you will need to consider revisions to your proposal, to address the concerns or issues raised by the review committee. Quite often specific issues are raised by ethics review committees that require just minor changes that can be addressed quickly. For more substantial concerns that require additional time to address, we recommend the following steps in responding to the concerns. Get as much information as possible from the ethics review committee about the concerns, preferably in writing (via letter or email). Consult with supervisors (if relevant) and colleagues about the ethics concerns raised and how the concerns might best be addressed. Draft a revised version of the ethics review application, or the specific sections or document about which concerns were raised. Show this draft to other people for comment and then send it back to the contact person for the ethics review committee.

Key ethical procedures to cover in a research proposal

If your project intends to collect information directly from research participants, your research proposal will need to describe how you plan to protect the safety, dignity and privacy of these people. In particular, at least four main ethical issues will need to be addressed:

- how potential research participants will be identified and initially contacted or approached
- how research participants will be informed about the project
- how consent will be obtained from research participants
- how the privacy and safety of research participants will be protected during the course of the project and after the project is finished.

Approaching and recruiting potential research participants

The methods you intend to use to find, contact and recruit research participants should be ethically sound and not breach privacy or confidentiality requirements. The procedures should also be culturally appropriate for the research participants you intend to recruit. For some types of research, it may be cost-effective to recruit participants from existing client databases. Many organisations and businesses, including insurers, hospitals, health clinics and government departments, maintain databases of personal information about their clients or service users. Potentially these databases could be used for selecting and contacting prospective research participants. However, access to these databases is usually restricted to staff within the organisation or business. Special procedures need to be used before any information on the client database can be passed on to a researcher (see Box 6.6).

Box 6.6   Recruiting research participants from health care services

According to most ethical guidelines, it is inappropriate for a doctor to provide a copy of his or her patient database directly to a researcher so that the researcher can phone or write to the patients and invite them to take part in a research project. If a patient finds out that their personal information has been given without permission to a person for whom it was not intended, this could undermine the person's trust in their doctor or willingness to reveal personal information to a health professional in future. A more appropriate method is for the doctor (or a member of his or her staff) to approach each of the patients individually and ask if they would be willing for their personal details to be given to the researcher. This method retains patients' control over how their personal information is used. If patients agree to their details being forwarded to the researcher, the researcher can then contact them and provide them with a clear description of the project's intended research procedures and seek each patient's formal consent to become a participant in the research.

From an ethical standpoint, this two-stage consent process is generally the most suitable way of recruiting research participants from health or social services, including the client or patient databases operated by these services.

When recruiting participants from communities, especially if the researchers are 'outsiders', special provision may need to be made to contact an appropriate group or organisation in the community to obtain their approval before attempting to recruit individual research participants. Sometimes it may not be clear whether any specific group can 'represent' the community. In these cases, longer-term planning may be needed to contact and carry out discussions with various groups and organisations in the community. Of course, extensive prior consultation will not necessarily guarantee community-level approval. Some communities may have a history of negative experiences with research groups and may be unwilling to participate in any further research projects.

Informing potential research participants about the study

Another key ethical requirement in research is informed consent. This is the principle that potential research participants should receive a thorough briefing on a research project's aims and methods and be free to choose whether or not they take part in the project.

Everybody invited to participate in a research project should be given a good, easy-to-follow explanation of the objectives, methods, potential risks and benefits, expected outcomes and intended uses of the project. Normally, a written project information sheet will be given to prospective research participants in conjunction with an oral explanation of the project. Ideally, people should be able to take the information sheet away, think about their involvement and discuss it with others. Prospective research participants should also be given plenty of opportunity and encouragement to ask questions about the project (cf., Barata, Gucciardi, Ahmad, & Stewart, 2006).

The project information sheet should outline in plain language, and concisely (ideally on one side of a page), all the important information research participants should know about the project. If the project intends to recruit research participants whose first language is not English, then the sheet should be translated into other languages as well. A typical information sheet will include the details shown in Box 6.7.

Box 6.7   Topics to cover in an information sheet for research participants

- Title of the project.
- A brief description of the project, including its aims and methods, who is conducting the project and why.
- A clear invitation to the person to consider taking part in the project.
- Statements covering the following points, where relevant to the project:

  - how research participants are being selected (and how many)
  - what participation in the project will involve (e.g., where interviews will be held, how many meetings, how much time altogether, samples taken, taping of interviews, etc.)
  - that the study is voluntary and participants can withdraw from study without any disadvantage to them
  - that interpreters will be available for participants if requested by participants
  - whether participants will be reimbursed or recognised for their contribution to the project (e.g., gift or voucher)
  - whether participants can have support people with them during the research
  - how information collected from research participants will be kept anonymous and/or confidential, how it will be stored and for how long, and who will have access
  - whether and how the results of the research will be available for participants
  - that an ethics committee has approved the study (if applicable).

- The name, professional designation and contact details of the researcher (plus those of other researchers in the project, where relevant).
- Date on which the information sheet was compiled or updated.

During an ethical review of your project proposal, some ethics committees may want to see copies (draft or finalised) of the project information sheets you plan to give to prospective research participants.

Getting consent from research participants

Integral to the ethical principle of informed consent is the requirement that people should be free to choose whether to take part in a research project. Prospective research participants should not be coerced or pressured into joining a research project. Rather, they should be told plainly that they are free to accept or decline the invitation to participate. They should also be informed that if they do elect to participate in the project, they can still choose to leave the project at any time. They do not have to continue taking part if they do not want to. In the project information sheet, research participants should be told about any possible negative consequences of withdrawing from a study. If there are no foreseeable negative consequences, this should also be stated in the project information sheet.

Ethical guidelines often indicate that offering payment to people to take part in a research project can act as a form of inducement. This may result in some people agreeing to participate in a project when otherwise they would not have. Normal practice is to avoid offering straight financial payment to research participants. However, some remuneration for incidental expenses such as travel, food or childcare is usually considered appropriate (see Box 6.8).

Box 6.8 Ethical dilemmas in providing payment to research participants

One of this book's authors (DRT) was a member of a research team conducting interviews with 'at-risk' parents. Given that these parents were financially disadvantaged, the research team discussed whether it should provide some type of cash payment to the parents to cover the interview time (about 1 hour). However, some of the team worried that this payment might act as a financial inducement or be seen as 'coercion' to participate in the interviews. After further discussion, it was decided to offer the participating parents the choice of a petrol voucher or a supermarket voucher and not to tell them about this offer until after their interview was completed. While this satisfied most of the ethical issues discussed, it did not address one issue, which was to avoid providing a payment that could be used to purchase alcohol or cigarettes.

Most ethical guidelines emphasise the importance of clearly documenting that research participants have freely agreed to take part in a project by asking them to fill in and sign a printed consent form (see Box 6.9). Typically, the consent form will consist of a series of statements, which participants sign or mark in some other way to verify they:

- have received, read and understood the project information sheet
- have had an opportunity to discuss the project with members of the research team and ask questions
- understand that taking part in the project is voluntary and that they may withdraw at any time without being disadvantaged

- understand that participation in the study is anonymous and that any information which may identify them will be kept confidential
- agree to take part in the project.

As with the project information sheet, it is important to ensure research participants are able to read and fully understand the contents of the consent form. For some projects it may be necessary to provide a translated version of the form or an interpreter.

Box 6.9   Example of a consent form

University or other organisation letterhead

CONSENT FORM
Title of Research Project
Researcher: W. B. Jones

☐   I have been given and have understood an explanation of this research project. I have had an opportunity to ask questions and have them answered.
☐   I understand that the information I provide will be anonymous and I will not be identified in any analyses or reports resulting from the data collection.
☐   I understand that I may withdraw myself, or any information traceable to me, without giving a reason, for up to one month from the date of my participation.
☐   I agree to take part in this research.

Signed:
Print Name:
Date:

When reviewing a research proposal, an ethics committee may want to see copies of the consent forms you plan to use. Some ethics committees provide sample consent forms indicating the information they like to see in a consent form and how to present it.

In some cases it may not be possible to obtain written consent from research participants, perhaps because they are too young or too affected by a serious health problem or disability. In these situations, an alternative approach is to obtain 'third-party' consent from a close family member or caregiver. This could be done in conjunction with efforts to obtain either written or verbal consent from the actual research participant.

For telephone surveys, or brief face-to-face interviews in public places, it is sometimes impractical to obtain written consent. Nonetheless, it is important that all research participants are informed verbally about the aims of the project, have an opportunity to ask questions, and are told plainly that they are free to agree or decline to take part in the research. In some cases it may be feasible or necessary only to record a person's oral agreement to participate, such as at the start of an audio or video interview session.

For more sensitive telephone surveys where obtaining written informed consent is regarded as crucial before the survey can proceed, one solution is to send information sheets and consent forms to the research participants by post or email several days or weeks prior to the telephone interview. Research participants can then return their signed consent forms by mail, either before or after research team members have contacted them by phone to discuss the study and answer any questions.

Informed consent from individual participants might also be supported by broader declarations of consent by communities or organisations. This might be achieved through formal meetings with relevant community representatives or officials.

Protecting the privacy and safety of research participants

Ethical guidelines repeatedly stress the need to ensure that the identities and personal information of research participants remain protected and confidential. Essentially, this means any information that could identify individual research participants, or any information given by research participants in confidence (i.e., with the expectation that it will be kept secret), must not be revealed to anyone except members of the research team (see Box 6.10).

Box 6.10   Maintaining confidentiality

Methods for protecting the identities and confidential information of research participants include:

- limiting the number of research team members able to access files containing names of research participants and other identifying material
- using code numbers or pseudonyms (false names) instead of people's real names in questionnaires, databases, interview transcripts and other project materials
- ensuring all sensitive or confidential project files are securely locked away or password protected when not in use
- when publishing research results, ensuring information such as case studies or verbatim extracts from interview transcripts are presented in such a way that individual research participants cannot be identified.

In many instances, especially if a project is investigating a sensitive or controversial topic, research participants may not want other people (family members, friends, work colleagues) to know they are contributing information to the project, or find out about the kinds of opinions or personal experiences they are reporting. For this reason, it is crucial to set up systems for securely storing away all research participant information so that only authorised people can access it.

Similarly, when a research project's findings are presented in research reports, it is vital that none of the information in these reports, such as direct quotations from interviews or biographical sketches and commentaries, can be used to personally identify any of the project's research participants or reveal private information research participants do not want disclosed (cf. Wiles, Crow, Heath, & Charles, 2008). This is likely to be especially important in projects covering sensitive or controversial topics. If the identity of a research participant can be determined from clues given in a research report and linked to information or opinions the participant has given about a topic, this can potentially expose the person to a range of negative consequences.

Note, however, that in some research projects – especially where the research participants are already well known in their community or have a high profile in their occupation or profession – some individuals may be prepared to waive their rights to privacy and confidentiality. These people may be happy to be openly identified as participants in the research and to have their names associated with opinions, experiences or other personal information described in reports. However, when quoting participants who can be identified, it is important that the researcher shows the research participant a copy of the information to be included in the report prior to the report being finalised, and that the participant agrees to the information being included (see Box 6.11).

Box 6.11   Participant confidentiality: a brief case study

In a draft report describing the results of a survey on community needs for youth facilities, the researchers include a quotation from an interview with the manager of a youth facility. In the quote, the manager is highly critical of a government agency that provides funding for youth services. When the manager sees the report, he threatens to sue the researchers unless they remove the quote from the report.

The researchers made two errors when including the quote in their report. Firstly, they did not check with the manager whether the quote could be included in the report. Secondly, they used the manager's name in the report without getting his explicit approval to do so.

Some ethical guidelines advise that research participants should be given an opportunity to review the information they supply to a project (e.g., interview transcripts, notes from focus groups). This helps ensure research participants are happy with the information in its current form and that confidential information is not being revealed inadvertently. Research participants should also be given a copy of a project's final report (or a summary), or at least told where they can access the report if they want it.

Health and social research projects often deal with sensitive or controversial topics that can be disturbing or upsetting for some research participants. As well, certain types of research, such as clinical trials, involve administering health treatments like surgery or drugs, or asking people to provide samples of body fluid or tissue. These kinds of procedures have the potential to cause undesirable side effects, pain or discomfort, especially in more vulnerable groups such as children, older people and people with pre-existing health conditions. At all times, researchers should try to anticipate the many different ways in which the data collection procedures they plan to use could be upsetting or harmful to research participants. Steps should be taken to try to minimise the risks of these negative effects occurring, as well as putting in place strategies for managing any problems if they arise. These strategies might include, for example, making counselling services available to research participants who get upset by topics covered in interviews, or having experienced health practitioners on hand to respond quickly to any negative side-effects of medicines or other risky treatments.

More broadly, ethical guidelines often stress the importance of ensuring the research procedures chosen for a project are appropriate to the prevailing cultural and social expectations or norms of the research participants. For example, people from some cultures or social groups may find it uncomfortable, challenging or distressing to be expected to participate in research involving highly individualised data collection techniques, such as one-to-one, face-to-face, tape-recorded interviews. Group-based forms of research inquiry may be more appropriate in these contexts.

In addition, representatives of the communities or cultures in which a research project is being conducted may need to be involved in the design and implementation of the project. This can help build trust between the research participants and researchers and ensure the use of culturally or socially appropriate research techniques from the very start of the project. As indicated previously, ethics committees often require researchers to show they have consulted with recognised representatives of relevant cultural or social groups and communities in the locations where they plan to do research.

In projects involving large numbers of research participants, it may be important to set up a clear project contact point (e.g., telephone number and email address) and a formal complaints process so that research participants can formally draw attention to any problems they are experiencing with a project. Some ethics committees require all research participants in a project be given the name and telephone number of a person they can contact to make a complaint. Sometimes it is also required that research participants have the option of taking complaints directly to the ethical authority.

Safety of indigenous peoples and disadvantaged ethnic groups

In some countries, ethics committees now require researchers to consider the potential impacts of their proposed research on the health and well-being of indigenous and ethnic minority groups, particularly groups that historically have been disadvantaged or experienced racism and discrimination. This reflects concerns that research by people in dominant ethnic groups has had negative impacts on specific groups, or that the research has only benefited certain dominant ethnic groups. As a result, in some countries it has become increasingly difficult for researchers to gain access to indigenous communities or to recruit participants from ethnic groups that have traditionally been disadvantaged. As well, many people in non-dominant ethnic groups may be distrustful of researchers from dominant groups (Barata et. al., 2006).

Assessing research involving non-dominant ethnic groups

As a matter of good practice, researchers should familiarise themselves with issues likely to arise when doing research with ethnic and cultural groups different from their own group, especially when researchers from dominant ethnic groups intend recruiting participants from non-dominant ethnic groups. The following questions provide an initial checklist for thinking about the ethical dimensions of these kinds of research projects.

1. *Reducing inequalities.* In what ways might the research lead to a reduction of inequalities among ethnic groups? Disadvantaged groups may justifiably be reluctant to participate in research that will not lead to any benefits for them. Research that simply aims to document already well-known inequalities among ethnic groups might justifiably be rejected if it is unlikely to contribute to reducing these inequalities (cf., Braveman & Gruskin, 2003).
2. *Developing research workforce training and experience.* How can the research project be planned so it provides training and research experience for members of disadvantaged groups, so they develop their own research skills, participate as researchers in ongoing research projects, and initiate their own research?
3. *Ensuring the use of culturally appropriate data gathering procedures.* Research involving ethnic or cultural groups different from those of the project team should ensure the data-gathering

procedures are culturally appropriate for the research participants. Some of the writing about this topic refers to the need for 'cultural competence' in the research team, especially team members who have direct contact with participants, such as interviewers (cf., Donovan & Spark, 1997; Skaff, Chesla, Mycue, & Fisher, 2002).

4. *Multiple interpretations of research findings.* In what ways can the analysis and interpretation of the project data allow for multiple perspectives? Can the project team avoid culture-bound interpretations of the data that may perpetuate inequalities (cf., Jones, 2001)?

5. *Avoiding victim-blaming or deficit explanations.* Social and health research contains many examples of disadvantaged groups being portrayed as responsible for their own disadvantage. Researchers need to avoid blaming disadvantaged groups for outcomes that are more likely to be the result of exclusion or discrimination. Deficit theories of disadvantage are especially suspect.

6. *Disseminating findings through indigenous networks.* Worldwide, there are also many examples of research projects that have included research participants from indigenous and ethnic minority groups, but where the researchers have neglected to communicate their project findings directly back to the local people and communities involved. When planning any new project that includes people from indigenous or non-dominant ethnic groups, it is important to identify how the project findings will be reported back to these people through local or indigenous networks, so the people have an opportunity to consider and use the results. Project proposals and ethics applications should include a section discussing the steps that will be taken to do this.

Conclusion: Maintaining a personal commitment to ethical research

Preparing an ethically watertight research proposal is really only the beginning of a researcher's ethical responsibilities. Even more important is the need to successfully meet and uphold these ethical principles and standards in practice once a project starts, and in all activities related to the project from then on. Each new project will have its own set of unique ethical problems and challenges. By taking the time to read, reflect on and discuss the information outlined in this chapter, hopefully readers will be in a better position to understand these ethical problems and challenges, as well as identify appropriate procedures to resolve them.

It is important to stress in closing that there is continuing debate in research circles about the value and practicality of some of the ethical principles and procedures discussed above (Alderson, 2007). For example, some researchers contend that it is unrealistic to expect all potential research participants to read, let alone understand, the details supplied on a project information sheet, even if it has been written with care. Some researchers, too, even question whether it is a good idea to have formal ethics committees reviewing research proposals. They argue that the review process can often be too complicated, time-consuming and costly for researchers and in some cases a genuine barrier to getting more innovative or exploratory styles of social research up and running. A better approach, some say, is to focus primarily on educating and encouraging individual researchers to think deeply about the potential ethical dimensions of their work and to learn as much as possible about the range of practical strategies available for getting their work done with the minimum of risk to their research participants and others.

Exercises for ethics and research

1. Submitting a research proposal for ethical review often involves following complex instructions and filling in lengthy application forms. To develop your knowledge of ethics review submission processes, find the website of the main human research ethics authority in your institution, district or discipline. Read through the authority's instructions about the types of research requiring ethical approval and how to submit an application for review. Then go to some of the university research ethics authority websites listed in Appendix 5.2 (or others you can find on the Internet). Compare the ethics review application processes described on the websites you locate. How similar are they to the application process of your local ethics authority?
2. You are hired by your local department of justice to conduct a research project looking at people's perceptions of different types of crime and criminal behaviour. The main method of data collection is face-to-face interviews with a representative sample of the general adult population. The interviews will be held mainly in people's homes. You anticipate some proportion of the research participants will have been involved in criminal behaviour at some time in their lives. They may even want to discuss illegal things they have done, or are doing. What ethical considerations do you think should be included in the project's research proposal to cover these people? What safeguards do you think should be put in place for the researchers carrying out the interviews?
3. Recent years have seen a steady increase in the use of the Internet for conducting research on people's opinions and experiences, such as by way of online questionnaires, virtual interviews, or by participating in chat rooms or other online forums. Do a brief literature search on the ethics of online research. What are some of the special ethical problems or challenges associated with doing research in the online environment? What practical strategies do you think could be used to promote more ethical online research?
4. You intend to do research with a group of people who are usually hard to contact and recruit for participation in research. To expedite your project you intend to offer them some payment or a gift. Do a literature search to identify the advantages and disadvantages of offering payment or other inducements to participate. Then identify three key ethical principles that are relevant to payment of participants.

References and further reading

Alderson, P. (2007). Governance and ethics in health research. In: M. Saks & J. Allsop (Eds), *Researching Health: Qualitative, Quantitative and Mixed Methods* (pp. 283–300). London: Sage.

Barata, P. C., Gucciardi, E., Ahmad, F., & Stewart, D. E. (2006). Cross-cultural perspectives on research participation and informed consent. *Social Science & Medicine, 62*(2), 479–490.

Braveman, P. & Gruskin, S. (2003). Defining equity in health. *Journal of Epidemiology & Community Health, 57*(4), 254–258.

Dixon-Woods, M., Angell, E., Ashcroft, R. E., & Bryman, A. (2007). Written work: the social functions of Research Ethics Committee letters. *Social Science & Medicine, 65*(4), 792–802.

Donovan, R. J. & Spark, R. (1997). Towards guidelines for survey research in remote Aboriginal communities. *Australian and New Zealand Journal of Public Health, 21*(1), 89–95.

Hammersley, M. & Gomm, R. (1997). Bias in social research. *Sociological Research Online, 2*(1). Retrieved May 12, 2009, from: www.socresonline.org.uk/socresonline/2/1/2.html.

International Committee of Medical Journal Editors (2008). *Uniform Requirements for Manuscripts Submitted to Biomedical Journals: Writing and Editing for Biomedical Publication* (Updated October 2008). Retrieved April 20, 2009, from: www.icmje.org/.

Jason, L. A., Pokorny, S., & Katz, R. (2001). Passive versus active consent: a case study in school settings. *Journal of Community Psychology, 29*(1), 53–68.

Jones, C. P. (2001). Invited commentary: 'Race,' racism, and the practice of epidemiology. *American Journal of Epidemiology, 154*(4), 299–304.

Madge, C. (2007). Developing a geographers' agenda for online research ethics. *Progress in Human Geography, 31*(5), 654–674.

Mertens, D. M. & Ginsberg, P. (Eds) (2008). *Handbook of Social Research Ethics.* London: Sage.

National Health and Medical Research Council (2007). *National Statement on Ethical Conduct in Human Research.* Canberra: Australian Government. Retrieved May 21, 2009, from: www.nhmrc.gov.au/guidelines/ethics_guidelines.htm.

Richardson, S. & McMullan, M. (2007). Research ethics in the UK: what can sociology learn from health? *Sociology: the Journal of the British Sociological Association, 41*(6), 1115–1132.

Sismondo, S. (2008). How pharmaceutical industry funding affects trial outcomes: causal structures and responses. *Social Science & Medicine, 66*(9), 1909–1914.

Skaff, M. M., Chesla, C. A., Mycue, V., & Fisher, L. (2002). Lessons in cultural competence: adapting research methodology for Latino participants. *Journal of Community Psychology, 30*(3), 305–323.

Tinker, A. & Coomber, V. (2004). *University Research Ethics Committees: Their Role, Remit and Conduct.* London: King's College London.

Wiles, R., Crow, G., Heath, S., & Charles, V. (2008). The management of confidentiality and anonymity in social research. *International Journal of Social Research Methodology, 11*(5), 417–428.

APPENDIX 6.1

Examples of Statements of Professional Ethics and Codes of Practice

Australia

Australian National Health and Medical Research Council: National Statement on Ethical Conduct in Human Research, 2007
www.nhmrc.gov.au/health_ethics/ahec/guidelines/index.htm

Australian Psychological Society: Code of Ethics
www.psychology.org.au/aps/ethics/default.asp

Australian Sociological Association: Ethical Guidelines
www.tasa.org.au/ethical-guidelines/

Australasian Evaluation Society: Guidelines for the Ethical Conduct of Evaluations
www.aes.asn.au

Canada

Canadian Sociology and Anthropology Association: Statement of Professional Ethics
www.csaa.ca/structure/Code.htm

Canadian Psychological Association: Code of Ethics for Psychologists
www.acposb.on.ca/code.htm

New Zealand

New Zealand Psychological Society: Code of Ethics for Psychologists Working in Aotearoa/ New Zealand
www.psychology.org.nz/Code_of_Ethics

Sociological Association of Aotearoa: Code of Ethics
http://saanz.rsnz.org/ethics.html

Association of Social Anthropologists of Aotearoa New Zealand: Principles of Professional Responsibility and Ethical Conduct
http://asaanz.rsnz.org/codeofethics.html

United Kingdom

Social Research Association: Ethical Guidelines
www.the-sra.org.uk/ethical.htm

Royal College of Nursing's Guidance for Nurses: Research Ethics
www.rcn.org.uk/development/researchanddevelopment/rs/publications_and_position_
   statements/research_ethics_guidance

British Sociological Association: Statement of Ethical Practice
www.britsoc.co.uk/equality/Statement+Ethical+Practice.htm

British Psychological Society: Code of Conduct and Ethical Guidelines
www.bps.org.uk/the-society/code-of-conduct/code-of-conduct_home.cfm

RESPECT Code of Practice for Socio-Economic Research
www.respectproject.org/code/

United States

American Psychological Association: Ethical Principles of Psychologists and Code of Conduct
www.apa.org/ethics/code2002.html

American Sociological Association: Code of Ethics
www.asanet.org/page.ww?section=Ethics&name=Ethics

American Evaluation Association: Guiding Principles for Evaluators
www.eval.org

American Anthropological Association: Code of Ethics
www.aaanet.org/committees/ethics/ethcode.htm

American Educational Research Association: Ethical Standards
www.aera.net/AboutAERA/Default.aspx?menu_id=90&id=222

APPENDIX 6.2

Examples of University Websites Containing Research Ethics, Review Instructions and Application Forms

Australia

Charles Sturt University
www.csu.edu.au/research/committees/human/index.htm

University of Western Sydney
www.uws.edu.au/research/ors/ethics/human_ethics/apply_to_human_research_ethics_committee_guide1

University of Western Australia
www.research.uwa.edu.au/welcome/research_services/Ethics/human_ethics/forms_guidelines_policies2/eligibility_criteria

Flinders University
www.flinders.edu.au/research/info-for-researchers/ethics/committees/social-behavioural.cfm

Canada

McMaster University
www.mcmaster.ca/ors/ethics/index.htm

McGill University
www.mcgill.ca/researchoffice/compliance/human/

University of Toronto
www.research.utoronto.ca/ethics/

New Zealand

University of Auckland
www.auckland.ac.nz/uoa/about/research/ethics/human-ethics-committee/university-of-auckland-human-participants-ethics-committee.cfm

University of Canterbury
www.canterbury.ac.nz/humanethics/apply.shtml

University of Otago
www.otago.ac.nz/administration/committees/human_ethics_cmmttee.html

United Kingdom and Ireland

City University London
www.city.ac.uk/research/ethics/research_ethics.html

Queen Margaret University (Edinburgh)
www.qmu.ac.uk/research_knowledge/ethics.htm

Oxford Brookes University
www.brookes.ac.uk/res/ethics/review

Swansea University
www.swan.ac.uk/registry/PostgraduateResearchstudies/Researchethics/

University of Bristol
www.bristol.ac.uk/research/support/governance/ethics/ethics.html

University College Dublin
www.ucd.ie/researchethics/ethical_review.html

University of Reading
www.reading.ac.uk/internal/res/ResearchEthics/reas-REethicshomepage.asp

University of East Anglia
www.uea.ac.uk/foh/research/ethics

University of Glasgow
www.gla.ac.uk/lbss/research/ethics/

University of Greenwich, Research Ethics Committee
www.gre.ac.uk/research/research_ethics_committee

United States

Fresno Pacific University
www.fresno.edu/irb/

Stanford University
http://humansubjects.stanford.edu/index

University of Florida
http://irb.ufl.edu/

University of Illinois
http://irb.illinois.edu/?q=home.asp

University of Iowa
http://research.uiowa.edu/hso/index.php?get=irb_main

University of Maryland Eastern Shore
www.umes.edu/IRB/Default.aspx?id=18988

University of Massachusetts Boston
www.umb.edu/research/orsp/compliance/irb.html

University of North Dakota
www.umb.edu/research/orsp/compliance/irb.html

Vanderbilt University
www.mc.vanderbilt.edu/irb/index.php

7 Doing a Literature Review

Topics covered in this chapter

- What is a literature review?
- Types of literature review
- Getting to grips with technology
- Preliminary thinking and scoping your review
- Using electronic search engines and databases
- Using key words in electronic searches
- Widening the literature search
- Storing your search results
- Getting hold of publications
- Critically appraising the literature
- Writing and organising your review

This chapter describes the steps involved in preparing a literature review, from initial searching through to final report writing. While the chapter is mainly written for people who are setting out to do a literature review for the first time, researchers with some experience of preparing literature reviews may also find the guidelines helpful.

What is a literature review?

A literature review is a systematic study of existing research and other published information on a specific topic. Literature reviews can be used to:

- identify key information relevant to a topic
- assess the status or quality of existing research
- critically examine support for alternative theories or arguments
- evaluate research methods used in previous studies.

When planning a new research project, such as a thesis or dissertation, a literature review can be used to:

- identify possible research topics to focus on
- find out what is already known about a topic
- highlight questions or issues that need further study
- select suitable research methods to use in a project.

Literature reviews can also be used to assist the formulation or evaluation of policies, programmes or services by:

- updating basic knowledge
- reviewing research assessing the effectiveness of specific applications or interventions
- identifying best practice principles.

Doing a literature review usually involves four main steps:

- developing and refining the topic and scope of the literature to be reviewed
- searching for and retrieving copies of relevant research material
- reading through the studies located and assessing them
- writing a report summarising the key information found.

Often these steps will overlap. In most reviews, several rounds of searching, reading and writing may be needed before a review is complete.

Types of literature review

Literature reviews can be long or short, cover a wide or narrow range of studies and be aimed at a broad or specialised audience. Two general types of literature review are summarised in Table 7.1. These are:

- a general or conceptual literature review (which may be brief or extended)
- a systematic review that provides evidence regarding best practice.

TABLE 7.1   COMMON TYPES OF LITERATURE REVIEWS

	General, conceptual literature review		Systematic review
Length of review	Extended review	Brief review	Usually extended and highly focused
Format for the review report	Chapter in a thesis, section in a research technical report or a stand-alone document	Introduction section for a journal article, research proposal or funding application	Review report summarising outcomes from best available evidence
Purposes	Conceptual or narrative overview and summary of findings related to research topic	Justification of how the research project addresses a topic needing further research	Assess quality of evidence supporting use of specific practices or interventions
Analytic strategy	Mainly narrative, qualitative or thematic analysis	Concise focus leading to research questions or hypotheses	Mainly quantitative, using 'hierarchy of evidence' assessment to identify best quality reports
Scope	Extensive, may include some history and context for topic	Primarily research studies that are pivotal or central to the proposed research	Review only best quality studies that have assessed specific practices or interventions
Focus on design and methods in studies reviewed	Topic is primary focus but may include information on methods	Both topics and methods are usually relevant	Research design and methods a crucial part of quality assessment. RCT studies are preferred
Outcomes highlighted in review	Knowledge of a range of literature related to research topic	Identifies key questions needing further investigation	Selection criteria for inclusion of studies, synthesis of evidence from highest quality studies
Potential audiences	Specialist researchers, thesis examiners	Other researchers interested in the topic	Practitioners and service managers, other researchers

RCT = randomised controlled trial

A general extended literature review for a technical report, or a thesis or dissertation, is likely to be about 15–30 pages long. It will usually be included as a separate chapter in the report or thesis. Normally the review will provide a *conceptual overview* of the research topic, be organised into several sub-topics or themes and include a discussion of how research in the area has developed over time. A conceptual overview is a framework or organising structure that helps make sense of the multiple topics included in the review. A thesis literature review needs to demonstrate knowledge about the key features of the research topic, and assess the strengths and weaknesses of the various research studies on the topic. The review should note the types of research reported and identify any gaps in the research. Sometimes the review of research methods related to a thesis topic may be written as a separate chapter. Box 7.1 shows an example of a general, conceptual review.

Box 7.1   Example of a general conceptual literature review

Outsourcing and the Changing Nature of Work (Davis-Blake & Broschak, 2009)

This sociology review, published as a journal article, is 20 pages in length. It defines outsourcing and describes the key features of outsourcing arrangements likely to affect the nature of work. The primary purpose of the article is to 'review and organise the growing but fragmented body of research that suggests that outsourcing is indeed associated with important changes in the design and functioning of jobs, work groups, internal labor markets, and key intra- and interorganizational structures' (p. 322). The main topics covered in the article include, types of outsourcing arrangements, dimensions of outsourcing arrangements, effects on job design and work group dynamics and effects on organizational design. It concludes with a section on 'Directions for future research'.

The article is an example of a general, conceptual literature review. Its primary purpose is to clarify the nature of outsourcing and its links with other features of work. The article does not include any detail about the search procedures or the databases or other sources used to locate relevant literature, nor does it mention the research designs or methods used by the authors of the articles reviewed.

A brief conceptual literature review, such as one included in the introduction to a research proposal, funding application or research report (e.g., manuscript for a research journal) is typically about 3–5 pages long and aims to provide a context and justification for the research proposed or reported. The review needs to be brief for space reasons, as funding agencies and journal editors often strictly limit the number of words or pages allowed in a research proposal or manuscript. The review should focus only on the most relevant literature and be clearly linked to the aims and objectives of the research being proposed or reported.

A systematic review is a special type of literature review that aims to provide a synthesis of the main trends or findings in a carefully selected group of studies on a topic, using procedures intended to limit bias and random error (see Cooper, 2009). Selection of research reports for inclusion in a systematic review involves assessing the quality of each study and its research methodology according to specified criteria such as: (a) the type of research design used, (b) the population or sample used in the study, (c) the type of intervention (or group differences) reported and (d) the outcomes from the study. Many systematic reviews include only quantitative studies and often limit inclusion to only those using randomised controlled trials or experimental studies. A meta-analysis is a type of systematic review that combines the statistical results from several studies to produce an overall summary estimate. Box 7.2 outlines an example of a meta-analytic review that has used a systematic review approach. Further information about systematic reviews in health care interventions is available from the Cochrane Collaboration (www.cochrane.org).

Box 7.2   Example of a meta-analytic review

Perceived Discrimination and Health (Pascoe & Richman, 2009)

This review tested the hypothesis that perceived discrimination is significantly related to mental and physical health outcomes. The review used a meta-analysis and research synthesis to examine the relationship between perceived discrimination and several health outcomes. The most common forms of discrimination covered are racial or ethnic discrimination (examined in 65 per cent of research articles covered by the review) and gender discrimination (14 per cent of articles). The meta-analysis identified the ways perceived discrimination can affect health, such as through psychological and physiological stress responses and health behaviours. The review concludes that perceived discrimination has a significant negative effect on both mental and physical health and leads to heightened stress responses and participation in unhealthy behaviours.

The review is based on a Masters thesis by the review's first author and is 24 journal pages long (16 pages of text and 8 pages of references). To be included in the research synthesis, an article had to contain data relating discrimination to a health outcome. The review reports the search terms and databases used for the review, as well as the specific criteria for inclusion of articles in the review. The sample consists of 192 articles of which 134 are included in the quantitative meta-analysis.

Getting to grips with technology

Before starting work on your review, make sure you are familiar with the range of electronic search technology available today. This chapter assumes you will be using some type of computer-based search technology.

Recent years have seen a shift away from doing literature reviews using paper-based library catalogue systems, manual browsing of library shelves and the photocopying of hard copies of research studies. The wide availability of computer-based search technology, coupled with the facility to download digital copies of studies straight from electronic databases or publisher websites, have made it potentially much easier and quicker to do literature reviews.

Some of the more popular ways to electronically search for and/or download published studies include using general Web-based search engines (e.g., Google), specialist research-focused search engines (e.g., Google Scholar at http://scholar.google.com/) and research literature databases accessible through university libraries. Features of these three methods are summarised in Table 7.2.

TABLE 7.2 SEARCHING FOR RESEARCH LITERATURE USING ELECTRONIC SOURCES

	General Internet search engines	Research-focused Internet search engines	Research literature databases
Examples	Google, Yahoo	Google Scholar	Medline, PsycINFO
Access	Public	Public	Via university library or other subscription service
Advantages	Quick and easy to use Can access 'grey' literature such as technical reports not covered in other research databases	Quick and easy to use Access to a wider range of research literature than other databases	Provides more in-depth coverage of sets of journals in a subject area Often provides full text access. Sometimes provides access to books in electronic format
Disadvantages	Many hits are likely to be irrelevant. Some sources may not be trustworthy	Many hits will be to articles requiring a subscription for full text access	Requires access through a subscriber service May require specialised search procedures

Preliminary thinking and scoping your review

Begin by thinking carefully about your review's scope and purpose. Are you aiming to do a general review or a briefer, more focused review? How much time do you have to do the review? How comprehensive or thorough does the review have to be? What are the key research questions or topics you want to cover? Are the research questions and objectives specific enough to guide the research design and data collection?

At the same time, try to get an initial idea of how much literature is out there on your topic. This can be especially important if you are planning to commit to completing your review within a fixed timeframe or budget. Start with a small preliminary search of an easy-to-access database like Medline or Google Scholar. Enter a brief description of your topic in the search area of the database and see how many articles it finds. Look at the abstracts for the articles. If there seem to be many studies all relevant to your topic, then potentially your review may need to be quite complex and require a lot of time to complete. Alternatively, if only a few relevant studies appear, there is a chance that your review could be done quite quickly.

If there is a lot of literature available, and if there are already published reviews on the topic you are reviewing, you might consider setting a date limit for your review when using electronic databases. For example, if you are doing a search in April 2011, you may specify a date limits of 2000 to 2011 (or 2000 to current). In this case, only articles from January 2000 to the current date will be retrieved. An example using date limits is shown in Table 7.3 (p. 112).

A useful procedure in the planning stage of a literature review is to talk to people who are knowledgeable about the topic you wish to review. Ask them about current controversies in the field, what are some key papers or articles on the topic, and which research centres or teams have been publishing or reporting on the topic, or related topics. Discussions with key informants can alert you to some of the key ideas you need to consider when planning your literature review.

Sometimes a literature review may be done as part of a team project. In this case, it may be possible for specific members of the team to focus on topics with which they are most familiar. However, when integrating the individual contributions and bringing the review together as a single document, coordination of the team and the writing styles used becomes important (See Box 7.3)

Defining and refining your topic

In the early stages of the literature review, it is quite common to experience a shift in specific areas of interest once you start reading relevant literature. For this reason, be flexible in the early stages when reading relevant articles and be prepared to revise any specific objectives for your review during the early stages of the review. While this flexibility may not be possible during a systematic review (clear objectives for systematic reviews are expected to be set in advance), it is common during thesis research to spend several weeks or months clarifying the specific areas of focus for a review. During the early stages of reading relevant literature, a good strategy is to note emerging themes and ideas, and develop and revise a set of specific questions, or sub-topics to create an overall framework for the review.

Box 7.3   Doing a large literature review as a team

Agencies and businesses often commission researchers to do literature reviews on selected topics. In some cases these literature reviews (sometimes called 'systematic reviews' or 'evidence-based reviews') can be very wide-ranging and include hundreds or even thousands of studies or published reports. Such extensive reviews are usually done by a team of researchers rather than just one person. The team may include people with special training in the use of electronic bibliographies and online search software. Often particular criteria will be used to define what kinds of studies will qualify for inclusion in the review. For example, a study might have to use a certain kind of research design, such as a case–control group or comparison group, before it is considered 'strong' enough evidentially to be included in the review.

Some literature reviews specify very stringent criteria for the studies that will be included. In these cases the research team may have to check through numerous papers and reports before finding perhaps only a handful of studies that actually qualify for inclusion in the review. This work is sometimes aided by the use of a standard checklist or question sheet which is filled in for each study report or paper being assessed.

Managing the process of reviewing many hundreds or thousands of individual study reports as a team is a significant logistical challenge that should not be under-estimated. The challenge will be greater if research team members are located in different parts of the country or have never worked with each other before. Ideally, there should be one person in the research team who takes overall responsibility for co-ordinating the work of the team. This includes making sure each research team member is receiving the correct studies to review and the criteria for excluding studies is being applied consistently by everyone in the team.

(Continued)

<table>
<tr><td>

(Continued)

When reporting the findings of the review, normally the review topic is broken down into separate sub-topics. Different members of the research team can then take responsibility for writing-up the findings relevant to each sub-topic. Sometimes key features or data from individual studies are summarised in 'evidence tables', rather than trying to describe each study in detail in the actual text of the report.

Team members working together on a large-scale literature review should have opportunities to check and critique each other's work before it is reported or published. In the end, everyone should be happy to have their names associated with the final review report.
</td></tr>
</table>

Using key words in electronic searches

To find the most relevant research reports on a topic, you will need to be creative and to think broadly about the key words and subject headings that could possibly be related to the topic in which you are interested. Authors of research reports, or the people preparing reports for entry into literature databases, may conceptualise or describe the research topic in several different ways.

During your initial reading, start making a list of possible key words you could use in a systematic search of the literature. For example, if you are interested in smoking in adolescents, you could include key words such as *teenagers, youth, adolescents, students* in combination with *smoking, tobacco, drug abuse, substance abuse*. You could also perhaps look under *addiction* and *nicotine*.

If you do your literature search on an electronic literature database, most of these databases will have advanced search procedures allowing you to use more complex search sequences. Based on the example above, on an electronic database you might use the following search 'string.'

(teenagers <u>or</u> youth <u>or</u> adolescents) <u>and</u> (smoking <u>or</u> tobacco <u>or</u> nicotine)

The underlined words 'or' and 'and' in the above search string (sometimes referred to as *Boolean logic*) allow the creation of more complex search strings. These produce more targeted and efficient searches. Figure 7.1 shows a diagram of this search string.

If the initial search gives too many 'hits' (articles located), try restricting the search by adding a qualifier like the following:

(teenagers <u>or</u> youth <u>or</u> adolescents) <u>and</u> (smoking <u>or</u> tobacco <u>or</u> nicotine) <u>and</u> causes

After completing your initial search you might then want to focus specifically on studies that have attempted some type of intervention to help young people quit smoking. In this case you can either continue selecting from the larger pool of articles already located or start a new search. To reduce the number of articles located above, you could try an additional qualifier such as the following:

(teenagers <u>or</u> youth <u>or</u> adolescents) <u>and</u> (smoking <u>or</u> tobacco <u>or</u> nicotine) <u>and</u> (intervention <u>or</u> quit <u>or</u> cessation)

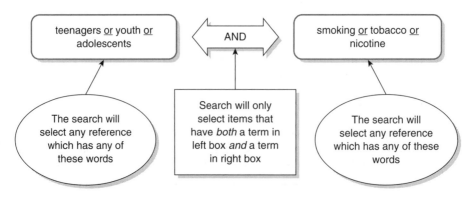

FIGURE 7.1   COMBINING TERMS FOR A LITERATURE SEARCH

Table 7.3 shows an example of a literature search history using the terms shown in the preceding text. The electronic database used for the search is called PsycINFO. See how imposing limits on the eligible articles dramatically reduces the number of articles located. The limits used were: (a) full text sources only, (b) English language sources only and (c) published between 2000 and 2009 (the most recent date) only. Also, see how the search procedures allow the progressive focusing of the search down to only those publications that include all the specified search terms. The final result of this search was 117 articles. The titles and abstracts of these articles can now be read to select the ones most relevant to the objectives of the literature review.

TABLE 7.3   EXAMPLE OF A LITERATURE SEARCH HISTORY USING PsycINFO

Search terms used	Hits (articles located)
1. (teenagers or youth or adolescents)	112,672
2. limit 1 to (full text and human and English language and yr="2000–2009")	4,402
3. (smoking or tobacco or nicotine)	28,830
4. limit 3 to (full text and human and English language and yr="2000–2009")	2,169
5. Combine 4 **and** 2	337
6. (intervention or quit or cessation)	109,941
7. limit 6 to (full text and human and English language and yr="2000–2009")	5,808
8. Combine 7 **and** 5	117

Note: This search was conducted using the PsycINFO database in April 2009.
The limitations (full text, English, 2000–2009) are shown for each search for illustrative purposes. In practice, the limitations need only be used once – on the first search string.

If you get to a stage where the search strategy produces too few articles, go back a stage and try alternative search strings until you get a manageable number of articles. You can also check more than one database to locate additional articles.

A good idea is to save a copy of your literature search history so you can use it when you write your report. It is becoming increasingly common in theses and dissertations to report the specific literature search terms used and the outcomes. An easy way to save your literature search history is to copy and paste it straight into a word processor document.

Widening the literature search

Extending the scope of your search will usually involve accessing not just one, but several of the major health and social science-related electronic databases listing research journals and books (see Table 7.4). Some of the more useful include Medline, Sociological Abstracts, PsycINFO and PubMed. With Internet access, you can also search many university library catalogues, as well as library catalogues in numerous public sector agencies throughout the world.

It is useful to develop some experience of using these and other databases yourself. However, if time is pressing, some library staff will conduct literature searches on request (usually for a fee). If the job is likely to be large, it might be worth hiring an experienced person to do the work for you.

Another useful source of information can be journals that specialise in providing research review articles on a particular topic or area. Go to these kinds of journals early in your search and see if you can find several reviews on your topic or on the broader area to which your topic is related. There are a number of review journals published each year which start with the title 'annual review of …'. To locate these journals, go to a university library and check its subscriptions using the search string 'annual review'. A recent check showed about 50 journals that start their titles with the words 'annual review'. As an example, the *Annual Review of Psychology* (2008 issue) had articles like:

- A comprehensive review of the placebo effect
- Children's social competence in cultural context
- Health psychology: the search for pathways between behaviour and health.

As well, remember to check the literature cited in the reference lists of the articles or books you collect. These lists often include studies regarded as essential reading by experts in the field.

Aim to obtain abstracts for as many of the references you find as possible. These are invaluable for assessing which publications are worth getting hold of, and which are not. It is quite common to use the abstracts for the initial screening of articles before deciding the ones you will try to obtain in full.

Sometimes, after searching various databases, you might find only a small number of publications on the topic in which you are interested. This could be simply because not much has been written about the topic (quite possible in specialised areas). Alternatively, you may not be searching the best databases (try others), or you may not be using the best key words or subjects for searching (tip: some databases have an index with cross-references to other similar key words and subjects).

Remember, too, that certain types of literature may not be included in some databases. For instance, some databases cover only scientific journal articles, not books. In-house reports are also often hard to find. For these sources, you may need to go directly to the relevant agencies involved. If in doubt about what to do at any stage, ask an information specialist or librarian, preferably one who is familiar with searching for social science, health or medical literature, as these areas include a range of specialised subjects.

If you are doing a systematic review, you need to be aware of possible bias in using only published sources of literature. Research journals are more likely to publish studies show-ing significant differences than studies showing no differences. As a result, studies showing no differences are usually under-represented in the published research literature.

TABLE 7.4   EXAMPLES OF ELECTRONIC DATABASES FOR LITERATURE SEARCHES

Discipline or subject area	Examples of databases	Description of specific databases*
Education	ERIC Education SAGE	*ERIC* Provides access to references and abstracts from over 750 journals, as well as documents produced by the Education Resources Information Centre and conference papers and reports
Health and medicine	Medline CINAHL PubMed Ageline Cochrane Library	*MEDLINE* includes bibliographic citations and author abstracts from more than 5000 biomedical journals published in the United States and 80 other countries *CINAHL* covers over 650 nursing, allied health, biomedical and consumer journals
Psychology	PsycINFO PsycEXTRA	*PsycINFO* abstracts over 1900 psychology journals as well as book chapters, books, dissertations and technical reports. The major database for psychology
Sociology and other social sciences	JSTOR Anthropology Plus Sociological Abstracts (Sociofile) Proquest Social Science Journals GenderWatch	*JSTOR* is a fulltext archive of scholarly journal literature, including key social science journals, back to their first issues *Sociofile* database provides access to international literature in sociology and related disciplines from approximately 2000 journals
General databases	SCOPUS Google Scholar ScienceDirect Web of Science Proquest Dissertations & Theses	*SCOPUS* is a large abstract and citation database of research literature and Web sources. It covers nearly 18,000 peer-reviewed journals from more than 5000 publishers, 600 trade publications, 350 book series, 3.6 million conference papers and 435 million scientific webpages

*These descriptions are taken from summaries on the database websites

One way of countering this potential bias is to contact research groups known to be doing research on the topics in which you are interested and requesting copies of unpublished research reports. Sometimes unpublished reports (often referred to as the 'grey literature' because it is usually not peer-reviewed) are available from the websites of research organisations. Other possible sources of unpublished reports include clinical research registries, clinical trial registries, and unpublished theses and conference paper listings. In addition, unpublished reports can sometimes be found on the websites of government agencies and agencies that fund research. An example is the website of the Centers for Disease Control and Prevention in the United States (www.cdc.gov), which has several hundred reports and links to research agencies on health and safety topics.

One of the most difficult things about literature searching is knowing when to stop. It is quite easy to extend your search in ever-widening circles and get bogged down with pages of references to literature that is only tangentially relevant to your topic. If you think this is starting to happen, reflect again on the purpose of your review and its key questions. Have you already got enough good material to answer the questions you are investigating? Certainly it is time to stop if you are turning up the same literature over and over again, with very few new references.

Literature reviews can become dated quite quickly. Specify the month and year in which the search was finished (e.g., August 2011) and use this as the end date for the search period. Save your electronic search terms so you can repeat the search towards the end of the project if needed, to check if any new articles have appeared since the date you conducted the main search.

Storing your search results

It is a good idea to store the results of your electronic searches on computer rather than printing them out on paper. This can save time later when you are writing up your review and needing to insert the reference details of the publications covered in your review.

You should also weigh up the potential benefits of using specialised bibliographic software to store your references and abstracts. Examples include programmes such as Endnote, Procite, Reference Manager and RefWorks. Using these programmes to create a personal bibliography takes some additional work in the early stages, but can save a lot of time in the later stages of a literature review when you are listing the publication details of all the material you have read (see Chapter 9, Software for Research, for more information on bibliographic software). At least one bibliographic package (RefWorks) has an online version that offers a free trial.

Bibliographic software has several advantages. It allows all references to be stored in one file that can be easily copied and backed up. It speeds up the insertion of reference citations in the text of documents (when you write your review or report), and saves a lot of time when you compile your reference list for your review or report. Many online journals now provide a facility for you to download the reference details directly to several types of citation manager software. Clicking on the button provided (e.g., 'Download to citation manager') on the article webpage allows you to select and open your software and download the reference details directly into your bibliographic database.

Getting hold of publications

Once you have compiled a list of potentially useful references (including abstracts), a good idea is to prioritise the publications that look most relevant and try to get hold of these first. Some journal articles will be available electronically as online, full-text articles. These are mostly in pdf format and can be read on a computer or printed out using Adobe Acrobat reader software, which is widely available as a free download.

A few journal sources are free for public download, but usually you have to pay a fee. Accessing the journal through a university library system (requiring individual logon) may allow you to open or download full-text options if the library has a subscription to the journal.

Other key publications may not be available online and will need to be retrieved manually from different sources. In many instances you will be able to access books and articles from local libraries, photocopying parts that are relevant (while remaining aware of copyright restrictions). If you are not in a position to do this work yourself, many libraries also offer literature retrieval and photocopying services. However, doing your own document retrieval and copying means you get another chance to work out which publications are likely to be worthwhile, which can save time in the long run.

Do not expect to get everything you need quickly. Some hard-to-get publications may have to be obtained from libraries outside your local area or country. This can take several days or even weeks in some cases.

Critically appraising the literature

Once you have collected a reasonable selection of relevant journal articles, book chapters, technical reports or other material, you can start reading and assessing the literature. At this stage, it may be useful to sort the literature into groups. For example, as an initial sorting procedure you may wish to distinguish several types of literature documents. These could be categorised as: published research reports that include original findings based on data collected; unpublished research reports (which could also include theses and dissertations); reviews of previous research, theoretical papers and commentaries expressing views about a specific field or topic; and papers written to advise practitioners on good practice. If you are using bibliographic software, you could add a key word to the listing for each document (e.g., 'review', 'commentary') to distinguish these types.

When assessing the quality and suitability of original research reports, there are likely to be several criteria you will need to consider. Several authors have provided detailed advice on how to critically assess research literature (e.g., Attree & Milton, 2006; Girden, 2001; Greenhalgh, 1997; Hunt & McKibbon, 1998). Probably the first criterion is to assess the *relevance* of each item for your research topic. Relevance may be assessed in several ways. Most commonly, relevance is assessed in terms of how close an article is to the topic or subject. A second type of relevance might be in terms of the sample or population group that was the focus of the research. A third type of relevance is in terms of how similar the research methods or specific data collection techniques are to your topic. Sometimes studies may be on a different topic but are relevant because the data collection methods are similar to what you plan to use.

A suggested procedure for sorting literature is to do an initial scan through the items and sort them into three groups; (i) *definitely relevant*, (ii) *possibly relevant* and (iii) *definitely not relevant*. Put aside or discard the 'not relevant' group, read the 'definitely relevant' group in more detail to clarify your ideas and identify key words commonly used. Then go through the 'possibly relevant' group and try to allocate items into either the 'definitely relevant' or 'not relevant' group. Once you have identified sufficient items in the 'definitely relevant' group, go through them individually in more detail and assess their quality.

Assessing the quality of literature is a technical task that takes some experience and familiarity with research procedures and reporting conventions. However, even beginning researchers should be able to form some idea of the quality of the research and how well it is reported. Box 7.4 lists some questions to bear in mind when reading articles. These criteria can help in assessing the overall quality of the research reports you are reviewing.

Box 7.4   Guide for critical appraisal of research reports

- What is the purpose of the research reported?
- Are the aims and objectives clearly stated and specific enough to link directly to the data gathering and findings?
- Are the sources of information cited credible? (such as literature sources)
- Is the rationale for the research design clear?
- Are the research methods described in sufficient detail to allow another researcher to replicate the research?
- Are the research methods justifiable and defensible given the research objectives?
- Are there clear links between the findings reported and the conclusions?
- Is the report clearly written and easy to understand?
- Is the report published in a reputable journal or by a well-known publisher or is it from a credible Internet source?
- Are the authors already known for their work on the topic reported?

Remember that not all articles published in refereed journals are necessarily of high quality. Conversely, not all unpublished technical reports are necessarily inferior to published versions. Critical evaluation of literature from all sources is essential. Literature from the Internet can especially be a challenge; there are fewer gatekeepers in electronic publishing compared to print publishing, and author and copyright information can be hard to locate. It is worth checking out publications that give guidance on how to critically assess sources of information from the Internet and evaluate the credibility of websites (e.g., Callahan & Thornton, 2007). Much of the information available on the Internet, that might seem to be research-based, may be misleading or false.

Another point to bear in mind is that different critical appraisal systems tend to be used in reviews of quantitative research studies (i.e., studies where the results are analysed and reported as numbers) compared with reviews of qualitative research studies (i.e., studies where the results are interpreted and described in words). For example, systematic reviews of quantitative studies assessing the effects of health treatments often include only research studies that meet specified criteria for quality. Generally, according to these criteria, the 'best' or highest level of evidence (Level I) is that obtained from a properly randomised, controlled trial. Level II evidence refers to studies that have used well-designed controlled trials without randomisation or well-designed cohort or case–control studies (cf., Concato, Shah, & Horwitz, 2000). More specific quality criteria used to assess whether or not a trial is well designed include:

- the extent to which the study reports steps taken to minimise bias in relation to sample selection and treatment conditions
- whether the study reports details of its sample size, power calculations for statistical analyses and the magnitude of reported treatment effects.

A checklist approach for reviewing qualitative studies is described by Attree and Milton (2006). Their *Qualitative Appraisal Checklist* covers eight quality categories: background; aims and objectives; context; appropriateness of the research design; sampling; data collection; data analysis; reflexivity; and usefulness of the research. It uses a scoring system, based on yes/no ratings on 23 specific attributes, with four summary assessment categories for each study:

A – no or few flaws
B – some flaws
C – considerable flaws but the study is still of some value
D – significant flaws that threaten the validity of the whole study.

Writing your review

How much time and effort you put into writing up the results of your review will depend to some extent on the purpose of the review. If you are intending to use the review mainly as a basis for preparing a research proposal, or as a starting point for developing some new research objectives, then it may not be necessary to prepare an extensive report. On the other hand, if the review will be widely published or circulated, and perhaps used by many different people to support important decisions, then preparing a well-organised and comprehensive report will be vital.

No matter what the size or importance of your literature review, at the beginning of your report you should always clearly state the specific objectives of the review and the topics it covers. You should also indicate why you conducted the review.

After this, it is usually good practice to include a paragraph setting out how you conducted your literature search. This might include listing the key words used, the electronic databases searched, the search sequences used (see the example in the key word section above) and the number of articles located at each stage.

The main sections of your review should describe, compare and discuss the different themes or topics covered in the literature you examined. Usually this is a straightforward narrative account. Occasionally, a more quantitative approach may be appropriate, for example in a meta-analysis where data from several studies are aggregated. This kind of review may contain multiple tables summarising statistical trends in the datasets reviewed.

Aim to organise relevant information from the literature under a series of headings or topics. Initially, it can be difficult identifying discrete topics and determining what order to present them in. Topics can overlap, and the same articles or books can cover several different topics. Drawing diagrams showing the interrelationships of topics can be helpful in planning a logical structure for your literature review. For larger reviews, it may also be helpful to use qualitative analysis software packages, to assist with the organisation of your review and the identification of key themes (see Box 7.5).

When summarising a specific study in the main body of your review, it is usual to indicate very briefly when and where the study was done, who the subjects were, how the study was done, its results and the author's conclusions. You may also need to include your own assessment of the limitations of the study methodology, and how the results of the study compare and contrast with other evidence.

Read the full-text of articles, not just abstracts, and aim to reflect the full range of opinions or ideas you have found, rather than just concentrating on material that supports your own theories or arguments.

Aim for a high level of accuracy when summarising other people's research. Try to reflect the authors' intentions and meanings as precisely as you can, and make it clear when you are expressing your own point of view, rather than other people's. When directly quoting another author, indicate this clearly (for example, by using a different font or text

Box 7.5   Using qualitative analysis software in a literature review

Raoul has to carry out a literature review in which he knows there are likely to be a large number of papers to analyse, perhaps more than 100. Based on previous experience of doing a literature review for his doctoral thesis, in which he reviewed about 60 papers, he decides to use qualitative analysis software to do the analysis. In the previous review, it had taken him several weeks to locate, download and read the papers, then about two months to do an initial draft of the review. He wants to speed up what to him seemed to be quite a slow process. There are no detailed guidelines that he can find indicating how to do a literature review using qualitative analysis software. He has some previous experience of using the QSR NVivo software when he did an analysis of 18 qualitative interviews. He considers himself familiar with the basic operations of the software but not an expert at using it.

After he has located the papers to be included in the review (a total of 110 papers), he starts downloading the full text copies of the papers (mostly pdfs) and creating internal documents in the qualitative software. Putting in the citation details and abstract for each paper is straightforward as he copies this text direct from the journal webpages. An initial difficulty is that for some of the pdfs the text cannot be copied and pasted into NVivo. He goes back to the journal websites and finds some have full text in webpage format (html) that can be copied and pasted directly into NVivo. However, some do not have full text. He checks with a colleague and finds that a recent new version of Adobe Acrobat writer software has an optical character recognition (OCR) function that can convert scanned text in pdfs into a version in which the text can be copied. After purchasing a copy of the new Acrobat software, Raoul is able to copy the relevant text into NVivo for the remaining pdfs. To get to this stage takes him about three weeks.

After another two weeks, Raoul completes the initial analysis of the 110 articles. He is able to use the top-level categories and sub-categories from the analysis as headings in his literature review report. Using the text from the articles that have been coded into specific categories, he is able to write directly about each category. One outcome he discovers in using the qualitative analysis software is that it focuses the review much more directly on the text of the findings reported in the articles he has reviewed. Although quite a bit of time was needed initially to get the text of the articles into the software, Raoul estimates that using the qualitative analysis software reduced by several weeks the total amount of time he spent on the analysis and report writing for his review.

style, indenting, or quotation marks) and always include the page numbers of the article or book from which the quote is taken.

If you are compiling your references manually (without using bibliographic software), insert the references you wish to use into both your text and reference list at the same time as you are drafting your review document. It can be very tedious inserting references into your document after you have finished writing all your text. If you are using bibliographic software, use the software to insert the reference list when you have finished writing the paper.

The concluding section of your report should summarise the main findings of the review and indicate what, in your view, the balance of the evidence suggests. It can also include your assessment of the rigour and overall quality of the available information, as well as identify gaps in the literature, implications for social or health-related policy and services, or ideas for further studies.

Structure of your review

The central objective of a review is to write a report that reveals the current state of knowledge on the selected topic. If the review is to provide a context for developing a new research study, the review report should provide a rationale for the new study. It can do this by ending with a series of findings that lead into the proposed research.

An example of an organising structure or writing plan for a literature review is shown in Table 7.5. This hypothetical review is on the topic of 'The influence of neighbourhoods on social support'. Note how the plan divides the review into sections and lists questions to be addressed in each section of the review.

Develop a clear structure for the review using headings and sub-headings and sections that flow in a logical sequence. Box 7.6 outlines a general format for a literature review. Identify the main themes of the review near the beginning. Re-assess the sequencing of your sections and headings after you have written the review to make sure you have a sequence that follows a logical pattern. This can be adapted to suit the particular purposes of your review.

TABLE 7.5   EXAMPLE OF A LITERATURE REVIEW PLAN FOR A RESEARCH PROPOSAL 'THE INFLUENCE OF NEIGHBOURHOODS ON SOCIAL SUPPORT'

Research topic	Examples of literature to be reviewed
Relevance of topic to proposed research	Why are neighbourhoods and social support important? What evidence is available in published sources that make plausible links between support, neighbourhoods and well-being?
Social support	What are the main types of social support? How is social support measured? Existing social support questionnaires Advantages and disadvantages of each type of measurement
Neighbourhoods	Physical features of neighbourhoods How do neighbourhoods vary within cities and across a country? Features relevant to social support Which features are associated with higher or lower levels of support?
Interventions to increase support	What studies have been done on changing physical and social features of neighbourhoods to increase support? What types of interventions have been reported? How successful were they? What components of interventions seem to work across a range of different environments?
Relevance to proposed study	Pull together the key ideas from the earlier parts of the review which provide a convincing rationale for the proposed study

---

Box 7.6   General format for a literature review

Cover Page (if not included in a research report)
   Title of review, Author, Author's affiliation and address
   Date, Review prepared for (name of organisation or person, if relevant)
Summary (if not included in a research report)
   About 150 words describing the topic and main conclusions
Introduction: State the specific objectives of the review. Describe the search proce-dures, key words used and databases accessed in sufficient detail so that a reader could replicate your search. Outline the topics to be reviewed. Describe the sub-topics or themes to be covered and how they are related to the overall topic of the literature review.
   Topic A – Review themes and findings relevant to a specific topic
   Topic B
   Topic C etc.
Conclusions: Summarise the most important findings from the review and state the impli-cations of the literature reviewed in relation to the objectives of the review.
References: List all references cited in the review at the end of the document you are writing.

Remember to find out what length is expected for your review. While 20–30 pages may be suitable for a dissertation or thesis, about 4–7 double-spaced pages might be appropriate for manuscripts to be submitted to journals. For a research proposal of about 12 pages, a 2–3 page literature review would be suitable, unless there is a specific reason for a longer review.

The review should point out both consistencies and contradictions in the literature as well as offer possible explanations for these (e.g., use of similar or different theoretical conceptualisations or research methods). Studies that are particularly relevant should be described in some detail. However, reports that present very similar or comparable find-ings usually should be grouped together and briefly summarised.

The writing plan you develop for your review will probably need to be revised several times as additional ideas occur to you after reading and re-reading the literature and as the conceptual framework for your review evolves. To help with this, look at some of the most relevant journal articles you have located and think about how the authors have written their review section.

A single section from a literature review is shown in Appendix 7.1 at the end of this chapter as an example of a writing style commonly used in literature reviews.

Writing style and formatting

Using an appropriate writing style for a literature review is something that does not come easily to many people. Expect to go through several drafts of the review and get feedback from other people. The written review should not consist primarily of a series of quotes or a series of abstracts.

When writing literature reviews, a common error is to review a number of articles sequen-tially, giving prominence to the authors' names. Avoid patterns like: '*Brown said that …, Jones reported that …, Smith concluded that …*'. Remember to focus the discussion on issues, topics or themes, not individual articles or authors. For example:

> *Several studies have reported that parenting programmes relying primarily on lecture presentations were ineffective in changing parent behaviours towards children.* (Brown, 2003; Jones, 2001; Smith, 2004)

Multiple citations (such as those shown in brackets above) should be listed alphabetically by first author, and by earliest to most recent year for citations having the same author.

Use of quotations

When using quotations from another report or publication be careful about using them appropriately. Be selective about using quotations in a literature review and use them very sparingly. Most published reviews use very few quotations or none at all. If you do wish to use a quotation, make sure you introduce each quotation in the text prior to the quotation and note the source immediately following the quotation. Occasions when it would be appropriate to use quotations include:

- where a source has expressed a key point especially well
- quoting the actual text from a source which you are critiquing
- when noting a controversial statement made by another author
- to illustrate the language style used in a specific source.

Text that includes long strings of quotations is inappropriate for a research review and indicates a poor writing style. Especially avoid putting together long strings of quotations with just brief sections of your own text in between. Unfortunately, some thesis students tend to use long strings of quotations in their literature review in the mistaken belief that quoting large chunks of text from another source shows their familiarity with the topic.

A quotation written into the text should have quotation marks before and after the quotation. If the quotation is longer than about three lines, indent the quotation as a separate block quote without quotation marks. An option is to use italics or another altered font to make quotations stand out from the main text. Ensure that the appropriate reference details including the page number of the source are cited at the end of the quote (e.g., Smith, 2005, p. 26). Where the source is an online document with no page numbers, put the paragraph number or the section heading where these are shown in the source (e.g., Smith, 2008, Conclusion section, para. 3).

In terms of copyright, note that if longer sections of text are quoted, or if tables or figures from another source are used, copyright permission may need to be obtained. Copyright prohibits use of lengthy quotations or use of any item that is seen as a stand-alone entity, such as a table or figure, without the permission of the author or copyright owner.

While there is no specific word limit relating to potential copyright infringement when using quotations, be careful if you are quoting more than about 300 words from a single passage in a source. The concept of fair use or fair dealing allows the use of quotations from other sources providing it is in the context of reviewing or critiquing the original source. For fair dealing use, it would be expected that the quotation would be introduced in the preceding text and comments made about the quotation in the accompanying text.

Citing references

Settle on a standard referencing system for citing literature in the text of the review and for setting out references in the reference list at the end of the document. For *research* reviews, do not use the label 'bibliography' – unless you are compiling a general bibliography that lists all the research publications located on a particular topic. Which referencing system you use may depend on your academic subject's usual practice or the requirements specified by a publisher, client or funding agency. Look at journal articles on your topic to find examples of how to apply these standard referencing systems, or read a style manual.

Harvard and APA citation styles

One standard referencing system, called the Harvard style, is used in psychology and many other disciplines and journals. In this system, text citations (references to specific research literature in the text of a review) uses the 'author, date' format, e.g., (Smith, 1998). A version of the Harvard system is used in the present book. The *Publication Manual* of the American Psychological Association (APA) sets out the formatting for a commonly used version of the Harvard system, and gives detailed examples.

Vancouver citation style

The Vancouver system is commonly used by medical journals and some other journals. In this system references are numbered consecutively in the order in which they are first mentioned in the text. References in text, tables and legends are cited using Arabic numerals in parentheses, or in some journals by using superscript numbers. References cited only in tables or figure legends are numbered in accordance with the sequence established by the first identification in the text of the particular table or figure. In this system, the titles of journals are abbreviated according to the style used in the Index Medicus.

Documents from Web sources

Increasingly, documents cited in proposals and reports are being accessed from webpages on the Internet. If you are using documents from the Internet, you need to note the URL (webpage address) and the date you accessed the document. Box 7.7 shows a standard set of APA formats for citing Web documents.

Box 7.7   Citing references from online sources

Online periodical (APA style)
Author, A. A., Author, B. B., & Author, C. C. (2000).
   Title of article. Title of Periodical, xx, xxx–xxx. Retrieved month day, year, from: source
   (URL or DOI).

(Continued)

(Continued)

Example of article from online journal that also produces a print version
   Brandon, P. R., Taum, A. K. H., Young, D. B., Pottenger, F. M., III. & Speitel, T. W. (2008). The complexity of measuring the quality of program implementation with observations: The case of middle school inquiry-based science. *American Journal of Evaluation, 29*(3), 235–250. Retrieved September 11, 2008 from DOI: 10.1177/1098214008319175.

Example of article in an Internet-only journal
Fredrickson, B. L. (2000, March). Cultivating positive emotions to optimize health and well-being. Prevention & Treatment, 3, Article 0001a. Retrieved November 20, 2000, from: http://psycnet.apa.org/?fa=main.doiLanding&doi=10.1037/1522-3736.3.1.31a.

Online document (APA style)
Author, A. A. (2008). Title of work. Retrieved month day, year, from source (URL or DOI).

Example
   Chou, L., McClintock, R., Moretti, F., Nix, D. H. (1993). Technology and education: New wine in new bottles: Choosing pasts and imagining educational futures. Retrieved August 24, 2000, from Columbia University, Institute for Learning Technologies from: www.ilt.columbia.edu/publications/papers/newwine1.html

If a document is contained within a large and complex website (such as that for a university or a government agency), identify the host organization and the relevant programme or department before giving the URL for the document itself. Precede the URL with a colon.

Source: American Psychological Association Electronic Formats, Retrieved May 20, 2009, from: www.apastyle.org/elecref.html.

Given the rapid development and continuing restructuring of webpages, many specific URLs cited from the Internet are likely to change after several months or years. This means that specific Internet addresses (URLs) may not work in the future. To get round this problem, many academic publishers have begun assigning a Digital Object Identifier (DOI) to journal articles and other documents. A DOI is a unique alphanumeric string assigned by a registration agency. When a DOI is available, include the DOI instead of the URL in the reference. As well, a good safeguard is to clearly cite the title of a paper and the website organisation's name (e.g., Columbia University Press). A browser search on key terms from the title or organisation provides another way of locating a specific paper.

To keep your online sources up to date, check all URLs in your reference list prior to the submission or publication of your report. If the document you are citing has moved, update the URL so that it points to the correct location. If the document is no longer available, you may want to substitute another source or omit it from your report. For sources whose full text is accessible by subscription only, give a higher level URL such as the home page, the contents page of a journal or publications page of an organisation.

Plagiarism and acknowledging sources

Plagiarism refers to the use of other people's text or ideas without appropriate acknowledgement of the source from which the text or ideas has been taken. With the development of the Internet it is relatively easy to find sources from which text can be copied into a document on a word processor. Unfortunately plagiarism is quite widespread, but with the growing sophistication of Internet search engines it is also relatively easy to detect (Braumoeller & Gaines, 2001). An example was reported by a faculty member teaching a research methods course. For this course, the students were required to do a brief literature review. In the first year in which all reviews were required to be submitted electronically for checking for plagiarism, four out of 45 students had copied substantial sections of text without appropriate acknowledgement. As a result, the four students were penalised by having their grades reduced. With the development of very efficient checking systems for plagiarism, such as *Turnitin*, it is now relatively easy to detect unacknowledged copying, or edited copying where just a few words from the original source are changed.

When describing in your own words specific ideas or key points taken from other sources, use citations to acknowledge the source of the idea. If you use the actual text from another source, make sure you format the text as a quotation with the source details appropriately acknowledged. Examples of citing literature and using quotations are shown in Appendix 7.1 at the end of this chapter.

Plagiarism is taken very seriously by academic institutions and there are often severe penalties for students engaging in plagiarism (see Box 7.8). Researchers also are likely to suffer negative consequences from engaging in plagiarism.

Box 7.8   Example of plagiarism in a Masters thesis

Tina completed a research project for her Masters thesis in public health. When her supervisor was reading drafts of her literature review chapter, he noticed the style changed in one section that consisted of nearly three pages of text. He went to a search engine, typed in a phrase from this text (about five words) as a quotation search and quickly found a technical report from which the text had been taken. Tina had made only a few minor changes in the text and had not acknowledged the source of the material.

The supervisor highlighted the copied text and wrote a warning message in margin. Tina subsequently submitted the thesis without sending it to the supervisor for a final check. When the thesis was sent for external examination, one of the examiners noted that some of the literature review chapter contained plagiarism and recommended a fail grade for the thesis. As a result of the plagiarism, Tina's thesis failed the examination and two years' work she spent on her thesis topic was wasted.

Specific points regarding writing style

Given the range of mistakes that people commonly make when trying to do a literature review for the first time, the following are some additional points to note when writing a review.

Use a title or chapter heading which indicates the topic

For a thesis or dissertation, avoid using a title or chapter heading such as 'Literature Review.' This gives no indication of the review topic. Instead, use a title that shows the actual topic, for example 'Review of literature on youth smoking'.

Provide a context for the research reviewed

When reviewing research literature, make it clear whether each literature source refers to research in your own country or research from other countries. Do not assume that research carried out in other countries can be generalised to your own country, even if you share a common language. Much social science and public health research is likely to be context-specific and not necessarily applicable to multiple locations, communities or peoples.

Review substantive topics separately from research methods

A common error in literature reviews is to include a great deal of discussion of research methods or approaches at the expense of discussing the findings of studies. It is best to review methodological approaches in a separate section of your review, following the primary review of your main topic. For example, if your are reviewing literature about the most successful interventions for smoking cessation among young people, first review what types of interventions have been tried and which are the most successful. In a separate section, review the methodological issues, such as types of measures used in research relating to smoking cessation and their advantages and disadvantages. It is certainly important to cover methodological issues in a review where they are relevant to supporting or discounting the findings of a particular piece of research, or a specific method of research.

If your literature review is part of a report describing the methods and findings of a research project, it may be useful to include a review of the methodological literature to provide a context and justification for the research methods used in the project. Ideally, this methodological review should be included in a section at the end of your main literature review. It should not be included in the report's methods section or chapter. For a thesis or dissertation, if the methodological review is quite long (e.g., more than 10 pages) it may be best to put it in a separate chapter, following the main literature review chapter.

Use of secondary citation sources

Do not routinely use secondary citations when referring to literature sources. For example, a commonly used (*and incorrect*) format is:

> The study by Smith (1975); cited in Brown (1984)…

Cite only the source you have seen. Secondary citations are rarely used in research reports and literature reviews. When used regularly they are usually an indication that the writer has used only a small number of original sources. Secondary citations should only be used in the following circumstances:

- when you include a quotation reported in the secondary source that was originally quoted in an earlier source
- when you report specific data from a secondary source where the data came from an earlier study
- for classic or well-known sources or ideas.

The *correct* citation format for a secondary citation in the text is:

The study by Smith (as cited in Brown, 1984, pp. 56–58) ….

Only the date for the source seen by the writer is noted (see the American Psychological Association *Publication Manual*, 2001, p. 247). Note that some books on writing styles give incorrect information about the APA style for citing secondary sources.

Separate document or part of a report?

If your literature review is to be a separate document, remember to present it so it can be read on its own, without reference to other documents. Include a cover page and summary. Literature reviews presented as separate documents can be longer (e.g., 15–20 pages double-spaced), compared to a literature review included as part of a research report.

If your literature review is to be part of a research report, check how much detail is needed in the review. In a brief research report, and manuscripts intended for journal publication, it is often appropriate to include a literature review section of about 2–4 pages double-spaced. A more detailed review, for example in a longer technical report, may go up to 5–6 pages single-spaced. If the review is longer than about six pages (single or double-spaced), check whether this will be appropriate for the intended audiences of the report. Many people who are interested in reading the findings of a specific research project may not be interested in reading a lengthy literature review.

Literature reviews that are part of research carried out for Masters or PhD theses are often between 15–30 pages long (double-spaced) and are usually presented as a separate chapter.

Exercises for literature searching and reviewing

1. Develop a set of literature search terms for a research project focusing on depression among people living alone.
2. Briefly describe the two major formats used for citing references and formatting reference lists at the end of a research report.
3. Using your Web browser, find the articles from these DOIs (Digital Object Identifiers)
   DOI: 10.1161/CIRCULATIONAHA.107.725101
   DOI: 10.1177/1098214008319175
4. Find four electronic databases that would be relevant to a literature search on a topic in which you are interested.
5. Locate three recent journal articles that are research reports on a topic in which you are interested and note the following points about their literature review sections (usually the first section after the abstract):
   (a) Approximately how long are the reviews? (e.g., words, pages)
   (b) What sub-headings were used to structure the reviews?
   (c) What was reported about the search procedures used?
   (d) How did the authors start and finish their literature review (first and last paragraphs)?

References and further reading

American Psychological Association (2009). *Publication Manual of the American Psychological Association* (6th edn). Washington, DC: APA.

Attree, P. & Milton, B. (2006). Critically appraising qualitative research for systematic reviews: defusing the methodological cluster bombs. *Evidence & Policy, 2*(1), 109–126.

Braumoeller, B. F. & Gaines, B. J. (2001). Actions do speak louder than words: deterring plagiarism with the use of plagiarism detection software. *PS: Political Science & Politics, 34*(4), 835–839.

Callahan, C. & Thornton, L. J. (2007). *A Journalist's Guide to the Internet.* Boston, MA: Pearson.

Columbia University Press (2006). *Guide for Authors.* New York: Columbia University Press. Retrieved September 11, 2008, from: http://cup.columbia.edu/static/161.

Concato, J., Shah, N., & Horwitz, R. I. (2000). Randomized, controlled trials, observational studies, and the hierarchy of research designs. *New England Journal of Medicine, 342*(25), 1887–1892.

Cooper, H. (2009). *Research Synthesis and Meta-Analysis: A Guide for Literature Reviews* (4th edn). Thousand Oaks, CA: Sage.

Davis-Blake, A. & Broschak, J. P. (2009). Outsourcing and the changing nature of work. *Annual Review of Sociology, 35*(1), 321–340.

Dochartaigh, N. O. (2007). *Internet Research Skills: How To Do Your Literature Search and Find Research Information Online* (2nd edn). Thousand Oaks, CA: Sage.

Fink, A. (2004). *Conducting Research Literature Reviews: From the Internet to Paper* (2nd edn). Thousand Oaks: CA: Sage.

Girden, E. R. (2001). *Evaluating Research Articles: From Start to Finish* (2nd edn). Thousand Oaks, CA: Sage.

Greenhalgh, T. (1997). How to read a paper: assessing the methodological quality of published papers. *British Medical Journal, 315*(7103), 305–308.

Hart, C. (2001). *Doing a Literature Search: A Comprehensive Guide for the Social Sciences.* London: Sage.

Hunt, D. L. & McKibbon, A. (1998). Locating and appraising systematic reviews. In: C. Mulrow & D.J. Cook (eds), *Systematic Reviews* (pp. 13–22). Philadelphia, PA: American College of Physicians.

Index Medicus – Abbreviation of Journal Titles. Main Library of Poznan University of Medical Sciences. Retrieved May 18, 2009, from: www2.bg.am.poznan.pl/czasopisma/medicus.php?lang=eng.

Machi, L. A. & McEvoy, B. T. (2008). *Literature Review: Six Steps to Success.* London: Sage.

Pascoe, E. A. & Richman, L. S. (2009). Perceived discrimination and health: a meta-analytic review. *Psychological Bulletin, 135*(4), 531–554.

Ridley, D. (2008). *Literature Review: A Step-by-Step Guide for Students.* London: Sage.

Robinson, T. N. & Sirard, J. R. (2005). Preventing childhood obesity: a solution-oriented paradigm. *American Journal of Preventive Medicine, 28*(2S2), 194–201.

Taylor, D. & Procter, M. (2008). *The Literature Review: A Few Tips on Conducting It.* Retrieved September 11, 2008, from: www.utoronto.ca/writing/litrev.html.

APPENDIX 7.1

Example of a section from a literature review

Source: Thomas, D. R., Dixon, R. & Thomas, Y. L. (2001). Evaluation of home visiting programmes: research methods literature review. (report prepared for the Evaluation Management Group, Wellington). (pp. 15–18). University of Auckland, New Zealand: Centre for Child and Family Policy Research.

Evaluation of Home Visiting Programmes:
Research Methods Literature Review

Structure and content of home visits

A key aspect of home visitor programmes is the structure and content of home visits. Several evaluators have commented on the difficulty of providing detailed information on the content of home visits (e.g., Gomby, 1999; Hauser-Cram, 1990). While a lot of attention has been focused on the intensity (frequency and overall number) of the visits (e.g., Duggan et al., 1999; Olds et al., 1999), most evaluations have relied on programme plans to identify content (Olds et al., 1999) as well as other data sources such as observation (or video) of home visits, reports from mothers/caregivers and reports from home visitors (Gomby, 1999).

The Elmira, New York programme of prenatal and early childhood home visits by nurses was focused on reducing several events. These included: number of subsequent pregnancies, use of welfare payments, alcohol and drug abuse, child abuse and neglect, property crime by mothers, reported serious antisocial behaviour and emergent use of substances by adolescents in high-risk families. The programme produced most benefits among the neediest families. It had few effects on children's development and birth outcomes (Olds et al., 1999).

One common objective in home visits is facilitating access to other services and resources needed by families. Having a home visiting programme does not ensure effective linkage between families and community resources. If families can access other community resources it can potentially amplify the positive impacts of the visiting programme. As was noted in the Hawaii Healthy Start Program,

> *For program administrators it means establishing clear working relationships with other community-based programs. For program supervisors it means ensuring that home visitors provide the support and education services that they are best equipped to provide, and that they are encouraged to collaborate with other providers as needed to help families achieve their goals.* (Duggan et al., 1999, p. 88)

The other services to which client families could be referred are a crucial element in the success or failure of home visiting programmes. As they are often difficult and expensive to track, evaluations may not effectively assess the full impacts of these other services (Gray, 2001, pp. 25–26). The Hawaii Healthy Start Program (HSP) identified 14 other areas in which at-risk families often needed services. These were: adult health care, child care, respite care, transportation, adult education, housing, nutrition, counselling, substance abuse treatment, support groups, women's shelter, legal assistance, material assistance and financial assistance. For each of these areas the mother's perceived need for services and her experience in obtaining them were measured (Duggan et al., 1999, p. 77).

Visitors can find it difficult to move beyond crisis intervention to help families develop and work towards long-term goals (Gray, 2001, p. 20). It can be difficult for the visitor to decide what to focus on with a family because of limited time and the complexity of problems faced by the family. Some common reasons for deviating from the planned programme during visits have been noted (Gomby, 1999). Visitors may need to attend to immediate crises or other issues.

> ... participants have more positive impressions of workers who provide immediate and concrete options for a family's presenting problem in a non-judgemental manner. (Daro & Harding, 1999, p. 171)

Responding to a mother's or a child's immediate needs is a strength in a programme. However, deviating regularly from the programme means the visitor is not providing the service as the programme designers originally intended. In some cases more effective in-service training may be required. However, options for visitors need to be incorporated in visiting programmes so that the programmes are consistent with the realities that visitors and mothers face.

Variations across sites and programmes

Process evaluations have indicated that service provider organisations differ in programme implementation and this can lead to differences in the outcomes they achieve. In Hawaii, some HSP agencies succeeded in promoting certain aspects of family functioning and child development while others did not, even though all home visitors received the same initial six-week training and same contract requirements. Evaluating only one agency would give an inaccurate picture of system-wide performances (Duggan et al., 1999).

References

Daro, D. A. & Harding, K. A. (1999). Healthy Families America: using research to enhance practice. *The Future of Children*, 9(1), 152–176.

Duggan, A. K., McFarlane, E. C., Windham, A. M., Rohde, C. A., Salkever, D. S., Fuddy, L., Rosenberg, L. A., Buchbinder, S. B., & Sia, C. C. (1999). Evaluation of Hawaii's Healthy Start Program. *The Future of Children*, 9(1), 66–88.

Gomby, D. S. (1999). Understanding evaluations of home visitation programs. *The Future of Children*, 9(1), 27–43.

Gray, A. (2001, February). *Family Support Programmes: A Literature Review*. (Prepared for the Ministry of Education). Wellington, New Zealand: Gray Matter Research Ltd.

Hauser-Cram, P. (1990). Designing meaningful evaluations of early intervention services. In S. J. Meisels & J. P. Shonkoff (eds), *Handbook of Early Childhood Intervention* (pp. 583–602). Cambridge: Cambridge University Press.

Olds, D. L., Henderson, C. R., Kitzman, H. J., Eckenrode, J. J., Cole, R.E., & Tatelbaum, R. C. (1999). Prenatal and infancy home visitation by nurses: recent findings. *The Future of Children*, 9(1), 44–65.

8 Managing a Research Project

Topics covered in this chapter

- Writing a project task list
- Time planning and timelines
- Identifying resource needs
- Drawing up a project budget
- Managing day-to-day project activities
- Information management
- Project completion

After preparing a research proposal and obtaining any necessary ethical approvals and funding, it is possible to start work on the main information gathering and analysis stages of a project. This is usually the time when a research project really starts to get up and running, as research plans are translated into real, practical action.

Normally the work will begin with a period of data collection, using one or more of a range of techniques, such as face-to-face interviews, focus groups, telephone surveys or document searches. After this will come a period of review or analysis of the data collected. Then a project report will be written describing the results of the study. As a whole, this data gathering, analysis and report writing work is likely to be the most time-consuming and demanding part of most research projects.

This chapter looks at some key project management strategies and tasks that usually form the core phases of a project. In particular, it highlights a range of techniques for structuring the work of a research project and keeping it on track. These techniques will be relevant to anyone likely to be responsible for running a research project, from graduate students doing Masters or PhD research, to more experienced researchers in universities, government departments and the private sector.

The first part of the chapter looks at several project planning tasks. A key aspect of project planning involves identifying all the tasks that need to be accomplished during a project, as well as when and where they will be done, and by whom. It also includes anticipating the resources that will be needed to carry out these tasks.

The second part of the chapter looks at project management skills. These are skills likely to be important for running the ongoing, day-to-day work of a project. Four broad skill areas are covered: people skills, safety and risk assessment, managing unanticipated events and equipment skills.

Writing a project task list

Before starting work on the data collection phase of project, it is a good idea to set down in writing, in as much detail as possible, all the different tasks to be accomplished to complete the project. At the same time, it may also be useful to identify likely personnel requirements and other resource needs. Effort put into detailed project planning at this stage should pay off later, once the data collection, analysis and writing up phases get properly under way. There should be fewer surprises and a greater sense of control over the research process.

One useful planning technique is to draw up a project task list. This is a list detailing all the different tasks that need to be done to complete a project, and in what order. An example of a task list is shown in Box 8.1. Normally the list will show an expected start and finish date for each task (where relevant). If the project involves a team of researchers, the list will also usually indicate which team members are responsible for completing each task.

Box 8.1   Example of a task list

Task List for the Woodlands City Community Survey
(first page)

March 3	Project meeting 11am
March 6	3–4pm Briefing on survey for undergraduate students Recruit students as interviewers Explain project, distribute information sheet and circulate sign-up sheet for names and contact phone and address

March 9	Project meeting 9am
	Notify print shop regarding date for Interview schedule printing
	–760 copies × 15 pages (deliver to print shop on 20 March)
	Distribute 12 copies of draft of interview schedule
	Mike Brown to arrange:
	    letter from Mayor, maps showing 29 city divisions,
	    publicity for Survey

March 13–16	1st Pilot testing: 4 people × 3 interviews Jenny and three graduate students
March 16	Project meeting 9am Review 1st Pilot testing Finalise lists of interviewers Fix dates, times and venues for five interviewer training sessions between 21–31 March (Jenny) 1st draft of training package available for discussion (Tim)
March 20	Final revision of interview schedule Finalise coding boxes, print final version on laser printer Completed interview schedule delivered for printing Photocopy 60 copies for interviewer training sessions Meeting 3.20pm for all interviewers to go through interview schedule prior to training session Announce dates, time and venues of training session and have sheets available to sign up for these sessions
March 21	Training sessions commence Ensure training session includes assessment of competence. Students failing must do another training session Give detailed instructions for returning interviews, whom to contact if any difficulties, and notifying Jenny when finished interviewing Completed summary sheet with last interview schedule

---

Ideally, a task list should also identify task interdependencies. This is when one task is not able to be started until another task has been completed. For example, in a large-scale survey involving an interview questionnaire, the pilot testing of the questionnaire should be completed before the final version of the questionnaire can be prepared. Where paper copies are required, the final version of the questionnaire is then sent for printing or copying. The survey data collection can only start once copies of the final questionnaire are ready. If a printing or photocopying service requires several days or weeks to complete the copying, then time for this will need to be built into the task list.

If a research proposal or funding application has already been prepared for a project, it might be possible to use these as a starting point for developing a task list. Key project activities, timelines and staff responsibilities may already be defined to some extent in these documents. However, normally the information will need to be expanded considerably to make it useful for project management purposes.

Time planning and timelines

Another useful project planning technique is drawing up a timeline. A timeline shows the expected start and finish dates, and duration, of each major project phase or task. One kind of timeline is known as a Gantt chart (see Figure 8.1). In a Gantt chart a standard unit of time (e.g., a day, a week or a month) is given to each cell or block in the chart. Each column in the chart is labelled with a specific date, while the main project tasks are listed in the left-hand column. Start and finish dates for specific tasks are indicated by inserting

	Jun 2010	Jul 2010	Aug 2010	Sept 2010	Oct 2010	Nov 2010	Dec 2010	Jan 2011	Feb 2011	Mar 2011	Apr 2011	May 2011
Planning and development												
Prepare draft letter and consent forms for participants	xx											
Develop and pilot questionnaire	xx											
Prepare ethics committee application	xx	xx										
Obtain ethical approval			xx									
Finalise letter and questionnaire				xx								
Recruiting research participants												
50 clients recruited from health service				xx	xx							
Questionnaire mailed to clients				xx	xx							
Participants mail back questionnaires				xx	xx	xx	xx					
Follow-up if questionnaire not returned							xx					

(Continued)

(Continued)

	Jun 2010	Jul 2010	Aug 2010	Sept 2010	Oct 2010	Nov 2010	Dec 2010	Jan 2011	Feb 2011	Mar 2011	Apr 2011	May 2011
Data collection and analysis												
Enter qnn data into stats package					xx	xx	xx					
Set up data analysis procedures						xx	xx					
Run data analyses								xx				
Prepare tables from data analyses								xx				
Report writing and dissemination												
Initial draft of full research report								xx	xx	xx		
Presentation at departmental seminar									xx			
Presentation at conference											xx	
Prepare a journal article										xx	xx	xx

FIGURE 8.1   EXAMPLE OF A GANTT CHART TIMELINE

'xx' in the appropriate cells. Shading can also be used to indicate start and finish dates, but 'xx' is easier to insert and change.

When preparing a task list or timeline, an important skill is estimating the total amount of time (hours or days) likely to be needed to complete each project task. This is not an easy skill to learn. Usually it develops only after working on a number of research projects and getting a feel for how long different tasks can take to do in practice. A related aspect of time planning is juggling multiple tasks and projects. Project coordinators are often responsible for several research projects operating at the same time. In such cases, additional planning and coordination strategies will be needed (see Box 8.2).

Box 8.2   Juggling multiple projects

Juanita is a junior researcher employed in a university social survey unit. The unit does surveys for other parts of the university as well as government agencies, the private sector and community groups. The unit has five full-time research staff, including Juanita, as well as a small team of part-time interviewers. Juanita's job responsibilities include designing survey questionnaires, organising the work of the interview team, and writing and presenting research reports.

When Juanita was doing her Doctoral degree, she could focus fully on just one research project. However, in her new role with the survey unit she is expected to work on several overlapping projects at the same time. Each year the survey unit normally does around 30 different projects and at any one time there may be 5–10 projects requiring some kind of ongoing input.

(Continued)

(Continued)

For Juanita, one of the most critical events in the month is when she and the unit's other researchers meet to review the unit's work programme and timetable. This is a key occasion when responsibilities for different project tasks are discussed, negotiated and agreed. It is therefore important that each researcher comes to the meeting with a clear idea of what their existing work commitments are for the months ahead and how much spare capacity they have for new work.

To help prepare for these meetings, Juanita has found it useful to draw up a chart indicating her personal work plan. This shows all the different research projects and project tasks she expects to be working on in each week of the forthcoming two or three months. Below is a brief extract from Juanita's work plan for October 2010.

Using her personal work plan, Juanita is able to see where tasks scheduled for one project may clash with tasks scheduled for other projects. She can better anticipate potential bottlenecks in her work programme, as well as identify relatively quiet periods when it could be possible to take on some new work. Armed with this information, Juanita is in a better position to perhaps argue for more assistance to be given to her by other team members for certain project tasks, or for the completion dates for certain tasks to be rescheduled.

		October 2010			November 2010
	Mon 4 – Fri 8	Mon 11 – Fri 15	Mon 18 – Fri 22	Mon 25 – Fri 29	Mon 1 – Fri 5
Project 1: Survey of Consumer Preferences	Draft project report	First draft project report due to client			
Project 2: Attitudes to Antibiotics	Second round of home-based interviews continues	Second round of home-based interviews continues	Second round of home-based interviews due to be completed	Data processing and analysis of home-based interviews	
Project 3: Use of Public Transport	Revision of final project report following client and peer review feedback	Revision of final project report following client and peer review feedback	Revision of final project report following client and peer review feedback		
Project 4 Unpaid Work Survey	Initial questionnaire design	Initial questionnaire design	Submit initial questionnaire to client for feedback		
Project 5 Illicit Drug Use Survey	Continuing data analysis and report writing	Continuing data analysis and report writing	Continuing data analysis and report writing	Continuing data analysis and report writing	

(Continued)

		October 2010			November 2010
	Mon 4 – Fri 8	Mon 11 – Fri 15	Mon 18 – Fri 22	Mon 25 – Fri 29	Mon 1 – Fri 5
Other				Monthly planning meeting	5 days leave – family wedding overseas

(Continued)

Try to be realistic about how long it will take to complete a project task. Initial estimates can be wildly optimistic. Some tasks can take twice or even three times as long as initially anticipated, even when everything goes smoothly.

If you want to estimate the total number of person hours or days likely to be needed for a project as a whole, a good rule of thumb is to take whatever total you first work out to be a viable estimate and multiply it by two. This is likely to come somewhere close to the actual number of hours or days that will be needed in practice.

Identifying resource needs

Along with drawing up a task list and timeline, another key project planning technique is identifying in detail the resources needed to complete a project. This includes people resources (e.g., project staff) and material resources (e.g., office facilities and equipment). Typical resources that might be required in a research project are listed in Box 8.3.

Box 8.3   Examples of common project resources

Staff
   Project director
   Project coordinator
   Specialist advisers
   Interviewers
   Data entry assistants
   Local liaison or contact people
   Secretarial services
Travel and accommodation
Office accommodation and furniture
Computers and software
Stationery
   (e.g., photocopying, printing)
Communications
   (e.g., email, telephone, fax, postage, courier)
Other resources
   (e.g., books, journal articles, Internet access, access to data)

People resources

In smaller projects, it may be possible for all data collection, analysis and writing tasks to be carried out by just one person. However, in most medium- or large-scale projects, several people are likely to be needed to complete different aspects of the project. How many and what kind of people will be needed, and when, will depend on the specific data collection, analysis and writing up tasks to be performed.

A reasonably common staffing arrangement in medium- or large-scale research projects is to have two core staff members: a project director and a project coordinator (sometimes called a project administrator). The project director is the leader of the project and has responsibility for key decisions and expenditure.

The project coordinator has responsibility for organising the day-to-day operation of the project. This includes ensuring all key tasks are completed and deadlines met. Specific tasks of the project coordinator might include arranging and chairing project meetings, preparing information sheets for research participants, preparing procedure sheets for interviewers, and setting up project information storage systems.

Other people that may need to be brought into a project at certain times include statistics or other data analysis experts, interviewers, translation specialists, data entry operators, audio-recording transcription staff, specialist editors, illustrators and so on. The list is potentially quite long. The more complex and varied the type of skills needed to complete a project, the more important it is that the project planning quickly identifies how and from whom these skills will be obtained.

Facilities and equipment

It will also be important to identify all the different facilities and equipment the project will need, as well as who will use it and when. Some kinds of research require hardly any equipment at all. For example, a project mainly analysing existing literature or file materials may need only a laptop computer and appropriate software. Other kinds of projects will need to access a large amount of specialised equipment. For example, studies relying on focus groups or interviews for collecting research information will typically require audio and/or video recording equipment, as well as equipment for transcribing or editing raw recordings into a suitable form for analysis. Clinical health studies may need access to expensive medical technology or equipment for diagnosing, monitoring or treating research participants.

On top of this, even the most rudimentary research project will need some kind of physical base or office setup, even if it is just the kitchen table at home or a corner table at the local cafe. The larger the project, the more likely the need for some kind of dedicated office space where project material and equipment can be accessed and stored. For team-based projects, ideally the space should include workstations and meeting areas for use by project staff.

Other project resources

It is important not to overlook how many incidental resources can be needed to do a research project. These include telephone and Internet connections, a project-specific email address, access to courier facilities, postage, specialist library resources, efficient photocopying equipment and (for larger team-based projects) cafe and meal services. In many cases, these resources are vital for completing a project in good time and with the minimum of hassle. Trying to do without them may seem to save money initially, but prove costly in the long run.

Drawing up a project budget

Another potentially valuable project planning skill is knowing how to draw up a detailed project budget. This basically involves allocating a monetary cost to all the different tasks and/or resources a project will undertake or use. For example, it might be estimated that the total cost of the payments for the contract interviewers hired for a project will (or should be) $10,000.

In settings where a research project is being carried out on a commercial basis and funded by a sponsoring organisation or client, it is normal practice before the project starts to draw up a budget indicating how the money allocated to the project will be spent. The level of detail in these budgets can vary. In some projects they can be very detailed, right down to indicating the costs of the last box of audio tapes or postage stamps.

Figure 8.2 shows one way of setting out a relatively simple budget estimate for a research project. The cost estimates shown are for a hypothetical nine-week project involving face-to-face quantitative and qualitative interviews with a sample of 250 adults. The project team includes a full-time project director and project coordinator, as well as temporary contract workers.

Generally, the main reason for drawing up a detailed budget is to try to reduce the risk of a project running out of money before it is finished. Calculating what share of the total project funds are to be allocated to which particular tasks, personnel, services and equipment should, hopefully, make it easier to monitor and control expenditure as the project goes along. Using the budget, an estimate can be made of how much money should, in theory, still be available after certain project tasks have been completed. If, after these tasks are done, the total funds available are less than predicted, this indicates a need to cut back on the costs of future components of the project, or find extra funding.

In team-based projects the project director will normally have main responsibility for funding decisions and ensuring a project is completed within budget. However, the director may also rely on other team members or staff from the project's host institution to supply financial records and other data for monitoring project expenditure.

It can take some experience to work out realistic cost estimates for project components. Estimates often are not able to be precise and many budget figures are likely to be calculated mainly on the basis of educated guesswork.

One important financial planning skill a project director or coordinator should try to develop is the ability to foresee where cost savings can be made by arranging project tasks more efficiently or smartly. Achieving these efficiencies, without negatively affecting the quality or appropriateness of any project work, is a real skill.

Managing day-to-day project activities

Once the data collection, analysis and write-up work of a project starts, several other project management skills are likely to be required. These include:

- *people management skills* to deal with the personnel connected to the project, including recruitment, supervision and support
- *safety and risk assessment* to reduce potential risks and ensure the safety of all members of the research team
- *managing unanticipated events*: skills in problem solving are needed to manage unanticipated events to ensure a project stays on track
- *equipment skills* to effectively operate and troubleshoot technology and facilities needed during a project.

People management skills

During most research projects there will be a need to interact with a variety of people, all of whom may be vital to getting the project done successfully. In larger projects these could include research team members, research participants (i.e., the people being surveyed or interviewed), project sponsors, members of project advisory groups, and staff from the project's host institution. An ability to communicate effectively face to face, by telephone and in writing with these different people is a key skill that all project directors or project coordinators should aim to develop. Different communication styles and strategies are often necessary depending on who is being contacted, and for what purposes.

When leading a research team, key skills include an ability to negotiate the allocation of project responsibilities and workloads, and to resolve interpersonal differences. Another useful skill is an ability to generate and maintain enthusiasm for a project.

As a research team leader, it is also often necessary to monitor the work of team members and evaluate how well project tasks are being accomplished. Are scheduled project tasks being completed successfully, within the expected timeframes and resources allocated? Are project staff delivering on agreements? Is the work they are producing to a good standard? Effective monitoring is likely to be especially important during larger, more complex projects involving several researchers. In these situations, there is often potential for the project director or coordinator to lose touch with what different team members are doing.

Monitoring skills also include the ability to initiate systems for keeping track of the work being done by individual team members. For example, a computer or paper-based timesheet system could be used to track how many hours each team member spends working on different project tasks, as well as when work on a particular task started and finished.

Holding regular team meetings can help maintain group cohesion and commitment to a project. Meetings can also provide useful opportunities to:

- check on progress with key tasks
- resolve problems
- discuss funding issues
- make alternative arrangements if a project member is unable to meet their commitments.

Meetings could be held weekly, fortnightly or monthly, depending on the size and complexity of the research project and the amount of time available to complete it. In busy periods, meetings may be needed quite frequently. If a project is going through a quiet phase, meetings may not be required at all.

When hiring temporary contract staff to perform specialised roles, it is important the project director or coordinator has a good understanding of employment rules relevant to their workplace or employment setting. Projects can get into difficulty if the correct recruitment procedures are not followed, or if the people hired turn out not to have the right mix of skills for the job.

Safety and risk assessment

Risk assessment is another important aspect of research project management. This includes taking steps to ensure the safety and well-being of all research participants and project team members (cf. Craig, Corden, & Thornton, 2000) and to ensure the data collected during the project is of adequate quality.

In the following list are some examples of precautions to ensure the safety and well-being of people involved in a research project, such as team members and participants.

- When sending field interviewers out to do face-to-face interviews, check whether they might need to go to potentially high risk areas or neighbourhoods. If they do, consider asking the interviewers to work in pairs and for each to carry a mobile phone. It might also be necessary to ask the interviewers to avoid doing interviews at night and use their judgement to avoid settings that might be potentially risky (see Box 8.4).
- Arrange regular debriefing sessions with field interviewers, to discuss any challenging or difficult situations they have encountered.
- If interviewers are working with people from multiple ethnic or cultural groups, ensure they have adequate skills (i.e., cultural competence). In some settings it may be appropriate to arrange for interviewers to interview only people of the same ethnic or language group.

Box 8.4   Safety of interviewers in the field

During a survey involving knocking on the doors of homes to recruit people for a face-to-face interview, the instructions to interviewers included the following advice:

You are not expected to enter properties where you feel there is any risk or danger to yourself, or where interviewing might be otherwise inappropriate (e.g., properties with large dogs, noisy parties and/or other intimidating residents). If the person who answers the door seems to be under the influence of alcohol and/or other drugs, terminate the approach with a polite excuse.

Where fieldwork involves travelling, discuss possible risks and ways of reducing them with fieldworkers, especially where the fieldwork is in remote or potentially dangerous locations (cf. Kenyon & Hawker, 1999; Paterson, Gregory, & Thorne, 1999). When using a private vehicle for fieldwork travel, will the vehicle be covered by an insurance policy? Who is responsible for meeting the costs in the event of accident or intentional damage to the vehicle during fieldwork? Are fieldworkers insured for personal injury while engaged in fieldwork?

Occasionally during projects, crises or unfortunate events may occur. In such an event the project director or coordinator should call a meeting and get the research team to discuss what appropriate steps, if any, are needed.

In projects that employ teams of interviewers to assist with the data collection, two procedures are commonly used to ensure adequate quality during the data collection stage: training of interviewers and verification of the data collected to check it has not been made up by the interviewer. It is good practice to give interviewers sufficient training to ensure their interviews are of a suitable standard. In data verification checks, a proportion of participants are contacted again (e.g., 10%) to verify that the participants listed actually completed an interview. If verification checks are planned, usually only the interviewee's first name and phone number are collected. Where verification checks are used, they should be included in the employment briefing and interviewer training, so interviewers are aware checking is being done, and why.

Managing unanticipated events

In any project, there is always the likelihood of unanticipated events occurring. These may range from relative straightforward events such as a delay in the printing of a survey questionnaire, to the loss of a key project computer containing all the project documents and datasets or major overspending on the project budget. Project managers need to set up systems that will allow an effective response to or recovery from a range of unanticipated events. There are common types of problems that may need addressing during research projects. These problems include: delays or refusal of approval during ethical review, difficulty in obtaining access to potential research participants, low recruitment rates for research participants, data collection methods not working as planned, data processing and analysis being more difficult than anticipated, equipment failure or loss, projects running over budget and conflict or falling out among members of the research team (cf. Streiner & Sidani, 2009).

There are several strategies that can be used to avoid or reduce some of the potential problems that might occur during research projects. Carry out a small trial or pilot study to test recruitment procedures and check how well a survey or interview questionnaire is working (see Box 8.5). If employing people to assist with data collection (such as interviewers), set up monitoring systems to check how the data collection is progressing and schedule regular debriefing sessions with interviewers to discuss progress during the data collection phase.

Box 8.5 Recruitment problems

A Masters student was investigating the acceptability of reducing nicotine levels in tobacco using focus groups with smokers. She sought to recruit smokers through notices in workplace staff rooms and advertising in community newspapers. After several weeks, no one had replied to her recruitment attempts. As a result, she revised her recruitment strategy and contacted a number of smokers directly to conduct individual interviews. Fortunately, the qualitative study design, which involved key informant interviews and focus groups with smokers, could be revised without detriment to the project's integrity, following the initial recruitment difficulties experienced.

There are a number of other strategies to consider as well. Hold regular project meetings to identify any potential difficulties. Ensuring adequate communication among team members during a project can help reduce some of risks from unanticipated events. Use project team meetings for collective problem solving when difficulties do occur. Another aspect is to have someone responsible for monitoring project spending to ensure the project does not go over budget.

Equipment skills

As emphasised in other sections of this book, most research involves the use of a wide range of technology and equipment. This includes computer hardware and software programmes for capturing, storing and manipulating information in different formats. Other equipment commonly used in research includes:

- audio and video recording devices
- audio transcribing machines
- printing, scanning and copying machines
- binding machines
- handheld telecommunication devices such as mobile phones
- audiovisual presentation equipment.

Knowing how to use this equipment effectively can save a lot of time and frustration during a project. However, getting to grips with sophisticated technology is not always easy. It may sound boring, but spend an hour or so familiarising yourself with any new equipment obtained for your research project. Read the operating manual, or at least the bits indicating how to use the equipment's basic functions. Most importantly, store the operating manual in a safe place where you can find it when you need it.

When it comes to operating audio recording equipment for collecting information during interviews, it is especially vital that you understand how these devices work. Otherwise, there is a risk that important research information will be lost, perhaps forever. Do a practice interview prior to starting your main interview. Have someone help you by doing a mock interview. Learn how to detect and troubleshoot problems, perhaps by getting another person familiar with the equipment to alter the controls in different ways while you are out of the room.

Information management

A key aspect of project management is setting up and maintaining systems for efficiently collating, storing, retrieving and analysing project information. Most research projects involve a considerable amount of paperwork. Many also generate a substantial number of computer data files and other digital information. All this information needs to be organised and stored so it can be found easily when needed.

In most team-based projects, 'raw' research data collected in the field (e.g., interview transcripts, completed survey questionnaires, written notes from meetings) will be sent through to the project director or coordinator. Before storing this material in paper-based files or on computer, the director or coordinator should check it for completeness and legibility and make a note on a master list of all data collected and stored during the project. The list should include filenames and dates.

Another task for the project director or coordinator is to ensure that all written information sent out by the project team, including emails, is:

- appropriately written, presented and formatted
- uses a suitable letterhead (where necessary)
- indicates clearly the purposes for which any information requested will be used
- provides sufficient detail about the project to facilitate cooperation from key people.

Project directors or coordinators should aim to ensure that all paper-based project documentation is retained, collated, copied (where necessary) and filed. This includes signed-off ethical applications, project financial records, completed consent forms from research participants, completed questionnaires, interview transcripts, notes and memos documenting key project decisions, and all other sources of project-related data.

A golden rule is never to throw any project documentation away until the project's final report has been completed, no matter how trivial or irrelevant the documentation might seem at the time. Even when the project is finished, only discard or destroy material you are absolutely certain you will never need again. Projects can be thrown into disarray at crucial times because vital bits of information have been prematurely deleted from computers or despatched to the office rubbish bin or shredder.

All project-related electronic files, including emails, should be stored in an appropriate directory system on a secure, regularly backed up computer or server. A master file should be sent to all team members indicating how the electronic files are organised and coded, and how they can be accessed. Box 8.6 shows an example of a folder system for a research project. Once you have more than six or seven documents in a folder, create a subfolder to store older documents or earlier drafts of documents.

Box 8.6   Example of a project folder system on a computer

Community needs survey   (project title at top level folder)

Analyses   (analyses of raw data, outputs from software)
Archive   (to store older versions of project docs)
Communications and meetings   (e.g., email messages, meeting minutes)
Data files   (transcripts, text documents and quantitative data)
Ethics documents   (e.g., ethics application, information sheets)
Funding application   (applications for funding)
Questionnaires   (versions of all the question sets used)
Reports   (research reports and communication of findings)

When setting up computer backup systems, decide whether you want to keep permanent backup copies of earlier versions of certain files. Keeping copies of earlier versions of an important file can be useful if the current file you are working on becomes corrupted and then backed up in this corrupted state. If you can go back to the most recent uncorrupted version of a file it means that not all the work will be lost. Having earlier versions of a document also makes it possible to retrace editing changes over time. Some researchers routinely rename, save and backup versions of important documents they are working on, sometimes as a regularly as every day or even every few hours (see the suggestions for backing up files in Chapter 9).

Preparing project data for possible future use

As a project is nearing completion, consider possible arrangements for storing your research data for future use by other researchers (cf., Freedland & Carney, 1992). Possible uses include:

- re-analysis of the data to confirm the original findings
- additional or more detailed analyses, including analyses using different methods
- inclusion of the data in a meta-analysis or time series study
- linking the data to other datasets or research resources
- audit of the data to confirm it was collected as stated.

If you plan to store your data for future use, it is important to ensure that the types of analyses already performed on the data are adequately documented (e.g., in a codebook or other suitable document) and that clear links can be traced from the raw datasets to the reported project results. Some questions to consider, regarding possible future use of project data, are shown in Box 8.7. Most commonly, data will be stored electronically and multiple copies of data, project reports and other project documents can be held in several locations. A common choice is to select someone who is likely to continue working in the same organisation in the next few years to be the designated contact person for project information and resources.

Box 8.7   Future use of project data

Questions to consider when storing data and project documents that might be accessed, or used in future analyses, include the following:

- Where should the research data be stored?
- Are there any restrictions on who may access or use the data?
- Have all project documents that might be available to other people been screened to ensure no project participants can be identified?
- Who should be responsible for maintaining the ongoing availability of the data?
- Have codebooks or protocols been prepared that outline key information about the project datasets or databases and provide details about variables in the databases and the coding systems used?

Even if you decide not to make your project data available for future use by other people, it is good practice to nominate a person in your research team who will take ongoing responsibility for responding to requests for general information about the project and provide copies of project reports.

Project completion

The process of winding up a project is the final task in project management. During the closing phases of the project there needs to be a final check that all commitments made prior to and during the project are met. Where appropriate, send letters of thanks to people or organisations who have been especially helpful or have cooperated in ways that helped ensure the success of the project. For projects involving several people, the project completion could be marked with a social event or dinner together. If the project will involve finalising reports, finishing a thesis or preparing articles for publication, try to ensure that suitable information about the project outcomes is placed on an appropriate webpage if you wish to communicate the availability of the project findings to a wider audience.

Exercises for managing research projects

1. Write an initial task list for a research project you are considering carrying out. Put in a projected start date several weeks or months in the future and construct a summary timeline for the main tasks in the project (about 1–2 pages single-spaced).
2. Develop a project budget for carrying out 20 interviews (collecting both qualitative and quantitative data) with people experiencing financial distress in your current home location or city. Assume you will do the interviews yourself, there are no other project employees, and your budget will be part of an application seeking funding from a local agency or university.
3. Review a research project you have recently been involved in (or one you know something about). Identify 4–5 potential risks or safety issues in the project and write a brief risk assessment report (1–2 pages single-spaced) in which you describe the risks and how they might be reduced, or managed, if they occurred.
4. For a research project you have recently been involved in (or one you know something about), identify the various types of raw data and project reports from the project, and prepare a summary resource list (1–2 pages single-spaced) which would allow another research team to use the raw data as part of a later study *five years from the present time*. Indicate on which webpage(s) you would provide a summary of the project, a list of its datasets and reports, and the name of a key contact person.

References and further reading

Craig, G., Corden, A. & Thornton, P. (2000). Safety in social research. *Social Research Update, 29*. Retrieved November 27, 2000, from www.soc.surrey.ac.uk/sru/SRU29.html.

Freedland, K. E. & Carney, R. M. (1992). Data management and accountability in behavioral and biomedical research. *American Psychologist, 47*(5), 640–645.

Kenyon, E. & Hawker, S. (1999). 'Once would be enough': some reflections on the issue of safety for lone researchers. *International Journal of Social Research Methodology, 2*(4), 313–327.

Mitteness, L. S. & Barker, J. C. (1994). Managing large projects. In: J. F. Gubrium & A. Sankar (Eds), *Qualitative Methods in Aging Research* (pp. 82–104). London: Sage.

Paterson, B. L., Gregory, D. & Thorne, S. (1999). A protocol for researcher safety. *Qualitative Health Research, 9*(2), 259–269.

Phelps, R., Fisher, K. & Ellis, A. H. (2007). *Organizing and Managing Research: A Practical Guide for Postgraduates*. Thousand Oaks, CA: Sage.

Streiner, D. L. & Sidani, S. (Eds) (2009). *When Research Goes Off the Rails: Why It Happens and What You Can Do About It*. New York: Guilford Press.

Wright, L. (1999). Doing things right. In: E. R. Perkins, I. Simnett, & L. Wright (Eds), *Evidence-based Health Promotion* (pp. 277–287). Chichester: John Wiley.

APPENDIX 8.1

Example of a project budget estimate

Phases: PLANNING (Weeks 1–2) · DATA COLLECTION (Weeks 3–5) · ANALYSIS (Weeks 5–6) · REPORT WRITING (Weeks 6–8) · DISSEMINATION (Weeks 8–9)

	WEEK 1	WEEK 2	WEEK 3	WEEK 4	WEEK 5	WEEK 6	WEEK 7	WEEK 8	WEEK 9	TOTALS
PERSONNEL (SALARIES/ FEES)										
Project director	$1,200	$1,200	$1,200	$1,200	$1,200	$1,200	$1,200	$1,200	$1,200	$10,800
Project coordinator	$1,000	$1,000	$1,000	$1,000	$1,000	$1,000	$1,000	$1,000	$1,000	$9,000
Senior interviewer	$400	$800	$800	$800	$800	–	–	–	–	$3,600
Interviewers (4)	$900	$2,800	$2,800	$2,800	$2,800	–	–	–	–	$11,200
Data entry operator	–	–	$700	$700	$700	–	–	–	–	$2,100
Statistical specialist	$500	–	–	–	$2,000	–	–	$500	–	$2,500
sub total	*$4,000*	*$5,800*	*$6,500*	*$6,500*	*$8,500*	*$2,200*	*$2,200*	*$2,700*	*$2,200*	*$39,200*
FACILITIES AND SERVICES										
Rent (office)	–	–	–	$1,200	–	–	–	$1,200	$300	$2,700
Electricity	–	–	–	$220	–	–	–	$220	$55	$495
Telephone	–	–	–	$180	–	–	–	$180	$25	$385
Internet	–	–	–	$50	–	–	–	$50	$12	$112

(Continued)

(CONTINUED)

	WEEK 1	WEEK 2	WEEK 3	WEEK 4	WEEK 5	WEEK 6	WEEK 7	WEEK 8	WEEK 9	TOTALS
Catering	$200	–	$250	–	–	$300	–	–	$400	$1,150
Photocopying	$50	$100	$100	$50	$50	$50	$200	$400	$150	$1,150
Insurances	–	–	–	$120	–	–	–	–	$120	$240
Library access	–	–	–	$50	–	–	–	–	$50	$100
Printing	–	$250	–	–	–	–	–	–	$460	$710
Courier and postage	$300	$500	$50	$20	$20	$20	$20	$20	$200	$1,150
Vehicle hire	$80	$540	$540	$540	$540	$80	–	–	$540	$2,860
Air travel	–	–	–	–	–	–	–	–	$1,000	$1,000
Travel accommodation	–	–	–	–	–	–	–	–	$1,200	$1,200
sub total	*$630*	*$1,390*	*$940*	*$2,430*	*$610*	*$450*	*$220*	*$2,070*	*$4,512*	*$13,252*
EQUIPMENT										
Desktop PCs (3) leased	$120	$120	$120	$120	$120	$120	$120	$120	$120	$1,080
Laptops (8) leased	$400	$400	$400	$400	$400	$400	$400	$400	$400	$3,600
Audio recorders (5)	$1,200	–	–	–	–	–	–	–	–	$1,200
Mobile phones (6)	$800	–	–	–	–	–	–	–	–	$800
Transcription machine	$350	–	–	–	–	–	–	–	–	$350
sub total	*$2,870*	*$520*	*$520*	*$520*	*$520*	*$520*	*$520*	*$520*	*$520*	*$7,030*
Totals	$7,500	$7,710	$7,960	$9,450	$9,630	$3,170	$2,940	$5,290	$7,232	$59,482

9   Software for Research

Topics covered in this chapter

- Word processing software
- Spreadsheet software
- Database software
- Statistical analysis software
- Qualitative analysis software
- Bibliographic software
- Presentation software
- Other software
- General tips for using software

Health and social research has been transformed in recent years by the availability of comparatively inexpensive computer technology. In particular, a range of powerful computer software now makes it possible to collect, analyse, write up and disseminate research information much more quickly and effectively than in the past.

This chapter introduces the different kinds of computer software commonly used in research. It describes what the different software packages do and gives some tips on when and how to use them. This information should be particularly useful for newcomers to research who have little or no experience with computers (see Box 9.1).

Software technology is developing rapidly and detailed information about specific software packages can quickly go out of date. The chapter therefore focuses mainly on the broad functions of the different categories of software. The individual brand names of specific packages are mentioned only as illustrative examples of more general categories of software.

Box 9.1   Crossing the digital divide

Lianne is returning to university after taking a 15-year break from formal study to raise a family. Having previously worked as a registered nurse, she plans to do a post-graduate course in health research methods. Ultimately she hopes to develop her research skills and build a career as an academic researcher. Although looking forward to resuming her university studies, Lianne is concerned about her lack of experience with computer technology. Something of a traditionalist, she feels a bit fearful of computers and their capabilities, although her children and husband use them and there are desktop and notebook computers at home. Last time she was at university computers were only just starting to become the mass market item they are today. She could happily ignore them, simply handwriting all her assignments and reports. Now, though, she is worried she is on the wrong side of the digital divide and that her lack of computer skills could count against her in the competition for good grades.

(Continued)

(Continued)

Lianne decides she had better be proactive and try to fast-track her learning in this area. Initially she asks one of her teenage children, a bit of a computer geek, to teach her the basics. But it only takes a couple of sessions of this for Lianne to realise that her son doesn't really have much patience for the role. He assumes too much prior knowledge and can't put things into simple words that Lianne can understand.

Lianne asks around some of her friends and discovers that the local community college offers a basic computing course especially designed for older people with no experience of computers. The course runs twice-weekly for six weeks and includes sessions on how computers work and how to use different types of software. Lianne signs up for the course and within a week has started to get to grips with the basics of how to start up a computer and how to connect different devices such as the keyboard, mouse and printer. Soon she is learning how to use software for browsing the Internet, sending and receiving email, and creating reports, spreadsheets and other documents. All this proves a revelation for Lianne, who soon realises that using computer software isn't really as complicated or daunting as it first seems. She is also pleasantly surprised to find out how much helpful information is available on the Internet showing how to use different types of software.

By the end of the course, Lianne has enough of a grounding in the basics of computing to feel confident to continue exploring more for herself using the PC at home. She deliberately prepares all her course applications and other course materials on the home PC, to get some practice using her word processing software on a real project. To practise using spreadsheet software, she downloads her monthly bank statements, and works out how to use the transaction data to estimate the minimum income she and her family will need during her first year back at university. To learn the basics of how to use database software, Lianne catalogues the family's large record, CD and DVD collection.

By the start of Lianne's first semester she is feeling much more confident around computers. Although aware there is a lot more to learn, she is no longer daunted by the challenge.

The more common types of software used in research are shown in Table 9.1. The types of software listed in the table are described in more detail in the following sections of the chapter. While many of the specific examples of software packages refer to commercial versions available for purchase, some researchers may wish to consider using 'open source' software or free software. Such software is available from the Internet or for a small fee from companies that add additional features or provide the software on portable media such as CDs. Try a search on 'open source software' to locate relevant webpages.

Word processing software

Effective presentation of the written word is vital in research. In most projects, a range of research-related documents – proposals, funding applications, ethics review applications, information sheets, survey questionnaires and project reports – will need to be prepared and circulated. To do this you should have access to suitable word processing software and be familiar with its basic functions.

A key advantage of electronic word processing over handwriting is the scope it provides to efficiently draft, revise and lay out text. Used properly, this can be a major

TABLE 9.1   EXAMPLES OF TYPES OF SOFTWARE USED IN RESEARCH

Type	Examples of specific software*	Purposes of software for research
Word processors	Microsoft Word WordPerfect	Writing documents and reports Storing text data (e.g., interviews) Preparing text data for qualitative analysis software
Spreadsheets	Microsoft Excel Lotus 123	Storing data, simple statistical calculations, calculation of project budgets and costs, financial statements
Databases	Microsoft Access Corel Quattro pro	Storing small or large sets of data, designing forms for data entry, analysing data
Statistical analysis	SPSS SAS	Performing simple or advanced statistical analyses on quantitative data
Qualitative analysis	QSR NVivo Atlas/Ti	Storing qualitative data, analyses of qualitative data
Bibliographic	Endnote RefWorks	Storing and retrieving bibliographic references and literature sources
Presentations	Microsoft PowerPoint Corel Presentations	Preparing slide sets for presentations

*Some of the specific software features listed are usually sold or supplied as part of a bundled 'office' package containing several types of software.

timesaver. As well, it enables text to be sent quickly to other people electronically by email rather than having to print it or photocopy it and send it physically by post or courier. This can be especially important if research team members are based in different locations.

A few tips for using word processing software:

- When choosing a new programme, make sure it can easily transfer your text documents into file formats commonly used in other word processing packages, so you can jointly work on documents with colleagues. A common file sharing format is rich text format (rtf).
- Most popular word processing programs contain all the basic functions required for creating professional-looking documents. For some documents, though, it may be better to use a specialist desktop publishing software package, especially if the document has a complicated layout or numerous charts or illustrations.
- Specialist software can be used to convert a word processor document into more stable file formats enabling the document to be downloaded and read by anyone in the world via the Internet. An example of this is the widely used Acrobat pdf file format software. This software makes it possible for research reports to be disseminated quickly without having to rely on standard print publishing through journals (a process that can sometimes take months or years to complete).
- Not everyone may feel comfortable creating and drafting text on computer. Pen and paper can still be a great way to initially organise ideas and sketch out text.
- Dictation software can help with the hard work of drafting lengthy research documents. The user talks into a microphone attached to a computer. Their speech is then transformed into

text on screen ready for further editing. However, be aware that dictation software can take some practice to operate properly. It also may be hard to use in busy open plan offices with high levels of background noise (see AskJack Blog, 2008).

Spreadsheet software

Spreadsheet software (e.g., *Microsoft Excel*[1] *or OpenOffice.org Calc*) enables the electronic storage, sorting and analysis of different items or segments of research data. Data can be stored in the form of numbers or words. Because spreadsheet software is widely available and relatively easy to operate, many researchers use it for:

- compiling project budgets and timesheets
- storing information about research participants (e.g., contact details, who has been interviewed, when and by whom)
- performing basic descriptive analyses of project data
- creating attractive charts (bar charts, line charts, pie charts, scatter diagrams) illustrating project findings.

Spreadsheets can also be used to perform statistical calculations and tests on data, although usually not to the levels of sophistication possible with specialist database or statistics software.

An advantage of spreadsheets is that the data stored in them can be copied or exported into other software packages. For example, a budget estimate for a project compiled on a spreadsheet can be copied and inserted as a table into a research proposal being prepared on a word processor.

Spreadsheets are generally most suitable for working with small or medium-sized datasets. If you are working with a large dataset (e.g., more than 1000 cases/rows or more than 230 columns) you probably will need to use a more specialised database or statistics analysis software package (see below), not a spreadsheet.

Database software

Database software (e.g., *Microsoft Access* or *OpenOffice.org Base*) is used for storing and manipulating comparatively large amounts of diverse research information, such as data from in-depth quantitative surveys involving many hundreds of research participants. The software usually makes it possible for a variety of statistical calculations and tests to be performed on data.

Database software normally has to be set up and customised to suit the requirements of each project it is being used for. This can be a tricky job. Specialist training in the use of the software is often needed to do this effectively.

Most popular database packages include the option to set up a customised data input screen. This guides the way data is entered into the database and prevents data being entered incorrectly. This can help to maintain accuracy and consistency when several people are entering data into a common database. Customised data input screens can also be used to enable survey participants themselves to enter answers to questions straight into a portable or desktop computer. The advantages of this approach include greater confidentiality and less need for printed questionnaires, interviewers and data entry staff.

---

[1]The copyright of registered software titles mentioned in this chapter is acknowledged.

Statistical analysis software

For projects requiring the sorting of large amounts of quantitative data, or the use of complex statistical analyses such as regression or analysis of variance, it may be necessary to obtain a specialist statistical analysis program like *SPSS*, *SAS* or *EpiInfo*. These programmes enable users to apply a wide range of detailed statistical tests as well as create charts illustrating trends in data.

Some tips for using statistical analysis packages:

- If you are unfamiliar with statistics or statistical packages, get advice from a statistics or data processing expert. Find out which data analysis techniques are the most appropriate to use with your research data. Find out, too, which software packages are most commonly used by researchers in your field of study to perform these analyses. Ideally, seek this advice as early as possible in the planning stages of your project.
- Proper use of graphics software can greatly enhance the clarity and impact of research reports describing a project's findings. Take some time to study how to produce readable charts. Look at how charts are presented in top-class research publications. Identify the techniques you like and try to replicate them in your own reports. Remember that spreadsheet software programs (see earlier section) can be used to produce good quality charts. Often there is no need to purchase specialised statistics programs for this purpose.
- For small questionnaires with a sample size of perhaps only 10–20 people, and where time is short, it may not be necessary to input results into a specialised database or statistics package. Basic statistics can simply be calculated manually or by using spreadsheet statistical tests.
- When doing a series of statistical analyses, keep accurate records of the variables included, the date files used, the actual number or types of participants included, the specific analyses performed and any transformations or corrections applied to the data. Assume an accurate audit trail is needed. After a few months, it may be difficult to retrace or recreate the actual analyses performed (see Box 9.2).

Box 9.2   Worksheet and data table management

Brad is a member of a team of contract researchers who do social survey projects for different organisations. Since joining the team straight from university, Brad has put a lot effort into building up his knowledge of the different spreadsheet, database and statistical analysis software packages the team uses. He is now regarded as the team's 'go-to guy' for advice on data management and how to handle large amounts of quantitative survey data.

From bitter experience, Brad has learned how risky it can be to try to take shortcuts when analysing quantitative survey data. When he first started working for the survey team, he was very intent on trying to impress everybody with how fast he could produce survey results and attractive-looking data tables. However, one day this all turned to custard when an anonymous reviewer queried the accuracy of some of the data tables he had produced for a high-profile survey report. When Brad sat down to check back through his workings on the tables in question, he found it very difficult to identify his original worksheets and retrace all the different statistical procedures he had performed to create the tables. He realised that in the rush to create meaningful results, he had neglected to adequately document each step he had taken to produce the data. Eventually, Brad was able to confirm that his original data was correct, but only after spending several anxious hours one weekend redoing the analysis from the beginning.

(Continued)

> *(Continued)*
>
> Nowadays, Brad takes a far more methodical approach with each analysis job he works on. He tries to organise his data files so that anybody with some experience of quantitative data analysis should be able to retrace and check the procedures he has used to produce his results. He carefully labels each worksheet, and each data table in each worksheet, with a unique name that is logical and easy to follow. He also includes detailed written descriptions in each worksheet indicating the different analysis steps he has performed to produce the data tables. Although this approach means data analysis projects take longer to complete, it saves time and frustration further down the track when statistical findings are queried or need to be double-checked.

Qualitative analysis software

Qualitative data analysis software (commonly abbreviated as QDA), or textual analysis software, is intended to assist researchers to quickly and accurately sort the contents of large text files – such as a set of interview transcripts – into common themes or topics. In the past researchers may have done this by cutting and pasting text segments manually using a word processor, or by physically cutting up and joining extracts from printouts.

Although using qualitative analysis software is potentially much quicker than traditional hand-sorting methods of text analysis, considerable time is still required to acquire and set up the software, learn how to use it, import the raw data text into the software and code the text. The time taken to learn how to use the software adequately will vary depending on your level of computer literacy. If you are putting text from interviews into a word processing program first, make sure it is arranged in a suitable format so that it can be easily transferred into the qualitative analysis software package you want to use later.

If you are unfamiliar with qualitative analysis software, find out from other researchers what software packages are commonly used in the discipline or area you work in (for examples see the websites at the end of this chapter and the books by Bazeley, 2007 and Lewins & Silver, 2007). Get an idea of how much time it takes to learn to use the software, whether it is likely to make the types of analyses you are planning for your projects more efficient, and whether there are people who can help if you get stuck (see Box 9.3).

Remember that you need to know how to do qualitative analysis before using these packages. The packages will not teach you how to do the analysis or do it for you! Essentially, the packages are an aid to support the process of developing a framework for organising the key ideas, concepts, opinions, or themes evident in a large body of text. It is still up to you to work out what all the information finally means and what appropriate and defensible conclusions can be drawn following a detailed analysis of the raw text data.

Bibliographic software

Some larger projects, such as extensive literature reviews, can end up identifying and retrieving hundreds or even thousands of unique documents. Keeping track of the title, author and other publication details of these documents can be a major logistical exercise, as can compiling an accurate bibliography or reference list for the final project report. Fortunately, there are several good reference management software programs available that researchers can use to store, sort and format large lists of references.

Examples include *Endnote*, *Reference Manager*, *ProCite* and the *RefWorks* software which can be used online. A key advantage of these programs is that citation formats can be easily changed to suit the requirements of a particular journal or project client. This avoids having to manually retype or edit reference lists each time they are used for a different purpose. Table 9.2 lists other specific operations for which bibliographic software can be used.

Box 9.3   Learning qualitative analysis software

Jenny's research project for her Masters thesis involved an investigation of community workers' views and experiences regarding the setting up of neighbourhood support groups for young mothers. The primary dataset was interviews with 15 community workers. The interviews ranged in length from 40 minutes to 1.5 hours. After getting the interviews transcribed, Jenny ended up with 92 pages of single-spaced text. She decided to do a grounded theory analysis and approached her supervisor for advice on how she might do the analysis. Her supervisor had heard of someone using a particular type of qualitative analysis software package and she suggested to Jenny that she might like to consider using this package. Jenny was reasonably computer literate and knew how to use word processor, spreadsheet, database and several other types of software. Jenny found the website and purchased the software package, which she was able to buy at the student rate.

Once Jenny started to explore the software, she found that she was unable to work out how to do some of steps required to set up her project and analyse her data. For example, when importing documents, sometimes the formatting would change in unpredictable ways. When she tried to do some relatively simple operations, like search all the interview documents for key terms like 'making contact', she could not work out how to do this. Although the software had a help routine, it did not include some of the topics or key words she needed help with.

Getting concerned about the length of time the analysis was taking, Jenny tried to find someone who knew about the software to help her. She could not find anyone through her networks, but found another researcher using a different qualitative analysis package who offered to teach her how to use that package. As a result, Jenny abandoned the software package she originally purchased, bought the second package and was able to learn that software quickly, with guidance from the other researcher.

Jenny realised it was risky to buy a software package without first checking with someone who had already used it. She also realised how useful it can be having an experienced user show you how to operate the software, rather than simply trying to work it out for yourself.

A *bibliographic database* is a list of literature items or sources created in a separate file using bibliographic software. When using bibliographic software it is much better to store all your literature sources in a single bibliographic database rather than several databases grouped by topic. If a specific selection of literature items on a single topic is needed – for example to send to colleagues – this can be exported from your single database when required. Over several years you may eventually accumulate thousands of items in your bibliographic database. It thus becomes a very valuable resource for future research. The time spent entering items into the database will be saved later when you need to cite literature and create reference lists in research reports.

TABLE 9.2   COMMON OPERATIONS WHEN USING BIBLIOGRAPHIC SOFTWARE

Type of operation	Purpose and comments
Enter or download reference items into bibliographic software file	Items can be typed in directly. If you are linked to an electronic journal or database you can often download directly. Look for a button or function called something like 'export/download to citation manager'
Assign your own customised key words to each item	Some journal articles come with a key word list but normally it is better to develop your own key words that you frequently use in your own writing and research. The software will provide a list of the key words you have assigned
Select preferred citation style for use when exporting items to a word processor document	Most bibliographic software has hundreds of options for choosing citation styles, including specific styles for a number of well-known journals. You can reset the style whenever you need to. See Chapter 7, Doing a Literature Review, for more information about citation styles
Search for items having one or more key words in common	If you know you have reference sources about 'child care' and 'Canada' for example, you can quickly find all items with both of these terms. The search function makes locating specific items in a large bibliographic database very easy
Highlight items of interest	Select specific items using one or more key word searches. These can be marked for export or marked from inside your word processor document through an active link to the selected item in your bibliographic database
Link items to word processing document citations in text and export reference list	With both your word processor and bibliographic software open, you can export items into a word processor document (usually to the end of the document) in the selected citation style
Verify the exported reference list in a word processor document	You need to check the reference list has compiled correctly at the end of your document. Once you have finalised your text document, you may need to 'deactivate' the link with your bibliographic software. This allows you to send the document to other people in a format that will not try to automatically search for and open the bibliographic software on your colleague's computer

Presentation software

Presentation software is used for creating professional-looking slides or overheads for lectures or when presenting research proposals or findings at conferences and other meetings. Most researchers at some stage will need to prepare a presentation using one of the software packages available. One of the more commonly used packages is Microsoft *PowerPoint*. However, other presentation software packages offer similar functions. Most packages include the option to add special effects such as digital pictures or sound effects.

As occasional attendees at conferences, the authors have sat through some great presentations and a fair number of boring or poorly delivered presentations. If you are unfamiliar with presentation software and plan to use it at some stage, it is worth taking some time to learn how to construct a presentation in PowerPoint or a similar package. This should include learning how to edit and revise the slides to customise them for a specific presentation. Table 9.3 gives an overview of suggested steps for preparing a slide presentation.

TABLE 9.3   STEPS FOR PREPARING A VISUAL SLIDE (POWERPOINT) PRESENTATION

Step	Description
Finalise text	Confirm and finalise the text of the research report or other type of source document you intend to use as the basis for your presentation (if needed). Suitable extracts from the text can be cut and pasted into your slides as a starting point for constructing your talk. If you are not using a source document, text can be typed directly into the software as you develop your presentation
Choose a slide design template	Most software packages have several design templates Choose one that suits your presentation. This will create a common design theme for all your slides
Construct slides using presentation software	Create each slide to contain a key point or idea relating to your research report or other documents. Write the slide title, the body text and then add any visual or graphic features if needed
Sort slides into an appropriate sequence	The first slide will usually be a title slide that includes the authors' names and affiliations. The slides that follow the title slide should have a logical flow through to the final slide
Add special effects to specific slides	Special effects include slide transitions when moving from one slide to the next, additional images and any added audio files Be careful not to overdo transition special effects
Add speaker notes if needed	If you are not confident about speaking to an audience, or there are specific points you wish to remind yourself to emphasise in your talk, add these in the speaker notes box for the slide, which is outside the main body of the slide. Points in speaker notes boxes can be printed out so you can take them with you to the presentation. Your audience will not see the points in speaker notes boxes when the 'slide show' format is being used
Review the presentation using the 'Play slide show' mode	Start at the first slide and look at each slide in turn and consider how an audience might interpret or respond to what is on the slide. Make notes as you go
Revise presentation	Use your notes to critically review each slide's content, sequence and special effects (if used). Make any necessary revisions
Do a live practice with an audience	Recruit one or two people (e.g., friends, colleagues, fellow students) to sit through a practice presentation and give constructive feedback about your presentation

A typical structure for a slide presentation reporting research findings is shown in Box 9.4. If you are constructing a presentation for the first time to report your research results, this gives an idea of what to include.

Box 9.5 lists some general issues to be aware of when preparing and delivering a slide presentation describing a research project. Paying attention to these points should help make your presentations more professional and effective.

Box 9.4   Slide sequence for a research presentation

- Title slide
- Overview slide, with key headings to be covered
- Acknowledgements, members of research team
- Aims, objectives, research questions
- Background to research
- Research setting or location
- Sample and participants
- Data gathering methods
- Data analysis procedures
- Finding 1
- Finding 2
- Finding 3 etc.
- Implications (e.g., for future research or practice)
- Conclusions

Box 9.5   Tips for slide presentations

- Make sure the font size of the text on your slides is large enough. Use about 36–40 point font size for slide titles and 28–32 point size for body text in the slide.
- Shorten the text on your slides into key words and brief statements. You are not expected to write full sentences.
- Don't cram too much text onto a slide.
- Don't prepare too many slides for the speaking time available. Allow enough time for questions from the floor and discussion.
- Don't overdo special transition effects when moving from one slide to the next. It distracts people's attention away from the content.
- Check for spelling and typing errors.
- Don't spend more than the first 30 per cent of the time talking about the background and methods of your study. A common mistake in presentations is spending more than 50 per cent of the time on the introduction and methods before starting on the findings.
- Don't stand in front of the screen, obscuring the view of the slides.

Other software

Other types of software that can be helpful for researchers include:

- *Project management software* for helping to plan and run the different stages of a project or manage several projects at once.
- *Survey software* that allows development of a survey questionnaire that can be used for data collection in Web surveys or surveys using notebook computers or other electronic devices.
- *Internet and email software* for accessing the huge quantity of research information available on the World Wide Web and quickly exchanging notes with colleagues and clients, wherever you are working.

- *Concept mapping software.* This can be used to sketch out ideas and models relating to research. A concept map consists of a number of key labels or elements enclosed in circles or boxes. Links or relationships between concepts are indicated by lines connecting the concepts.
- *Voice recognition software* for transcribing recorded speech into written text (cf., Anderson, 1998).

A few final thoughts on software

- It is probably better to get to know three or four relevant software packages really well, rather than many different packages superficially.
- Establish a reliable system for backing-up your most vital files on both your main computer and on portable storage media such as memory sticks (see Box 9.6). Leave backup copies in at least two different locations. Hours of work can go into accurately transcribing a single face-to-face interview, but the effort can be completely wasted if the only electronic copy of the interview transcript is accidentally deleted from your computer. Remember, having only one copy of all your data on a single laptop computer is one of the biggest risks for data and document loss.
- If possible, choose compatible software packages, or packages that have other types of functionality enabling you easily to copy and paste text or data from one package into another (e.g., spreadsheet data into database software; charts and other graphics into word processing or desktop publishing software).
- Having a wide range of up-to-date research software on your computer will not automatically make it easier to do research projects. The software is really just a set of tools. You still need to have a clear understanding of how and when to apply these tools and what you are aiming to achieve with them.
- Getting advanced training on how to use specialist software can be a worthwhile investment. You learn how to make more effective use of the software, including how to tailor the functions of the software to your specific needs.

Box 9.6   Backing up key files and documents

Have you been backing up your computer files? Are you storing the backup copies somewhere safe? Stories like this one, which was reported on an email list, are unfortunately common.

> Melanie recently had her laptop stolen and with it all her thesis files. Fortunately some had been emailed to her supervisor but her other stuff has gone.

Here are some tips for backing up key files.

1. Make a backup at the end of each day or after every session of work when you have added new information.
2. Use a USB memory stick or other portable storage device that can be kept separate from your computer. Alternatively, store files in a secure Web location.
3. Email key files to a colleague or friend and ask them to save them in a folder created for the purpose (or email the files to yourself if your email is stored on a server).
4. Save each day's work with a dated filename. If a file becomes corrupted, you will have the previous file to retrieve. You can add the date to the file name using year-month-day (e.g., Introduction100326). That way, the versions will be ordered by date. Keep three or four of the most recent versions and delete the older versions when too many accumulate.

Exercises for software skills

1. Do a Web browser search on 'QDA software'. Locate websites for the publishers or distributors of three different software packages. Note whether the following details are provided: cost of the package, user reviews of the software package, options to access a free trial version, list of the package's operations or functions. Based on what you have found, how important is website information for accessing and trialling a software package?
2. Do a Web browser search on the phrase 'tips for powerpoint presentations'. Locate three lists that offer advice and tips. Make a summary list of up to 10 tips or specific points mentioned in at least two of the lists you find.
3. Make a list of the software packages you know how to use reasonably well. Make a second list of the types of software you would like to learn how to use (or learn how to use better). For the top two items on your 'to learn' list, type some relevant key words into your Web browser (e.g., 'statistics software', 'project planning software') together with the word 'reviews' and locate some reviews of relevant software packages. Based on these reviews, narrow your search to two specific software packages. Try to locate instructions or tips for learning how to use these two software packages.

References and further reading

Anderson, J. F. (1998). Transcribing with voice recognition software: a new tool for qualitative researchers. *Qualitative Health Research, 8*(5), 718–723.

AskJack Blog (2008, 21 February) Can speech-recognition software transcribe interviews? Retrieved April 21, 2009, from: www.guardian.co.uk/technology/askjack/2008/feb/21/canspeechrecognition software.

Bazeley, P. (2007). *Qualitative Data Analysis with NVivo* (2nd edn). Thousand Oaks, CA: Sage.

Durkin, T. (1997). Using computers in strategic qualitative research. In G. Miller & R. Dingwall (Eds), *Context and Method in Qualitative Research* (pp. 92–105). London: Sage.

Hahn, C. (2008). *Doing Qualitative Research Using Your Computer: A Practical Guide.* London: Sage.

Lewins, A. & Silver, C. (2007). *Using Software in Qualitative Research: A Step-by-Step Guide.* Thousand Oaks, CA: Sage.

Phelps, R., Fisher, K., and Ellis, A. H. (2007). *Organizing and Managing Research: A Practical Guide for Postgraduates.* Thousand Oaks, CA: Sage.

Examples of software websites

(Hint: Do a Web browser search on 'QDA software' or 'statistics software' or 'open source software'.)

Statistical software:
   www.statpages.org/miller/openstat/
List of qualitative analysis software:
   www.eval.org/Resources/QDA.htm
Online QDA:
   http://onlineqda.hud.ac.uk/Which_software/index.php

QSR Qualitative analysis software(e.g., NVivo):
  www.qsr.com.au/
ATLAS.ti software:
  www.atlasti.com/
Bibliographic software:
  RefWorks online software (annual subscription software). Trial version available at: www.refworks.com/

10   Working with Colleagues and Supervisors

Topics covered in this chapter

- Working with colleagues in a team
  - Forming a research team
  - Getting to know each other
  - Agreeing on roles and tasks
  - Progress reports and team meetings
  - Managing differences
  - Writing as a team
- Working with supervisors
  - Finding a supervisor
  - Clarifying expectations with a supervisor
  - Having more than one supervisor
  - Resolving differences with a supervisor
  - Publishing papers with a supervisor

This chapter looks at two situations many researchers are likely encounter during the early years of their professional training:

- working with colleagues in a team
- working with a supervisor for a postgraduate research qualification such as a Masters degree or a PhD.

Working with colleagues in a team

A research team can be defined as two or more people working together on a research project. Compared to when just one researcher does all the work, a team approach has the potential to get a project done more quickly and to a higher standard of quality. More people and a wider range of skills and knowledge can be called upon at different stages of a project. This can be especially important in complex projects involving large numbers of research participants and sophisticated data collection and analysis procedures.

However, doing research as a team also carries with it certain risks. Team-based research and other forms of close professional collaboration between researchers can be an intense activity, involving a lot of emotional investment. Team members can become very reliant on each other. A research project can get into serious trouble if team members do not work together effectively. It is therefore vital to try to anticipate these risks and think carefully about how to develop and maintain effective working relationships in a team.

Forming a research team: getting the right mix

The way a research team is first put together can be a major factor shaping its success. If a research team has the right mix of skills and personalities, this increases its chances of operating smoothly. If there are gaps in the team's skill-mix or if certain personalities clash, then the team is more likely to have a bumpy ride.

Box 10.1   How common is it for researchers to work together?

Counting scientific journal articles written by two or more people is one way to measure teamwork in research. A study of nearly 20 million articles published in the past 50 years in science and engineering, social science and the arts and humanities found a steady increase in the proportion of co-authored articles. In the social sciences, 51 per cent of research articles published in 2000 were co-authored compared to just 17 per cent in 1955 (Wuchty, Jones, & Uzzi, 2007). Co-authored articles were also more likely than sole-authored articles to be cited widely in other publications. This suggests co-authored articles generally spark more interest and may have greater scientific impact than sole-authored articles.

Research teams can be formed in a various ways. In some cases researchers with similar interests who already know each other professionally or socially will decide it might be a good idea to work on a research project together. This may be after perhaps months or years of informal meetings to share research ideas and knowledge.

In other cases, a general notice will be issued to all researchers in a particular agency or workplace inviting them to consider joining a newly developed or emerging project. Anyone who wants to become part of the project team can do so. Nobody is refused or excluded if they are keen to be involved.

In a third scenario, a research team might be assembled specifically with a view to tendering for a project requested or commissioned by a funding agency or sponsor. People considered to have certain skills needed for the project will be approached individually and asked if they want to join the team. Team members may not necessarily know each other well or even be based in the same organisation or place.

Each of these different approaches has certain benefits and risks. Forming a research team around people who already know each other well can help minimise the risk of friction or disharmony. People will trust each other and know what makes each other tick. However, people may get on so well together that socialising interferes with getting the job done.

Box 10.2   Reasons for researchers to collaborate

Benefits of researchers working together on projects can include:

- sharing of specialised skills and knowledge
- cross-fertilisation of ideas from other disciplines or research fields
- more access to tacit knowledge not available in print
- sharing of equipment or resources
- enhanced productivity

(Continued)

(Continued)

- improved internal quality control
- training opportunities for novice researchers
- enhanced professional networks and contacts
- camaraderie and intellectual companionship (research can be a lonely occupation)
- stimulation and enhanced creativity
- more scope to respond to a range of research funding opportunities
- improved success with competitive grant applications.

(Bozeman & Corley, 2004; Katz & Martin, 1997; Melin, 2000; Priest et al., 2007)

Issuing a general notice to all researchers inviting them to join a project team can increase the chances that the people who do volunteer are more likely to have a genuine interest in the study, and time available to contribute. However, the team as a whole may still lack certain skills or knowledge.

Hand-picking individuals and persuading them to join a team, if done well, can increase the chances of the team containing the right mix of skills, experience and personalities for a project. However, it may not necessarily mean that everyone in the team is enthusiastic about the work they are doing.

In practice, most research teams are likely to be formed using a combination of these approaches. Some team members will already know each other and be keen to work together more closely. Other people will volunteer to join the team because they are enthusiastic about the research topic. Certain individuals with vital specialist skills or knowledge will be shoulder-tapped and encouraged to come on board.

Recruitment of new team members is likely to be an ongoing feature of some projects, especially larger projects running for several years. Existing team members may quit or significantly scale down their involvement in a project and need to be replaced. As well, new people may need to be brought into a team temporarily to perform specialised tasks.

Getting to know each other

At the beginning of a team project, plenty of opportunities should be arranged for team members to meet each other and discuss the project. During these meetings, it will be important to check out to what extent everybody shares similar perspectives about the research topic and the project's research design. Especially in projects with multidisciplinary teams, some team members may hold quite divergent views about what research is for and how it should be conducted, or use quite different conceptual models or terminology to describe research (Loan-Clarke & Preston, 2002). This can be a source of misunderstanding or friction, especially in the early stages of a project where most team members have not worked together before.

Resolving these conceptual difficulties as soon as possible is important. Ideally, at least one or two team members should have a good working knowledge of the range of research-related concepts and terms applicable to different disciplines, and be able to act as a kind of interpreter and mediator for other team members. However, sometimes a newly created team of researchers working together to develop a proposal can run into difficulties if contrasting research values among team members are unable to be resolved (see Box 10.3).

Box 10.3   Preparing a research proposal with a group

Sometimes writing a research proposal as a group can get difficult.

Marcus is a researcher in the Health Department's regional evaluation unit that does research and evaluation projects for a range of health sector clients. One day Marcus is phoned by a diabetes educator from the local diabetes society. The society has developed a new diabetes self-management plan for use by people with type II diabetes. The plan is intended to help people better monitor their blood glucose levels, diet and body weight and reduce the incidence of diabetes complications.

The society wants to set up an evaluation project to test the plan's effectiveness. It has a small amount of money available that could be used to pay a researcher to coordinate the writing of an evaluation research proposal. This proposal could then be developed into a formal application to the Medical Research Council for financial support to do the evaluation.

The diabetes educator asks Marcus if he would be willing to help coordinate the writing of the evaluation proposal. After checking with his manager, Marcus agrees and a week later attends a meeting at the diabetes society convened by the diabetes educator. The meeting includes people from a range of different backgrounds interested in diabetes. During the meeting it is decided to set up a special committee of key people who Marcus will work with during the preparation of the proposal. The committee includes the diabetes educator, a person representing consumers of diabetes services, a senior lecturer from the local medical school with an interest in diabetes education and treatment, a practice nurse educator with an understanding of diabetes care in community settings, a senior lecturer in general practice from the local medical school, and a health promotion and marketing specialist from the local Health Department. This is the first time Marcus has ever had to work with such a large team of people to develop a project proposal and he is slightly apprehensive about how it will all turn out. He has no prior experience of working with any of the committee members and knows very little about their research interests and perspectives.

The first meeting of the committee is scheduled to be held in two weeks. Marcus agrees it would be a good idea to try to prepare an initial rough draft of the proposal so this could be sent to the committee members in time for the meeting. Having talked several times by phone and in person with the diabetes educator, Marcus is under the impression that the diabetes society thinks the evaluation should mainly look at the acceptability and appropriateness of the new diabetes self-management kit for people with diabetes and their families. This includes whether people with diabetes properly understand the information provided in the self-management kit and are willing to use the kit on a regular basis. With this in mind, Marcus prepares the first draft of the project proposal. It includes a section listing some tentative evaluation objectives plus a research design section outlining how telephone interviews with a sample of people with diabetes could be used to assess the kit's acceptability and appropriateness.

Marcus circulates his first draft to the other committee members by email before the next meeting. At the meeting there is a mixed response to Marcus's first writing efforts. The diabetes educator, the consumer representative and the practice nurse educator are positive the proposal is shaping up in the right direction. However, both of the medical school lecturers criticise the proposal for its lack of focus on outcomes, especially clinical outcomes. For them, the only proper test of the suitability of the diabetes self-management kit is whether or not it can be shown to improve people's clinical risk factors for diabetes complications.

This causes a dilemma for Marcus. Obviously there is potential to add new elements to the evaluation proposal so the project examines these clinical outcomes. But this will also turn the evaluation into a much more resource-intensive and complex project than the one originally

(Continued)

(Continued)

envisioned by the diabetes society. Preliminary calculations by a biostatistics specialist in Marcus's unit suggest a minimum of 420 people with type II diabetes would have to be recruited into the clinical outcomes phase of the evaluation to ensure any positive clinical benefits identified are statistically significant. On top of this, extra staff and equipment would be needed to manage tasks associated with taking and storing people's blood samples and performing other routine medical tests. Marcus calculated it may be necessary to find funding of about \$200,000–250,000 to pay for such a comprehensive evaluation. By contrast, the evaluation described in Marcus's initial draft proposal could be funded for about a quarter of this price. As well, it would only take a matter of a few weeks to complete, rather than the many months that would be needed to conduct a full clinical evaluation.

As Marcus begins to think more deeply about the different arguments and positions of the individuals on the committee, he realises he has stumbled rather blindly into his proposal writing role. For one thing, he had assumed that having a mixture of people from diverse backgrounds on the committee would be beneficial to the proposal writing process. The more people on the committee, he thought, the greater the pool of experience and knowledge there would be to draw on and therefore the better the proposal would be in the end. However, he had not counted on people on the committee disagreeing over what should be the priority objectives for the evaluation. He had naively assumed that all the committee members would simply accept the priority objectives identified by the diabetes society. In reality this was not to be; the clinicians on the committee sought to override the society's objectives, resulting in Marcus having to develop a number of increasingly complex, multi-layered evaluation designs in an effort to satisfy everybody's wishes.

Slightly spooked by this experience, Marcus is now more wary about agreeing to prepare research proposals or evaluation plans on behalf of committees or large teams, especially if the time and funding available to do the work are limited. He is especially careful at the beginning to check out to what extent committee or team members already agree on what should be the central goals or objectives of a research or evaluation project. If there is marked disagreement between committee or team members, he attempts to broker some kind of consensus. Only after this is achieved will he start writing up the first draft of the proposal.

Agreeing on roles and tasks

During preliminary meetings, team members should also discuss and agree on the timetable for the project and who will take responsibility for different project roles and tasks. Decisions on these matters should be noted down in writing and kept for future reference, to reduce the risk of later misunderstandings. This will be especially important if team members are already juggling large portfolios of work.

Team members should also agree on what kind of decision making structure to use during the project. Will it be better to adopt a relatively top-down, hierarchical, structure, or a more open, inclusive structure (see Box 10.4)?

Box 10.4   Team decision making: some options

In a relatively top-down team structure, decisions are taken mainly by one or two key team members. These people have responsibility for seeing the big picture and managing the flow

(Continued)

(Continued)

of information between other team members. This kind of approach can be effective in a rapidly changing or challenging research environment, where quick decisions are needed. However, because not everybody in the team may get a chance to contribute to decisions, some decisions can be based on partial or inadequate information. As well, the absence of a key decision maker for any reason, say ill-health or reassignment, can contribute to delays in making vital decisions.

In a more open, inclusive team structure, all team members are encouraged to think about the big picture and have input into major decisions. This increases the potential for decisions to be based on full information. It also means the loss of a key project member is unlikely to be too damaging to the project. Other team members will be familiar with the big picture. A disadvantage is that a lot of time can be taken up sharing information with each other and making decisions, especially if team members are located in different offices and have to communicate by phone or email, or travel long distances to meet (He, Geng, & Campbell-Hunt, 2009).

Progress reports and team meetings

Once a project starts, team members should keep each other informed about how the project tasks they are responsible for are progressing. Written or oral reports should be exchanged regularly, indicating:

- tasks accomplished to date
- any problems arising
- future plans
- questions or suggestions for other team members.

Different projects, and different phases of projects, are likely to require different levels of reporting between team members. During complex or challenging project phases, team members may need to report on progress quite frequently – perhaps weekly, daily or even hourly. Less frequent reporting (fortnightly, monthly, six-monthly) may be suitable during relatively undemanding, technically straight-forward phases of a project, especially if team members already have a good track-record of working together successfully.

Box 10.5   Diversity in research teams

Remember that team members can have different work habits and attitudes. Some people may be prepared to devote virtually all their waking hours to a project, whereas others may want to do only what is necessary and balance their project work with other responsibilities and interests. Some may have a real passion for the project. Others may regard it simply as a stepping-stone to more desirable work and have very little personal interest in the topic. Some team members may be analytical thinkers and details people. Others may be strategic thinkers, more interested in the big picture. Team members may also have different ways of communicating disagreement or complaints. Some may be very gentle and restrained when it comes to communicating problems or making observations that might be regarded as negative or critical. Others may take a more hard-nosed approach, not holding back with criticism.

Some team members may have contact with the rest of a project team only for short periods when their expertise is needed. A challenge in these situations is to ensure that these peripheral team members are kept up to speed with vital information about the study.

Similarly, if team members are based in different locations and unable to meet with each other on a regular basis, this poses extra challenges for building and maintaining close professional ties and trust. Face-to-face meetings are more likely to be effective for developing group cohesion than video and phone conferencing or emails (Hinds & Bailey, 2003).

Research by its nature tends to attract individuals with questioning, inquiring minds. In a team project, even the most inexperienced or junior team members are likely to be scrutinising how the project is going and forming their own views about the best ways to do things. Holding regular meetings, where all team members are encouraged to talk freely about these matters, can be important for identifying emerging disagreements about technical aspects of a project and jointly working out strategies for resolving them. Providing opportunities for team members to socialise together outside the regular workplace environment can also have positive spin-offs in terms of increasing people's willingness to be open and honest with each other during team meetings.

The enthusiasm of team members can wane at any stage in a research project, but especially in the middle or final stages. Some projects can run for several years, meaning there is scope for boredom to develop, especially if the work involved is quite repetitive and mundane. Other priorities may intrude and team members can get side-tracked. Team members can also lose heart if they are constantly battling difficult methodological problems or finding it hard to recruit research participants. In these situations it can be an advantage if there are at least one or two people in the team who can stay calm and optimistic in the face of adversity. This can help keep problems in perspective and re-motivate other team members.

Managing differences

In any team project, people can get offside or upset with each other. In some projects this happens frequently, in others hardly ever. Resolving major breakdowns in team relations can be time-consuming and costly to the progress of a project, especially if the underlying causes are complex and hard to define. The risk of major disharmony between team members can be reduced by being sensitive to the first signs of an emerging dispute and taking steps to defuse it amicably, before it has a chance to grow larger.

First signs of a possible breakdown in team relations can include slower than expected responses to requests for advice or assistance, reluctance to freely share crucial information, or escalations in the frequency and seriousness of petty disagreements or disputes. More obvious signs include open expressions of hostility or anger.

Box 10.6   Testing times for research teams

General conditions of the research environment and culture can increase the potential for friction in team projects. In some settings, colleagues may be working together in a team while also being rivals for research funds in other areas of their work. This can make it difficult for team colleagues to fully trust or be open with each other.

(Continued)

> *(Continued)*
>
> If a team is doing client-driven commercial or policy-orientated research, competition for research funds may be intense. Much attention may be given to ensuring research money is well spent and not squandered on low-performing or ineffectual studies. There may also be a big emphasis on completing research quickly, to meet client expectations and needs. These factors can all increase the pressure on team relationships, especially if a team includes novice researchers who are still developing their research skills through on-the-job training.

If disputes between team members do become so serious that they cannot be resolved internally by the team, it may be useful to seek help from an independent person with experience in mediation or conflict resolution. Restructuring the research team may also be a solution. Timetables and tasks could be re-organised so that the people in dispute with each other do not have to work together so often. In a worst case scenario, where all other options have failed, the only choice left may be to ask the individuals involved to leave the team.

Ultimately, though, it is probably unrealistic to expect harmony to prevail at all times between team members. It can even be argued that a certain amount of creative tension between team members can be good for a project.

Writing up findings as a team

There is no one, standard approach for writing up the findings of a team research project. In some cases, all team members will share responsibility for preparing project reports or articles for publication, with each team member working on different writing or editing tasks. In other cases, just one team member will take responsibility for writing up all project findings.

An advantage of the single-writer approach is that it is usually easier to achieve a consistency of writing style and language. However, the writer may need to spend a lot of extra time coming to grips with technical aspects of the project – aspects that other team members are already familiar with. As well, if the writer gets sick or is swamped with other work, progress on writing tasks can cease.

An advantage of the team-writing approach is that the specialised knowledge of each team member is likely to be incorporated into the written work more easily. However, the resulting draft material may be more likely to include a mix of different writing styles and terminologies. Quite a bit of extra editing may be needed to make everything consistent. This approach also relies on all team members fulfilling their writing commitments on time and to a good standard. If one team member cannot finish their work for any reason, this can jeopardise the whole process.

These days, word processing software and the Internet make it is possible for multiple authors to edit a single publication together with reasonable ease, even if the authors are located in different offices. However, when using this technology it is important to be very careful with the labelling and circulation of different drafts. It can be frustrating if team members find they are using the wrong version of a draft report, or if all their hard work revising a document is suddenly lost because of mistakes in the organisation of shared computer files.

Working with supervisors

A core responsibility of academic staff in universities and other higher learning institutions is the supervision of research projects by postgraduate students. This section looks at the special case of the supervisor–student relationship. What features should a student look for in a research supervisor or mentor? What kinds of help or advice should a research supervisor be expected to provide? What can a student do if he or she disagrees with their research supervisor's advice?

Finding a supervisor

When seeking a person to act as a research supervisor, take some time to carefully review the range of people available. Look around and consider all your options. Ask yourself, how many people do I know who may be able to perform this role? Ideally, which of these people would I prefer to be my supervisor, and why? They need to be willing to supervise your research and have the time for supervision. It also helps if they have a personal interest in your research topic.

Think about what style of supervision you are looking for (see Box 10.7). You may be a very capable, self-reliant and motivated student who requires only minimal contact with a supervisor. Or you may be a student who feels most secure when the details of your project plans and work are being regularly checked, with the supervisor acting almost as a kind of research director or manager. Some supervisors are very adept at providing light-handed, unobtrusive but highly effective mentoring. Some supervisors are also more willing than others to immerse themselves in the details of a student's research project or take an interest in the seemingly mundane or routine elements of a study.

Box 10.7　Different styles of research supervision

Studies have looked at the different styles of research supervision experienced by university students. Four common styles are evident:

1. *Traditional, laissez-faire style.* The student is expected to manage both the research project and him- or herself. The supervisor–student relationship is marked by formality and distance, intellectual sparring and challenge. The supervisor does not offer personal support.
2. *Empathetic style.* The student is expected to design and manage the research project but is recognised to need personal support and encouragement while doing this. The supervisor aims to develop a good interpersonal relationship with the student, sharing in the student's struggles and providing motivation.
3. *Directive, task-oriented style.* The student is assumed mainly to need guidance on how to design and manage their research project, not personal support. The supervisor provides structure for the research process, defines objectives, sets deadlines, devises timetables and issues instructions. The student aims to work largely within these pre-set frameworks.
4. *Open, flexible style.* The supervisor negotiates with the student about the kinds of assistance he or she requires with both project management and personal/

(Continued)

(Continued)

self-management. The supervisor aims to facilitate rather than direct or manage, emphasising shared creative problem solving.

Many students tend to prefer the latter, more open, flexible supervision style. The best supervisors are able to adjust their style to meet the technical and personal needs of the student at different stages of the research process.

Sources: Acker, Hill, & Black, 1994; Deuchar, 2008; Grant, 2005; Gurr, 2001; Kam, 1997

Are you wanting a supervisor who prefers you to work in areas closely aligned to their personal research interests? Or do you want a supervisor with a good general understanding of a range of topics who can guide you as you pursue your own research interests? Are you mainly looking for a person who will assist with theoretical and technical aspects of the design and execution of your research project? Or are you mainly looking for a person who will provide you with personal support and reassurance as you tackle the challenges of your study?

Talk with others who have already worked in a similar role with the people you are considering as possible supervisors. What do they think? How did it work out for them? Bear in mind that the supervisor–student relationship has the potential to be quite intense. Depending on the nature and duration of the intended research project, this level of intensity may have to be sustained over the course of several years. Some university staff will have heavy teaching, research and administrative workloads and may be unable to devote a lot of time to helping you solve problems with your project or reviewing drafts of your written material.

Remember that there is no one, set formula for a successful supervisor–student relationship. Rather, there are different styles of supervisor–student relationship, all of which have the scope to be successful. The trick is to recognise which style is most likely to work for you, then to find a supervisor who offers this approach. Bear in mind that the choices available for potential supervisors may be quite limited, especially in smaller academic departments. In some cases, students may be offered only one option for a supervisor, that they can either accept or not.

Clarifying expectations

Early in discussions with your supervisor, try to talk openly about what you each consider to be the objectives of the relationship and the processes and structures you would like to put in place to achieve them. It is easy to automatically assume you both share the same goals for the relationship and agree on what needs to be done to achieve them. However, in truth this may not be the case.

Take time to openly discuss and reach agreement on the basic ground-rules for the supervisor–student relationship. Cover issues such as:

- how often you would like to meet
- the extent to which you are wanting light-handed or close supervision
- how meetings might be structured

- the extent to which you or the supervisor will be expected to set the agenda for the content of meetings
- whether what is talked about in meetings should be recorded or noted down for future reference.

In particular, it is important to check out the limits of what the supervisor is prepared to do to help you complete your project. What aspects of your work do they regard as suitable for them to provide advice or assistance with? What other aspects are they unable or unwilling to help with? How much are they prepared to provide you with personal support during the project, as opposed to helping simply with technical aspects of your research design or project management?

Having more than one supervisor

In some situations, such as a PhD or a large Masters research project, it can be useful to have more than one supervisor. A second supervisor can provide extra ideas about how a project could be designed or managed. They can also provide advice or support in areas where the first supervisor is not qualified, such as knowledge of social and cultural practices appropriate for research with people from certain communities or ethnic groups.

In academic settings it is quite likely that a primary or sole supervisor may go on extended leave, retire or get a job at another university. Having a second supervisor in these circumstances can save a lot of disruption to the supervision process. A good strategy is to ask a potential supervisor about their availability over the next three or four years.

The potential benefits of multiple supervision should be weighed against its risks. In some cases supervisors may end up disagreeing with each other on fundamental points of theory or research practice. They may also give conflicting or inconsistent advice, which can leave a student wondering what to do next.

Resolving differences with supervisors

Disagreements between supervisor and student about aspects of a research project are not uncommon. Usually they are part and parcel of a healthy supervisor–student relationship, reflecting the principle that knowledge advances through the rigorous testing of people's beliefs and knowledge. Conducted in the right spirit, disagreements can be productive and beneficial.

Box 10.8   Successful supervisor–student relationships

Recent literature has identified the following elements to be important:

- the student takes an active role in selecting their supervisor, rather than simply having the supervisor assigned to them (Ives & Rowley, 2005)
- at the start of the relationship, both parties clarify their expectations and assumptions (Engebretson et al., 2008; McCormack, 2004)

(Continued)

> *(Continued)*
>
> - supervision meetings are held frequently and have clear objectives and goals (Engebretson et al., 2008)
> - the supervisor provides prompt, detailed, constructive feedback on the student's work (Engebretson et al., 2008)
> - the supervisor treats the student as an individual and adapts their style of supervision to suit the student's changing needs over time (Engebretson et al., 2008; Kam, 1997)
> - the student has a second supervisor to use as a backup if their principal supervisor is unavailable (Ives & Rowley, 2005).

Sometimes, however, disagreements can escalate and become so charged with emotion and ego that they begin to undermine the quality of the supervisor–student relationship. In this situation, it may be advisable to get another opinion about the issue from an experienced researcher respected by both parties. Another option could be for the supervisor and student to nominate a person they both trust to mediate the situation and help resolve their differences amicably.

In the end, if the level of disagreement is so intense that no resolution is possible, it may be best for all concerned if the student obtains a new supervisor. However, this option should be used only as a last resort. Changing supervisor can significantly disrupt and delay a project. The new supervisor will need to be briefed on work completed to date and will probably require time to fully absorb and come up to speed with relevant issues.

Publishing papers with supervisors

Once a research project such as a PhD or Masters thesis is finished, students will often involve their supervisor in the writing of journal articles or conference papers reporting the results of the thesis. In some cases, the supervisor's contribution may amount to nothing more than commenting on drafts or identifying potentially useful references. In other cases, the supervisor may be prepared to write sections of an article or presentation, so becoming a genuine co-author.

If the supervisor–student relationship has been generally positive to this point, the chances of maintaining a successful co-author relationship are reasonably good. However, things can still go wrong. The writing and pre-publication process usually includes a thorough critique of the methods and results of a project by experts in the field. This has the potential to reveal significant problems in a study's methodology or results, which by implication may reflect on the skills or knowledge of the supervisor or student. Challenges like this can amplify the pressures of the writing process and seriously test the character of the supervisor–student relationship.

Other potential sources of tension in the supervisor–student relationship include misunderstandings over the quantity and quality of writing and editing work each is expecting from the other. There may also be quibbles over academic status-related issues, such as who should be the first-named author of the publication.

Once again, clear, open communication from the very start of the writing process is important for preventing these kinds of misunderstandings from developing. Supervisor and student should agree together on what each intends to contribute in a practical way to the writing and publishing process. Some kind of reporting timetable should also be developed to ensure supervisor and student communicate regularly and stick to their agreements about the work they will do.

The publication stage of a postgraduate student's research project is when the results of perhaps many months or years of work are brought together and made available for the first time in the public domain. A breakdown in relations between student and supervisor at this critical stage can jeopardise all that has gone before. Interaction between student and supervisor at this stage must therefore be handled with special care, to ensure both parties have the best chance of coming through it with their respect for each other intact.

Exercises for working with colleagues and supervisors

1. '… the personal experience of research collaboration is necessarily imperfect, noisy, messy, and ultimately one of mixed emotions and outcomes …' (Butcher & Jeffrey, 2007, p. 1248). Evaluate this statement from the point of view of your own research experience. Do you agree with it?
2. Practise writing in a team. With a colleague or friend, choose a subject you are both interested in. It could be a research topic, an event you attended, or a leisure activity you both enjoy. Aim to write a one-page description of the topic, event or activity. Decide together how you will go about the process of drafting up your description. How will you identify what information to include? Will each of you write a separate draft description first? Or will you both work on the initial draft together? Will you hand-write or use a laptop? How will you edit and finalise your description? Will you use track-changes? What will you do if you don't like what the other person writes?
3. Pretend you are writing a job advertisement for the position of supervisor of your PhD or Masters research project. What personal attributes and skills will applicants for the position need? What would the ideal person for the job be like?

References and further reading

Acker, S., Hill, T., & Black, E. (1994). Thesis supervision in the social sciences: managed or negotiated? *Higher Education, 28*: 483–498.

Bozeman, B. & Corley, E. (2004). Scientists' collaboration strategies: implications for scientific and technical human capital. *Research Policy, 33*: 599–616.

Butcher, J. & Jeffrey, P. (2007). A view from the coal face: UK research student perceptions of successful and unsuccessful collaborative projects. *Research Policy, 36*: 1239–1250.

Deuchar, R. (2008). Facilitator, director or critical friend? Contradiction and congruence in doctoral supervision styles. *Teaching in Higher Education, 13*(4): 489–500.

Engebretson, K., Smith, S., McLaughlin, D., Seibold, C., Terrett, G., & Ryan, E. (2008). The changing reality of research education in Australia and implications for supervision: a review of the literature. *Teaching in Higher Education, 13*: 1–15.

Grant, B. (2005). Fighting for space in supervision: fantasies, fairytales, fictions and fallacies. *International Journal of Qualitative Studies in Education, 18*(3): 337–354.

Gurr, G. (2001). Negotiating the 'Rackety Bridge' – a dynamic model for aligning supervisory style with research student development. *Higher Education Research & Development, 20*(1): 81–92.

He, Z-L., Geng, X-S., & Campbell-Hunt, C. (2009). Research collaboration and research output: a longitudinal study of 65 biomedical scientists in a New Zealand university. *Research Policy, 38*: 306–317.

Hinds, P. & Bailey, D. (2003). Out of sight, out of sync: understanding conflict in distributed teams. *Organization Science, 14*(6): 615–632.

Ives, G. & Rowley, G. (2005). Supervisor selection or allocation and continuity of supervision: Ph.D. students' progress and outcomes. *Studies in Higher Education, 30*(5): 535–555.

Kam, B. (1997). Style and quality in research supervision: the supervisor dependency factor. *Higher Education, 34*: 81–103.

Katz, J. & Martin, B. (1997). What is research collaboration? *Research Policy, 26*: 1–18.

Lee, A. (2008). How are doctoral students supervised? Concepts of doctoral research supervision. *Studies in Higher Education, 33*(3): 267–281.

Loan-Clarke, J. & Preston, D. (2002). Tensions and benefits in collaborative research involving a university and another organization. *Studies in Higher Education, 27*(2): 169–185.

Magney, A., O'Brien, E., & Traynor, V. (2001). Assistants and mentors. In: C. Berglund (Ed.), *Health Research* (pp. 191–213). Melbourne: Oxford University Press.

McCormack, C. (2004). Tensions between student and institutional conceptions of postgraduate research. *Studies in Higher Education, 29*(3): 319–334.

Melin, G. (2000). Pragmatism and self-organization: research collaboration on the individual level. *Research Policy, 29*: 31–40.

Priest, H., Segrott, J., Green, B., & Rout, A. (2007). Harnessing collaboration to build nursing research capacity: a research team journey. *Nurse Education Today, 27*: 577–587.

Wuchty, S., Jones, B., & Uzzi, B. (2007). The increasing dominance of teams in production of knowledge. *Science, 316*: 1036–1039.

11 Communicating Research Findings

Topics covered in this chapter

- Developing a strategy for communicating findings
- Defining your audience
- Choosing your communication methods
- Implementing your communication strategy

You are finally coming to the end of the data collection and analysis phases of your research project. Some clear ideas about what your study has found are starting to emerge. These findings are exciting and suggest all your hard work has not been in vain. Can you now start to sit back and relax, content that the hardest part of your project is over? Unfortunately, no, you cannot. You still need to do one of the most important and potentially challenging phases of your study – communicating your research findings to others.

Most research should give a high priority to disseminating and publicising findings. Not only is this essential for spreading new ideas and knowledge, but it is also crucial for ensuring research findings are scrutinised openly to test their accuracy and fairness. If you do not communicate your research findings, nobody apart from you or others in your research team will know what you have found. Other people will not be able to review or discuss your research results, or use your findings in their own work.

Developing a strategy for communicating your research findings

Integral to any research project you are doing should be the development of a strategy or plan for communicating your research findings. The strategy should identify:

- the people and organisations you expect to be the main audience for your findings
- the methods or techniques you intend to use to communicate your findings to these people and organisations.

Aim to develop this communication strategy as early as possible in the research process – certainly no later than when your first project results are starting to emerge.

Ideally, write the strategy down and include it in a section of your research proposal or other project documents. Your project budget should also indicate any resources likely to be required to support your strategy.

Defining your audience

To start planning your communication strategy, make a list of all the different people and organisations you think will be interested in, or need to see, your research findings. Ask yourself:

- Who are the people and organisations to whom it will be most important to report my research results?
- What other people and organisations are likely to be interested in my research results, or find my research results useful?
- Who else should have an opportunity to examine my results?

If your research project is part of a graduate thesis or dissertation then in most cases the main audience for your work, at least in the first instance, will be your supervisor and the examiners who assess your project. Later, there may be scope to present your research findings to a broader audience of experts or other people with an interest in your topic.

If a key aim of your study is to contribute to academic theory, knowledge or argument, then it is likely that one important potential audience for your findings will be other scholars or researchers in your field of interest.

If your research project has a more practical or applied focus, such as investigating the impact of a new government initiative or policy, then your potential audience may be quite diverse. It could include policy analysts and other government officials, advocacy groups, community organisations, as well as other researchers in your field.

Similarly, if you are doing evaluation research, or action or participatory research – studies that often rely on developing close links with people in community groups, neighbourhoods, workplaces or businesses – then the potential audience for your research results will almost certainly include these people and groups.

If your research project has been commissioned by an agency such as a government department, private business or community group, then it is likely you will need initially to report your project findings to this agency. This may include reviewers or experts nominated by the commissioning agency. The commissioning agency may also have its own ideas about how your research findings should be communicated to others. In this case, your communication strategy will need to be developed in close cooperation with the commissioning agency.

Similarly, if you are a researcher employed on the staff of an agency, then your communication strategy will need to take account of your employer's existing guidelines and rules regarding the release of research conducted by its staff.

Choosing your communication methods

After defining (at least tentatively) the people and organisations you think should be the main audience for your research findings, the next step is to decide what methods of communication will be the best for relaying your findings to this audience.

Generally, there are two main ways that researchers communicate their research findings: presentations and written documents. Examples of different types of presentations and written documents are listed in Table 11.1.

TABLE 11.1   METHODS FOR COMMUNICATING RESEARCH FINDINGS

Type of communication	Examples
Presentations	Oral briefings during a research project
	Conference papers, seminars or lectures
	Talks to research participants, community representatives, professional associations, workplaces, or the wider general public
Written documents	Progress reports
	Technical reports
	Non-technical reports
	Theses or dissertations
	Journal articles
	Book or book chapter

Presentations can be 'live' or they can be recorded and distributed on various media, such as video or DVD. Consider using illustrative material such as slides or photos in your presentations to provide a context and increase interest.

Written documents can be produced and distributed either physically (printed hard copy) or electronically (computer files) by email or made available on websites for downloading. The tables below introduce these different ways of communicating research findings and provide more details about each of them.

Presentations

Presentations can be very effective in getting emerging or key findings directly to people who might make use of them. Table 11.2 outlines three types of presentations: oral briefings, conference presentations and talks or presentations to groups who might have an interest in the research, such as participants and community members.

TABLE 11.2   PRESENTATIONS

Oral briefing	An oral briefing is a short talk or discussion. It can be informal, such as a chat over coffee, or more formal, such as a telephone conference call or scheduled meeting in someone's office
Conference presentations	A conference presentation is a talk or lecture given at a formal meeting of people interested in a topic. Slides or other audiovisual material are also often included
Talks to research participants and community members	Talks covering the research findings given to research participants, community members and the general public

Oral briefings

Like progress reports, oral briefings are a useful way of relaying emerging project findings to people linked to a study. Because they often involve direct, face-to-face interaction, oral briefings can have more impact than written reports (Patton, 2002). Observing people's immediate reactions to project results can also provide an important validity check prior to finalising results.

Conference presentations

Conference presentations can be a good way to test people's reactions to project findings before reporting results more widely. Tentative conclusions about research data can be evaluated by other researchers familiar with the topic. For some conferences, presenters may be asked to submit a complete written version of their talk. This may be compiled and published in a report, known as conference proceedings. Conference presentations may also be taped or videoed live, so people can view or listen to them later. Many conferences also run poster sessions. Instead of presenting a talk, researchers can create posters summarising their research findings. These are displayed in a special area and people can ask questions about them.

Talks to community members

Research projects often depend on support and assistance from people in local communities, neighbourhoods, workplaces or voluntary organisations. These people help in various ways such as advising on research methods, supplying project information or recruiting research participants. Once a project is finished, it is common practice for researchers to give a presentation to these people to let them know what the project found. This is an important way of recognising and paying back people for the support and assistance they have given (Ezzy, 2002). Often the reporting back will be done as part of a larger community gathering or event involving perhaps food, music or dance, as well as speeches from local dignitaries and community representatives.

Brief reports

Brief reports during a project and at its conclusion can be an effective way of communicating findings quickly. Table 11.3 summarises the features of progress reports and short non-technical reports.

TABLE 11.3   BRIEF REPORTS

Progress reports	Progress reports are short written reports issued at regular intervals to people linked to a project, such as clients, sponsors, managers, advisory groups and research participants
Short non-technical reports	Short non-technical reports are usually no more than 10–20 pages long. They are typically used to communicate project findings to a non-specialist general audience

Progress reports

Such reports can include emerging findings, where available. Feedback on progress reports can help identify key issues to cover in subsequent reports, including technical reports.

Short non-technical reports

In these reports the main methods and findings of a research project are summarised in an easy-to-read, colourful and attractive format, using words and images most adult readers can understand. Unlike technical reports, non-technical reports usually do not contain enough detailed information to enable comprehensive assessment of a study's findings by specialists in the field.

Technical reports, theses and dissertations

Extended, detailed accounts of research project findings are commonly provided in technical reports and theses and dissertations. Table 11.4 summarises the key features of these types of report.

TABLE 11.4 TECHNICAL REPORTS, THESES AND DISSERTATIONS

Technical reports	A technical report is a document describing a research project and its findings in detail. Typically, a technical report is divided into chapters or sections covering topics such as: previous studies and literature, research aims, data collection and analysis, and research results. Tables, figures, pictures and other kinds of illustrative material may also be included, as well as appendices showing further information
Theses and dissertations	A research thesis or dissertation is typically written by a student as part of qualifying for a postgraduate degree like a Masters or PhD. It is usually expected to present original research findings or argue cogently for a particular position or theory. As well as detailing the design, methods and results of the student's research project, a thesis or dissertation usually includes a good review of previous studies and other literature presented in a well-ordered, scholarly manner

Technical reports

Technical reports can be reasonably short (e.g., 20–30 pages usually single-spaced) or quite long (100 pages or more). They usually start with a short summary, often labelled as an 'executive summary'. This presents the most crucial information about a study in a readily digestible form. Some executive summaries may be no more than 1–2 pages long; more extended summaries may be 5–10 pages (usually single-spaced). Ideally, an executive summary should be able to be read on its own and understood without reference to the larger technical report from which it is derived.

Depending on the type of research project, some technical reports will be published. Others will be kept confidential and only seen by the project's researchers and clients. In some instances a project's client or sponsor will take responsibility for arranging publication of a technical report. In other instances it will be the researcher.

Technical reports released to the public may be distributed in hard copy or electronic formats, including downloadable files from websites. Many agencies that conduct or commission research have websites from which it is possible to download or order copies of the agency's technical reports. Some technical reports may only be available electronically, to reduce costs or because the likely audience for a study is small. Detailed advice on how to prepare a technical report is provided in Chapter 13.

Theses and dissertations

Usually written under the guidance of a university supervisor (see Chapter 10), the finished thesis or dissertation is assessed by a small group of examiners who are usually specialists in the student's field of study. A feature of theses and dissertations is their relative inaccessibility compared to other types of research documents, such as journal articles. Normally, only a small number of printed copies of a thesis or dissertation are produced. These are lodged in the library of the student's university or other local libraries. In most cases theses and dissertations can not be physically removed from a library. Paper copies must be read at the library, sometimes in a secure room. Occasionally they can be accessed as Web documents on some university webpages or be read electronically via CD. Some websites now provide lists of dissertation titles and abstracts.

In a few cases, a student's thesis or dissertation will cover such an interesting topic, or be written in such an exciting and colourful style, that it attracts the interest of a publisher with a view to turning it into a book. As part of this process, the thesis may have to be revised or expanded so that it is less academic in format and more suitable for a wide audience.

Journal articles and books

The key features of journal articles and books as a means of communication are summarised in Table 11.5.

TABLE 11.5   JOURNAL ARTICLES AND BOOKS

Journal articles	A journal article is a research report published in an academic or scientific journal. Publishing research in a journal opens it to scrutiny by an international audience of researchers and scholars. Journals are issued regularly (e.g., monthly, quarterly) with each edition containing several articles. Most research journals are either produced by commercial publishing houses or academic and professional bodies. Publication costs are met through reader subscriptions and licence fees from libraries
Books and book chapters	A specialist book (sometimes called a monograph) is typically used to present extensive research findings on a topic. Compared with journal articles, books are typically a lot longer and cover a topic in more breadth and detail

Journal articles

Publication in a journal is one of the most effective ways to ensure a research report becomes accessible to a wide range of people, especially other researchers. In the peer-review process that usually precedes a journal article being accepted for publication the content of the article will be critiqued in detail by anonymous reviewers. Journal editors may request that an article be substantially rewritten before it is published. They may also decide not to publish the article at all.

With the growth of the Internet, many major journals are published online as well as in hard copy. There are also a number of journals published solely on the Internet (e-journals). The advantage of e-journals is that research results can be published relatively quickly and cheaply. However, some e-journals may not use rigorous peer-review processes, which devalues them in the minds of some people.

Probably for most social science and health research projects, a journal article will not be the first way the findings of the project are communicated (although it can be). Typically the results will be circulated first to a more limited audience via conference papers or technical reports.

Books and book chapters

Contributing a chapter to a book can be a bit like preparing a journal article. A publisher may decide to produce a book summarising research findings on a particular topic. People with expertise on the topic will then be invited to write a chapter summarising their knowledge of the subject.

Despite the growth in electronic publishing, most books are still published in hard copy form. Because they are expensive to produce and distribute, in most cases publishing a book is reliant on securing a contract with a recognised publisher. As with journal articles, it is uncommon for a book or a book chapter to be the first format in which social science and health researchers present their project findings. Results are usually presented in other formats first, such as technical reports and conference presentations.

Finalising your communication strategy

Boxes 11.1 and 11.2. give some idea of what the main components of a finished communication strategy might look like. The hypothetical example in Box 11.1 is for a student's PhD research project. In Box 11.2 the hypothetical example is for a study conducted on contract for a military training academy.

Box 11.1   Strategy for communicating findings from a PhD research project

*Topic: Beliefs about healthy food choices among
low-income residents of an inner-city district*

January–June 2010: Oral briefings to PhD supervisor. Include discussion of emerging findings.

June–September 2010: Write draft chapters for thesis. Will report and discuss all project findings. Chapters to be reviewed by PhD supervisor.

August 2010: Seminar presentation to invited university department staff and students. Will introduce and discuss the project's research methods and main findings.

October–November 2010: Completion of PhD thesis. Thesis will be read and assessed by examiners.

February 2011: Presentation of key research findings to a public meeting of residents from the inner-city district where the research was conducted. A short non-technical report will also be distributed describing the study's main findings in plain language.

(Continued)

(Continued)

March 2011: Presentation of key research findings to a meeting of officials and representatives from the health and education sectors. This will discuss policy implications of the project findings.

May 2011: Conference presentation to an expert audience at a prominent national or international public health conference. The conference paper will describe the project's research methods and findings to an expert audience.

March–June 2011: Prepare and submit three articles for publication in a prominent public health or nutrition journal. Each paper will report different aspects of the project findings.

In the end, the strategy you decide to use for communicating your project findings should be tailored to the specific context and goals of your research project. As well as reflecting the different information needs of the people and organisations in your intended audience, the strategy should also take into account:

- Your own preferences for how you would like to communicate your research findings. What communication methods do you feel most comfortable using? Which methods are you particularly skilled or experienced with already?
- Your personal goals and ambitions for publicising your research findings and for developing your reputation as a researcher. How important to you is it that you become well known in your field of study? Are you doing the research mainly for your own interest, as a form of personal development or learning? Or are you keen that your research results change other people's thinking or behaviour in some way?
- How much time, money and other resources you have available to support the dissemination of project findings. What communication methods can you afford? How committed are you to bringing your findings to the attention of others? If necessary, are you prepared to publicise your research findings at conferences, public meetings and other venues without any financial support?

Box 11.2   Strategy for communicating findings from a commissioned research project

Topic: Sexual harassment and discrimination in a national military training academy

June–September 2010: Confidential oral briefings to project client. Will include discussion of emerging findings.

September–October 2010: Write draft technical report (confidential). This will describe project background, aims, methods and findings in detail. Drafts of the report will be submitted to the client for review and comment. A draft will also be submitted to external reviewers nominated by the client.

December 2010–January 2011: Finalise technical report (including executive summary). Finished report will be sent to the client for acceptance and sign-off.

February 2011: Public release and launch of the technical report (assuming the client wishes to publicly release the project findings). In conjunction with client, participate in

(Continued)

(Continued)

press release and other media activities to publicise the technical report. Respond to media requests for interviews. Electronic copies of the technical report will be made available for download from client's website.

March 2011: With the client's permission, present a paper on aspects of the project methodology at a prominent social science research methods conference.

June 2011: With the client's permission, submit a paper assessing the strengths and weaknesses of the project's methodology to an internationally recognised qualitative research methods journal.

In some projects it may also be necessary for your strategy to consider how much control you will have over how the final research results are communicated. This will be especially relevant if you are employed as a researcher in a public sector agency or private business, or if you are doing research on contract for an agency. Agencies that commission research, or have researchers on staff, usually have established protocols for managing the publication of research results. These protocols aim to ensure that the agency's research is publicised effectively and reflects favourably on the competence and integrity of the agency and its researchers. People doing research for these agencies may be restricted contractually from using the research material as a basis for preparing papers for academic journals or conference presentations, at least until after a certain date. They may also be required to provide the client or employer with draft copies of any future papers or reports they intend publishing using the project data.

Box 11.3   Publish or perish?

In universities and other higher learning institutions, academic staff appointments and promotions are often determined partly on the basis of people's publication record. This includes not just the number of publications produced but also the type. In the race for status and recognition, more points tend to be given for research published in prestigious, independently peer-reviewed scientific journals or books. Fewer points are given for conference presentations, unpublished or small circulation technical reports, or for articles in non-peer-reviewed journals.

If you are doing a research project for a client, say a government agency or a private business, it will be crucial to clarify with the client, as early as possible, who will have ownership of the research results and what kinds of processes will be used to communicate them. Where appropriate, agreements on these issues should be included in written project contracts.

Remember that some clients may not want to release the results of a project to the public. Alternatively, they may want to wait and see the final results of a study before deciding whether or not to make the results public.

Research carried out by government agencies may be subject to freedom of information laws. In some circumstances, you or your research client may be legally required to release your research report into the public domain, even if you or the client do not want to.

Implementing your strategy: tips on communicating research findings

Reporting emerging or provisional findings

Think carefully about the information you include in oral briefings or written progress reports. Try to avoid releasing preliminary results too early in the analysis process. In fast-moving commercial or political environments, researchers may come under pressure to release project findings quickly, perhaps even before the results have been properly checked or verified. If you must report project results that could need revising later, make the status of these results plain in your briefing or report. Indicate clearly that they are provisional and could change. Ideally, any provisional results released to a project client should remain confidential to that client and not be circulated beyond this restricted audience.

Preparing conference presentations

Few people are able to deliver a well-structured talk completely unaided by notes or other written material. Most formal spoken presentations involve a good deal of written preparation. Often much of the content of the presentation will be written down beforehand. When the talk is delivered, the presenter will either read directly from their written notes or use the notes as the basis for a more improvised, off-the-cuff talk. Slides or overheads showing brief summary comments or small segments of key information may also be used to structure an otherwise note-free, off-the-cuff type talk (see the section on preparing slide presentations in Chapter 2).

Presenting research to non-researchers

Think creatively about the most effective ways to communicate your research findings to non-specialist audiences such as research participants or the wider general public. Traditional approaches like formal lectures may not be attractive to these groups. Try to use approaches that will generate some excitement and interest. For example, a researcher, after completing her thesis on a study of Maori identity, took her research participants on a bus trip (see Box 11.4).

Box 11.4   On the bus

In a study of Maori identity in the Bay of Plenty in New Zealand, Taima Moeke-Pickering used a novel approach to communicate the findings from her thesis to the 30-plus research participants whom she interviewed. She hired a bus for a day, which drove to important locations linked to local tribal and extended family identities. During the bus trip, she talked about her findings.

> ... it was felt that an exciting way to disseminate the finding would be to charter a bus for the day and take the whanau to significant places and tribal markers that were

---

> *mentioned in the thesis. A small booklet was composed for the trip. The contents included the background and purpose of the trip, whakapapa connections [ancestoral links] to each of the marae, an itinerary of places that were being visited and significant waiata [songs].* (Moeke-Pickering, 1996, p. 67)

Catering for people with a disability

Consider ways to increase the accessibility of your research material to people with disabilities. For example, documents intended for a broad audience, such as non-technical reports, could be published in Braille and large-print versions for blind or visually impaired people. The Internet has the potential to make research information more easily available to people with disabilities by removing barriers such as the need to physically travel to get documents from libraries. New technology such as screen readers and refreshable Braille can also improve the scope for disabled people to access text-based information on the Internet. Other Web design features, such as adding text summaries or transcripts of a webpage's audio or video material, can also improve the accessibility of Internet information to people with hearing or visual disability (Ritchie & Blanck, 2003; World Wide Web Consortium, 2008).

Working with editors and communications specialists

Larger agencies that carry out or commission research may have specialist editors or communications people who take responsibility for preparing the agency's research reports for publication. If you are doing research on contract or as an employee for one of these agencies, it is likely that your research reports will be reviewed and edited by these people. In some cases, changes to your report may be proposed that initially you may feel uncomfortable about or disagree with. If this happens, take some time to carefully assess the value of each of the proposed changes. Resist the temptation to simply reject all the proposed changes and demand that the document is left the way it is. Remember that you have probably been immersed in your research project a long time, making it perhaps harder to see obvious ways the report could be improved. Try to recognise the difference between changes that would compromise the accuracy or integrity of your research report and changes that would simply make your report easier for readers to understand and navigate through. The first type of change is something to guard against and oppose. The second type is something to welcome and applaud (at least in most instances). If, after calm reflection and discussion, you still disagree with some of the changes proposed, put your case clearly and firmly for retaining the status quo. In the end, editing or communications people may well accept your point of view, or at least be prepared to negotiate a compromise that everyone is happy with.

Communicating negative findings

Researchers are often the bearers of bad news. Evaluation studies may suggest certain services are not effective enough. Clinical studies may conclude there is no evidence supporting the use of certain health treatments or medicines. Surveys may indicate public awareness of a health promotion campaign is low. In these situations, special care should be taken when reporting project findings. Think carefully about ways to convey negative or critical findings sensitively and with consideration for the impact they may have on others. Avoid using emotive language or slogans. Aim for a balanced assessment of the situation. Although you may have strong feelings about your topic and the rights and wrongs of a situation, try not to allow your judgement to be overly coloured or swayed by these feelings.

Contact with the popular media: advantages and disadvantages

No matter what type of research project you are doing, and regardless of its stage or phase, there is always a chance you may attract interest from the popular media – newspapers, magazines, radio, television, news websites and so on. Many journalists pride themselves on their ability to break new stories and be first on the ground with information. They often attend conferences and scan the contents of research journals. At any time, you could be phoned out of the blue by a reporter or programme producer asking you for information about your research. Handling these situations effectively can be crucial for influencing public perceptions of your study.

Publicising your research through the popular media can be useful in some situations. Early in a project, if handled properly, it can raise a study's profile in the community and help generate public support. It can also assist with recruiting research participants. Later in a project, once research results are in, contact with the media can help disseminate the study's key findings to a wide general audience. This can be especially important if a researcher aims to publicise their results with a view to influencing public opinion, or altering the attitudes and behaviour of certain groups.

However, the potential downsides of contact with the media must also be recognised and managed. Not all media organisations will necessarily have your best interests at heart. Especially if your research is on a controversial or emotive topic, some sections of the media may have few reservations about reporting aspects of your study in sensationalist terms. This might even include misrepresenting or distorting your results. This can create a potentially dangerous situation that can damage the public profile of your study. In a worst case scenario the truth of what you have found may get completely lost in the controversy.

In every situation where a journalist or media representative makes contact with you, think carefully about how much you want to say to them. If you are at an early stage of your project and have no definite findings to report, state this politely but firmly. Do not be badgered or sweet-talked into saying more than you want to or should.

If you are a researcher in a university, government agency or private business, it is likely your employer will have guidelines or rules for handling contact with the media. You may be advised not to talk directly with journalists and to refer all enquiries and requests to your organisation's public relations people.

Ideally, any contact you do have with the media, especially if your project is likely to have a high public profile and attract considerable interest, should be managed by a specialist media liaison person or adviser – or at least someone with a good understanding of the internal workings of the news media. Skilled media liaison or public relations people understand how to arrange press conferences, frame press releases and manage interviews so that the findings of a research project are publicised in ways that draw attention to their importance, but without inviting undue criticism or controversy.

Conclusion: Communicating research findings

Communicating research findings is at the core of the research process. Thinking carefully about the right approaches to use to disseminate your findings is therefore vital. The key is to identify the main people you want to relay your research findings to, then select and implement suitable communication methods to reach these people.

Your communication strategy should not be treated as if it is chiselled in stone – an inflexible, rigid prescription. It should be an evolving plan, open to revision throughout the life of your project. Circumstances can change. Projects can develop in new directions. Findings presented to one audience can open doors to opportunities to present them to other audiences. Interest in your findings may snowball. Invitations to present or publish your results may start coming in from all directions. Suddenly, the process of communicating your research findings may take on a marvellous life of its own.

Exercises for communicating findings

1. Consider this statement: 'The last decade has witnessed a radical transformation of academic publishing. The metamorphosis was triggered by the introduction of the computerized networks that currently affect most sectors of western society. The significance of the Internet to academic publishing is comparable with that of the printing press and the scholarly journal: in the course of the process thus set in motion, the nature of the learned journal, as well as of scholarly communication more generally, may well be reconfigured altogether' (Bohlin, 2004: 366). How radically do you think the Internet will change the way you communicate your research findings in future? Will there be any room left for the traditional printed book or journal? What impact could a shift to purely electronic publishing have on the quality and reliability of research findings?
2. This chapter has mainly looked at formal methods of communicating research findings. But there are also many informal, low-key methods of disseminating your project results to colleagues and others. These include chats in the corridor, blogs and email networks. How many others can you think of?
3. Think about the last research assignment or project you did. Imagine you are a TV reporter for your local station. Prepare a brief news item on the research. What would you say at the start of the item to grab people's attention? What other key points would you cover? Where would the item be filmed? What other video would you include? Who would you interview and what would you ask them?

References and further reading

Allsop, J. & Saks, M. (2007). Writing up health research and getting published. In: M. Saks & J. Allsop (Eds), *Researching Health: Qualitative, Quantitative and Mixed Methods.* (pp. 387–408). London: Sage.

Berglund, C. (2001). Writing and publishing. In: C. Berglund (Ed.), *Health Research* (pp. 240–256). Melbourne: Oxford University Press.

Bohlin, I. (2004). Communication regimes in competition: the current transition in scholarly communication seen through the lens of the sociology of technology. *Social Studies of Science, 34*(3): 365–391.

Ezzy, D. (2002). *Qualitative Analysis: Practice and Innovation*. Crows Nest, Australia: Allen and Unwin.

Moeke-Pickering, T. (1996). Maori identity within whanau. Unpublished Master of Social Sciences thesis, Department of Psychology, University of Waikato, Hamilton, New Zealand.

Moffat, S., Phillimore, P., Hudson, E., & Downey, D. (2000). 'Impact? What impact?' Epidemiological research findings in the public domain: a case study from north-east England. *Social Science and Medicine, 51*, 1755–1769.

Patton, M. Q. (2002). *Qualitative Evaluation and Research Methods* (3rd edn). Thousand Oaks, CA: Sage.

Ritchie, H., & Blanck, P. (2003). The promise of the internet for disability: a study of on-line services and web site accessibility at Centers for Independent Living. *Behavioral Sciences and the Law, 21*(1): 5–26.

Vaughan, R. J. & Buss, T. (1998). *Communicating Social Science Research to Policy Makers*. Thousand Oaks, CA: Sage.

World Wide Web Consortium (W3C) (2008). How people with disabilities use the web. Retrieved March 14, 2009, from: www.w3.org/WAI/EO/Drafts/PWD-Use-Web/

12 Writing for Research: Some Guiding Principles

Topics covered in this chapter

- Why it's important to get the writing right
- Evaluating your writing skills
- Checking out how others do it
- Deciding what to cover
- Considering your audience
- Drafting and redrafting
- The writing context
- Writer's block
- Getting feedback and dealing with criticism
- Reaching that final draft

This chapter looks at the sometimes difficult task of writing research-related documents. It identifies key elements of effective writing for research and outlines strategies for helping research-related writing go more smoothly. The chapter is mainly designed for readers who are looking for ideas to develop their personal writing skills. Readers interested in issues that might arise when doing writing with a colleague or with several members of a research team should go to Chapter 10, Working with Colleagues and Supervisors.

Why you need to get the writing right

Writing is central to the research process. During any significant project, several types of documents may need to be prepared, including:

- literature reviews
- project proposals
- funding applications
- ethical review applications
- survey questionnaires
- information sheets for project participants
- progress reports to sponsors
- final project reports.

Research findings may also need to be written up in theses or dissertations, journal articles or books.

No matter what type of project document is being prepared, it is vital that it is well written and effectively gets its messages across to its intended readers or audience. Anything less than this can seriously jeopardise the quality of a research project. Even the most well-thought-out and executed piece of research can founder if its text-based documents are poorly written or confusing (see Box 12.1).

Box 12.1   When research writing goes wrong

Poor quality writing can affect a research project in a number of ways. Here are just three examples:

1. An information sheet for project participants uses language so complicated and specialised that the research participants cannot understand what the project is aiming to do, or why it is important to take part. As a result, the project only recruits a small number of research participants and has to be cancelled because there is insufficient data for analysis.
2. A research team has a brilliant idea for a research project but the team's research proposal is not well designed or presented. As a result, potential research sponsors and funders struggle to appreciate the project's distinctive elements and potential significance. The project is unable to secure enough financial backing to proceed.
3. The data collection and analysis phases of a research project go smoothly and reveal some exciting findings. But the study's final technical report is not well written. Readers find the description of the study's methods and findings hard to follow. Some media reports even misinterpret the study's conclusions. As a result, research team members have to spend a lot of time in media interviews explaining their findings.

Evaluating your writing skills

Some lucky people have a natural gift for writing research-related documents. They can produce near perfect documents at great speed and with little apparent effort. However, these people are rare. For most of us, writing good research-related documents is a skill that has to be developed and practised.

Anybody planning a career in social and health research should carefully assess their existing writing skills. How can these skills be further developed or sharpened to meet the specific requirements of research-related writing? This can be especially important if the researcher comes from a disciplinary background or training that emphasises verbal communication over written communication, or where written communication is largely in the form of short notes or bullet points, rather than long essays or reports.

Writing research-related documents can be a significant challenge for new and emerging researchers. Often problems arise not because there is anything fundamentally wrong with the person's core research methods or data, but because of difficulties with the writing process and effectively expressing ideas on paper. The novice researcher may start out feeling quite confident that they know what they intend to say and how to say it. But as the writing progresses, their confidence erodes as the pressure mounts to translate their ideas into a polished form suitable for circulation to a wide audience.

Checking out how others do it

Research-related writing is a distinctive style of writing, with its own special techniques and forms of expression. In particular, what sets good research-related writing apart from other kinds of writing is its emphasis on clarity and accuracy. Research-related writing aims to present information that is factually correct and to describe any associated theories, concepts, abstract ideas or arguments as precisely and unambiguously as possible.

As part of honing your research writing skills, the first thing to do, and perhaps one of the most important, is to carefully study the written work of other researchers. A lot can be learned by looking closely at the research documents produced by others, especially researchers with a successful track-record of publication or whose work you admire or respect. By analysing what you like (or do not like) about other people's research-related documents, you should be able to develop a better appreciation of the types of organising frameworks, formats, language and writing styles you could use in your own research-related writing.

Some of the best examples of research-related writing tend to be found in scientific and academic books. These are usually written by experienced researchers who have studied a topic for several years, are on top of their subject and confident with their material. For much the same reasons, articles in peer-reviewed scientific and academic journals can also serve as a useful guide.

In addition, try to spend some time studying examples of other types of research documents such as proposals, funding applications and participant information sheets. If you are a novice researcher in a university department or other kind of research organisation, you should be able to get permission to access examples of these kinds of in-house, limited-circulation documents without much trouble.

Other useful guidelines can be gleaned from style manuals issued by publishing houses, universities and government departments. These provide advice for writers and editors on how research documents should be written and formatted (e.g., Annandale, 2007; Gordon, 2000). Looking through these can alert you to potential issues in your own writing as well as offering possible solutions. The best style manuals are not too prescriptive and leave enough scope for researchers to add their own personal flavour to a document.

Deciding what to cover

No matter what kind of document you are preparing, before you start writing it is usually a good idea to start by:

- identifying the different pieces of information you want to include in the document
- deciding roughly in what order you think these pieces of information should be presented.

A common technique is to make a list or diagram showing all the key pieces of information or ideas that you think should be covered in the document. This 'brain-storming' process can be done on screen, on a large piece of paper or on a whiteboard. Start by listing bullet points or short sentences summarising all the points or items of information that you want to cover in the text. Ask yourself, what are the main segments of information I need to get across? Once you have identified these, decide in what order you think they should be presented so that they unfold logically and with a coherent shape.

An alternative starting point is first to brain-storm a preliminary structure for the document. This involves working out a list of section titles or headings for your document, then arranging them in an appropriate order. After this, dot-points or short sentences can be used to identify all the main points or items of information you want to include under each heading or in each section or sub-section.

Whatever approach you take, the ultimate goal is to end up with some kind of coherent list or diagram summarising the main points you intend to cover in the text of your document, and in what order. Some people will prefer to have this list or diagram fully developed before they begin writing their document. Other people will prefer to sketch out only a broad outline, with the actual process of writing the document being the main technique they use for identifying the points they want to cover and in what order (see Box 12.2).

Box 12.2   Writing the summary first

Elvira is a 22-year-old graduate student who has just finished the data analysis for her Masters research project. For the last few weeks, Elvira's supervisor has been encouraging her to start thinking about how to structure and present the final report of her research. This is the first time Elvira has ever had to write a full-scale research report and she is a bit unsure how she is going to handle the process.

Elvira has talked with other students in her department who have already finished their Masters or PhD research reports. Some of these students have lent her copies of their completed reports so she can see the organising frameworks they used to present their material. However, Elvira is not yet convinced she is ready to launch forth into writing the first chapters of her report. She is aware that she is still unclear in her own mind what her project results indicate and what her conclusions and recommendations might be.

As an experiment, to try to help concentrate and structure her thoughts, Elvira pretends she has finished writing her research report and has just the 2–3 page summary of her report left to do. Over the course of a day, Elvira drafts up an initial version of what she imagines the summary of her study would look like. By focusing her thinking on what to include in the summary, Elvira finds she is able to develop some very clear ideas about what her project has found and its implications. Having crystallised these thoughts, Elvira feels a lot more relaxed about the prospect of writing up her full report from the beginning. She now knows the important things she wants to say and in what order.

The next day, as she sits down to start writing up the first chapters of her report, Elvira keeps her draft summary beside her on the desk. Occasionally, while she is writing, new ideas occur to her about what to include in the summary or ways the summary could be altered. She makes these changes to the summary as she goes along, so that by the end of the report writing process she is able to cut and paste her completed summary straight into the front of her report.

Getting started

There are no particular rules about the order in which you should write the different sections of your document. The conventional approach is to start at the beginning of the document, writing each section or chapter, one after the other, in the order in which they will appear. However, in principle you can start writing any section of the document first, followed by any other section. Some people may prefer to start by writing their concluding sections, while others may prefer to start with the sections that they expect will be relatively easy or interesting – or conversely those they expect will be hard to write, to get them done and out of the way.

No matter where you start, the key thing is that by the end of the writing process all the different pieces of the document fit together relatively seamlessly. Ideally, each of the points you make should follow on from each other in a logical sequence, flowing from one to another in a way that seems natural and sensible.

Considering your audience as you write

At the start of the writing process, think about who are likely to be the main audience or readers of your document. Try to anticipate the needs and circumstances of these people. For example, a participant information sheet or survey questionnaire intended for a general audience will almost certainly require a different writing style compared with a research proposal or detailed technical report intended only for other researchers or experts.

As you write, try to imagine you are one of these readers going through your document for the first time. This can help to see if your text contains enough description and explanation, especially if the document is intended for a general audience. It can also encourage you to write more clearly and simply, leaving less room for confusion or misunderstanding.

Pay careful attention to sentence structure and word choice. Lengthy, convoluted sentences tend to be difficult to follow and should be used sparingly. Use shorter, simpler sentences as much as possible.

Similarly, paragraphs that are too long, or too information-rich, can quickly overwhelm and lose the reader. Aim for concise paragraphs that can be followed easily but still provide a good level of detail. The audience for your work should be able to quickly grasp the meaning of what you are writing, rather than having to read things over several times to work out what you are saying.

Drafting and redrafting

Constant drafting and redrafting is central to most research-related writing. Some of the best, most inspirational pieces of research writing can give the impression of having been produced quickly and effortlessly. Yet these elegant documents are often the result of many hours of painstaking, behind-the-scenes drafting and redrafting.

Typically, preparation of any project-related document, but especially documents intended for important audiences or wide distribution, will (and should) involve at least three or four drafts, and probably more, before the content and structure of the text will be up to a standard suitable for circulation to others.

Usually the first draft of a document forms the foundation or 'prototype' for the final version. Subsequent drafts aim to build on the prototype in several ways, including

- correcting errors or inaccuracies of fact and interpretation
- improving the sequencing of ideas and information
- improving sentence structure and word choice
- shortening unnecessarily long sentences and paragraphs
- adding extra material on certain topics to ensure all necessary detail is supplied.

When drafting a document, take a break from working on it for a few hours or days. When you come back later and read what you have written, you will probably be surprised by the number of obvious problems or deficiencies in your text that leap out at you from the page.

Good things take time

Do not underestimate the amount of time and effort required to produce well-organised, clear and accurate research-related documents. When planning the schedule of work for any research project, make sure that you build in enough time for writing tasks, especially in the final stages of a project (see Box 12.3).

Do not make the mistake of allocating only a small percentage of your total project time to writing work. It is a common misconception, especially among novice researchers, that the main work of any research project is the collection and analysis of data, and that once these phases are over the project is effectively finished. 'Just the writing up to go,' the researcher will observe with relief. Often, however, the work is really just starting.

As a rough rule of thumb, a research project can be divided into three parts: (a) designing, planning and securing resources, (b) data collection, information gathering and data analysis and (c) ongoing research-related writing tasks including final report writing and dissemination. Approximately equal amounts of a project's total time and resources should be allocated to each of these three important areas.

Box 12.3 Working overnight to a deadline

Although ideally a funding application or research report should be finished at least a week before it is due, in some cases this is simply not possible. Instead, it becomes necessary to do a lot of intense work in the final few days immediately before the application or report is due. In these circumstances, it is not unusual for researchers to work all hours of the day and night, and on some occasions overnight without sleep.

Trying to finish a lot of work in a short space of time, especially by working overnight, is a very high risk strategy. Lots of things can happen – a computer malfunction, not being able to find a crucial piece of information – that can easily disrupt the process. If you do find yourself in a situation where you have no choice but to work overnight on a project, remember to take a few precautions and plan ahead so that you give yourself the best chance of success.

Think about the environment where you will be working. Make sure you are doing your work in a place where you won't be distracted or interrupted. Make sure the temperature in the place where you are working can be controlled. Being too warm while working in the middle of the night can make you drowsy; being too cold can numb the mind.

Make sure you have plenty of water and nutritious snacks on hand so you can eat and drink whenever you feel the need. Some researchers who work right through the night prefer to briefly doze or catch a few moments of sleep from time to time. Others regard this as potentially risky, making them feel even sleepier or perhaps leading them to doze off for several hours. Only experience will show what is the best strategy for you.

Have backup equipment available in case any piece of vital equipment fails. If you are working on a computer make sure you have a second computer available in case the first one crashes irretrievably. Be obsessive about backing up your work as you go. Make new versions of the files you are working at least every 30 minutes and before starting each new stage of the writing process. Backup on to a pen drive or portable hard drive so that if your computer fails you can quickly resume work on another machine.

If you are working as part of a team on a proposal or report, consider the idea of doing the work in shifts. For example, one member of the team might work on the document from 9am to 5pm and then a second team member takes over, working from

(Continued)

(Continued)

5pm to 1am, while the first team member has a break. At 1am the first team member takes over the writing work again, while the second team member gets some sleep. This kind of arrangement can go on for several days and a lot of writing work can be completed in that time. However, for this technique to work properly, the team members must really understand and agree on what they are aiming to achieve with the work.

After working through the night on a piece of work, it is possible to experience an immense feeling of relief that the work is finally done and (hopefully) the deadline met. At the same time you are likely to be very tired and in need of sleep. Avoid driving at this time. Use public transport to get from the office to home, or get someone to pick you up. Block out your diary for the next two or three days. You are unlikely to be in great shape for doing much other work over this time. Several good nights' sleep may be required before you completely shake off the effects of the overnight working.

Your writing context

The context in which you do your research-related writing – the physical surroundings and the timeframes or schedules set for your work – can have an important influence on how well the work progresses (see Box 12.4).

Try to define which writing environments work best for you. Think carefully about times when writing for a project went particularly well. What features of the process helped to produce this positive result? Reflect, too, on times when you found research writing a major struggle and not a happy experience. What aspects of the writing context contributed to these difficulties? How could you avoid these problems cropping up in future?

Do you prefer to draft up the first versions of your text using a pencil or pen and paper, rather than a computer word processing programme?

Are you a person who does their best writing only when under the pressure of a tight or looming deadline, perhaps because of the adrenaline charge produced by the challenge of completing the work in time? Is the pressure of a deadline a positive stimulus to creativity, helping to focus the mind and producing a burst of energetic writing? Or do you write most effectively when under minimal time pressure? Do you like to begin a writing task as early as possible, so that you have a good draft of the entire work completed well before the planned finish date?

Box 12.4   Keeping on top of writing tasks

Katrina is a senior academic in a prominent university research centre. Much of her work is spent writing research-related documents. This includes research reports, project proposals, funding applications, reviews of other people's studies and manuscripts for journal articles. As well, there are numerous work-related emails she has to respond to on a regular basis.

Katrina normally finds it almost impossible to keep up with all the different writing tasks she has to do in a year. However, she has developed a few strategies so she feels more in control of her working week and doesn't fall too far behind schedule.

(Continued)

(Continued)

The first thing she does is set up an electronic diary for the year showing all the closing dates and deadlines for the different writing tasks she is working on. She uses colour coding to identify which of these closing dates and deadlines are fixed and non-negotiable, and which are more open to potential re-negotiation and change. This is useful for helping to prioritise which writing tasks to concentrate on as deadlines loom.

Another thing Katrina does is try to set aside certain periods of the day, or days of the week, for different kinds of writing work. For example, she tries to allocate mornings to writing up research results and findings from completed studies she has worked on. In the afternoons she tries to do writing tasks related mainly to planning or getting funding for new or existing studies. Later in the afternoons, or in the evenings, she aims to devote most of her time to reading and reviewing other people's work (students, colleagues) and responding to important emails from earlier in the day. This approach adds a degree of structure and predictability to Katrina's day, but also variety.

Another strategy Katrina uses is to keep a very well-organised collection of digital copies of all the previous research-related documents she has produced during her career. With this material at her fingertips, Katrina is able to quickly cut and paste relevant extracts from previous work she has done into documents she is working on currently, whether research proposals, funding applications, or reviews of other people's work. Although she may end up revising much of this material so that it is up to date and specific to the purpose, it still saves a lot of time when she can copy it from documents she has prepared earlier.

In terms of physical settings, do you write best in a quiet, secluded place such as a single-occupancy office or at home by yourself? Or do you get inspired only if your desk is in the middle of a busy open-plan office?

Are you easily distracted by background noise, phones ringing or the lure of checking your emails or text messages? Or do you slump into a state of creative inertia without regular stimulation from the gadgetry of modern office life?

Do you work best on writing tasks first thing in the morning, while you are fresh and before doing other things? Or do you do your best writing later in the day, in the evenings or late at night, once the day's other tasks have been completed and you can finally focus on the job at hand? Paying attention to these and other features of the context in which you write will help identify the particular routines and habits most effective for you.

When the going gets tough – writer's block

Occasionally, even with the best efforts to manage the uncertainties and pressures of the writing process, there will be days when your writing does not go well. Words will refuse to flow easily, if at all. Every sentence or paragraph you write will seem embarrassingly disjointed, convoluted or vague. Worse, you may even develop a full-blown crisis of confidence, questioning your ability to finish the document.

These kinds of difficulties are probably most likely to occur during longer, more challenging writing tasks such as preparing research funding proposals, final project reports, journal articles, or theses and dissertations.

To prevent these difficulties arising, a useful strategy can be to limit the amount of time you spend in a day working on writing tasks. Writing of any kind is best done when the mind is fresh and full of enthusiasm. Pushing on with a writing task if you are feeling tired or uninspired can be unproductive and ultimately self-defeating. You can soon become resentful of the writing project, even if you initially found it quite exciting and interesting.

Aim to conserve your energy and enthusiasm for writing. Begin each day by deciding how long you intend to work on major writing tasks and what you are aiming to achieve in this time. Try to stick to these self-imposed guidelines. Take proper breaks and aim to get at least some sense of accomplishment and satisfaction out of every writing session.

Avoid pressing on with writing if you are finding it hard to make progress or feel drained of creative energy. Stop and do something else for a while – ideally something that is totally absorbing and completely removed from your writing environment. This could be anything from physical exercise or sport to playing music, gardening or meeting friends for coffee or lunch (see Box 12.5). Getting fully engaged in these alternative activities can help clear the mind and improve your chances of returning to your writing with renewed vigour and enthusiasm.

Box 12.5   Brief walking helps maintain alertness

A study on the effectiveness of a sweet snack (candy bar) compared to 10 minutes of brisk walking reported that walking produced higher self-rated energy and lower tension compared to the sweet snack. A sweet snack by itself initially increased energy and reduced tiredness, however, this was followed by increased tiredness and reduced energy (Thayer, 1987).

Recognise, too, that difficulties with the writing process can be symptomatic of problems with the broader structure or plan for the document. In situations like this, sometimes the only solution may be a radical overhaul. This might even include putting aside all the writing work done to date and starting again with a fresh writing plan. Having the courage to make a completely fresh start on a writing project will usually pay off in the long run, provided the new writing plan is a significant improvement on the original. The second time round, you should have a clearer idea of what you want to say and how you want to say it. This should mean you get the job finished more quickly and to a higher standard than if you persisted and struggled on, patching up and adjusting your original sub-standard document.

Getting feedback and dealing with criticism

It is common during the preparation of most large-scale research-related documents to have the document reviewed by other people, to see what they like and dislike about the document and how they think it could be improved. This can help to ensure the document is easy to follow, accurate and complete.

Ideally, review work of this type should be done by people with some research experience and a good knowledge of the topic you are writing about. Asking a partner, family member or friend to review your work can be useful, although you may need to be careful that their feedback is not perhaps overly coloured by the nature of your relationship with them.

In some projects, it may be a contractual requirement that a draft of a project report be reviewed by an advisory group of representatives from different agencies. This advisory group may be quite large (10–15 people or more), with each member submitting their own set of comments and suggestions.

Regardless of whether it is just one person providing you with review comments, or a large group of reviewers, it is important to systematically work through and consider all the points raised in their feedback. Do not automatically assume that all the feedback you get (whether positive or negative) is necessarily accurate or appropriate and to be accepted without question. It is essential to sift carefully through all the different points raised to identify which ones you consider valid or useful, and which ones you consider irrelevant, unhelpful or even just plain wrong.

Remember that some reviewers, especially in a review process involving a large number of commentators, may not always have had time to examine your document thoroughly. Neither may they fully understand the finer points of all the material presented in your text. If you can see no good reason to accept certain critical points raised by reviewers, then put them to one side. Your main focus should be on responding to points that are likely to significantly improve and strengthen your document. You can always follow up with the reviewers later to clarify their reasoning behind points you do not agree with.

Reaching that final draft

Provided there is sufficient time available, the final editing and proofreading of a document can be one of the more satisfying and enjoyable parts of the writing process. Small revisions in key places can often make a dramatic difference to your document's overall quality and significantly improve its general impact on the reader. By the same token, failing to proof-read a document can result in a number of errors or presentational glitches appearing in your finished document. Not only can these distract readers from the main messages you are trying to get across, it can also cause readers to wonder if the entire research project is perhaps as error-ridden as the research document itself.

In larger research organisations, or for potentially very high profile projects, it is often standard practice to employ a professional editor to work on the final draft of a document, to correct writing errors and ensure the text is as easy to follow as possible. A sympathetic editor can improve a document in many different ways, including by ensuring complex technical language is explained and made more accessible to a wide audience.

In the case of research documents not intended for wide circulation, such as student assignments or in-house technical reports, normally it will be up to the researchers them-selves to finalise the document. In this situation, it is advisable to allocate at least 5–10 per cent of the total available writing time to final proofreading and editing.

Conclusion

Good quality writing is not the only ingredient for a successful research project, but also it is one of the most important. This is often overlooked when people first start out on research. Behind the scenes of any successful project, there is likely to be a considerable amount of effort devoted to working with words on paper or screen, drawing out and fashioning research-related ideas and information into a suitable form for presentation to others.

Perhaps in future, with the availability of relatively inexpensive multimedia technology, there may be greater scope for conveying research-related information to people in ways apart from text-based documents, such as movies or sound recordings. However, in the meantime, the principal method for organising and communicating research-related information remains the written word. Recognising this, and taking steps to develop and refine your research-related writing skills, should go a long way towards ensuring that any research project you are involved in has a good chance of success.

Exercises for writing for research

1. Think about the last time you really struggled with a major research writing task. What were the main reasons the writing was difficult? What did you do to try to help the situation? If you had to do the same writing task again, how would you do things differently?
2. 'Writing is about being able to convey issues, meanings, and feelings to others. You will not know if you have succeeded until others have been able to read your work, and let you know what they thought about it' (Berglund, 2001: 246). Think about the different ways you currently get feedback from other people on your research documents. How helpful is this feedback? Identify strategies you could use to get more regular or more extensive feedback from other researchers on your written work. One option might be to set up an informal writing group in your faculty or workplace.
3. Do a 'writing fitness' check on the area or place where you normally do your writing. What features of the area or place help you write better? What features make it harder for you to write? What changes could you make to the area or place so that when you are there you feel you can write more freely or effectively?

References and further reading

Allsop, J. & Saks, M. (2007). Writing up health research and getting published. In: M. Saks & J. Allsop (Eds), *Researching Health: Qualitative, Quantitative and Mixed Methods* (pp. 387–408). London: Sage.

Annandale, E. (2007). Editorial. *Social Science & Medicine, 64*(1), 1–4.

Belgrave, L. L., Zablotsky, D., & Guadagno, M. A. (2002). How do we talk to each other? Writing qualitative research for quantitative readers. *Qualitative Health Research, 12*(10), 1427–1439.

Berglund, C. (2001). Writing and publishing. In: C. Berglund (Ed.), *Health Research* (pp. 240–256). Melbourne: Oxford University Press.

Gordon, A. J. (2000). Guidelines for contributors to Social Science & Medicine. *Social Science & Medicine, 50,* 3–15.

Johnstone, M. J. (2004). *Effective Writing for Health Professionals: A Practical Guide to Getting Published.* Sydney: Allen & Unwin.

Thayer, R. E. (1987). Energy, tiredness, and tension effects of a sugar snack versus moderate exercise. *Journal of Personality and Social Psychology, 52*(1), 119–125.

Vaughan, R. J. & Buss, T. F. (1998). *Communicating Social Science Research to Policy Makers.* Thousand Oaks, CA: Sage.

Veit, R. (2004). *Research: The Student's Guide to Writing Research Reports* (4th edn). Upper Saddle River, NJ: Pearson Education.

13 Writing a Research Report: Organisation and Presentation

Topics covered in this chapter:

- Why write a research report?
- Types of research report
- Preparing to write research reports
- Writing a technical research report
- Writing manuscripts for journals
- Writing dissertations and theses
- General tips on producing research reports

Writing research reports can be one of the most difficult tasks researchers have to do. Often it involves long days struggling with tricky concepts, trying to produce a coherent description of how a research project was done and its findings. This chapter offers a set of guidelines intended to help researchers plan and write research reports that are well-organised, readable and presented in formats consistent with generally accepted practice.

Why write a research report?

A research report is a formal account of how a research project was conducted and what it found out. With it, people interested in the project can:

- read about the project's aims, methods and findings
- assess the quality of the project
- provide feedback to the project's researchers on what they like or dislike about the project
- incorporate aspects of the project's methods or findings into their own work or thinking.

For the researchers on a project, a research report provides a lasting record and reminder of the work accomplished and its outcomes. As well, feedback other people give on the report can help extend the researchers' knowledge and understanding of a topic. It can also hone their research design and management skills for future projects.

Potential readers of research reports include:

- other researchers, academics or knowledge workers
- managers in organisations who use research to inform decisions
- front-line staff delivering programmes or services (e.g., professional practitioners, clinicians)
- clients or consumers of programmes or services

- people living in communities and neighbourhoods where a research topic has special relevance
- research participants interested in the outcomes of studies they have contributed to
- journalists and other media representatives
- the general public.

Using information provided in research reports, people can increase their knowledge and understanding of a topic. This can lead to changes in people's thinking and behaviour, or to the design and operation of human services and systems.

Types of research report

Three of the most common types of research report are:

- technical reports
- manuscripts for journal articles
- theses and dissertations.

This chapter focuses on how to present research reports in these three different formats. A summary comparison of the three formats is shown in Table 13.1.

Technical reports

Technical reports describe a research project and its findings in detail. Usually they are intended to be read by people interested in all or most aspects of the project's design and execution. Full technical reports often begin with an extended description of the project's research aims and methods covering areas such as the stimulus for the project, sample selection, sample size, data gathering methods and data analysis procedures. The rest of the report then describes the project findings in depth.

Normally technical reports are divided into chapters or sections. Tables, figures, pictures and other kinds of illustrative material may also be included. Most technical reports are somewhere between 50 and 150 pages long (single-spaced). There is no set length or page maximum, although very long reports are probably less likely to be read from cover to cover. Often technical reports are of interest only to a reasonably narrow audience and so are not widely available or published in hard-copy form. If they are published, this tends to be electronically in pdf file format, with copies usually accessed by download from websites or via email on request.

Manuscripts for journal articles

A manuscript for a journal article is a research report presented in a form suitable for publication in an academic or scientific journal. Journal articles are normally a reasonably concise and tightly written form of research report. In contrast to technical reports, journal articles usually do not go into extensive detail about all aspects of a project. Instead, they concentrate on reporting certain key aspects or findings from a project. Journal articles

TABLE 13.1   FEATURES OF TECHNICAL REPORTS, JOURNAL MANUSCRIPTS AND THESES

	Technical reports	Manuscripts for journals	Theses/ dissertations
Expected length	No set length/Usual range: 50–150 pages*	Often a set maximum length (i.e., a page or word limit). Usual range: 10–30 pages for manuscripts	Expected length may be specified by university or other host institution (e.g., 50,000 words for a PhD). Usual range: 120–300 pages
Cover page included	Yes, for paper copies	Yes, showing title and author names	Yes
Title page included	Yes	No	Yes
Table of contents	Yes, good practice	No, not required	Yes, expected
Abstract or summary	Usually an extended summary (approx. 2–10 pages)	Brief abstract, usually about 150–400 words. Might have to be divided into sections with headings	Usually an extended summary (approx. 2–4 pages)
Expected level of detail for methods information	Considerable detail expected	Usually only brief information required	Considerable detail expected, including extended review and discussion of methodological options
Expected level of detail for findings	Considerable detail expected	Reasonable detail expected but concise, focused	Considerable detail expected, including extended review and discussion
Separate literature review?	Optional	No, literature briefly reviewed in the introduction section	Yes, expected
Text divided into chapters?	Yes, usually. In some cases may only use sections	No, only sections.	Yes, expected
Line spacing	Usually single spacing but may be larger spacing for initial drafts	Usually double-spacing for paper manuscripts. Some journals accept 1.5 or 1.3 spacing for electronic manuscripts	Usually double-spacing but some universities may accept 1.5 spacing
Option to include appendices?	Yes	No, not usually	Yes

*In North America the common page size used for reports is letter size (8.5 × 11inches or 216 × 279mm); in most other countries, the A4 size (210 × 297mm) is commonly used.

are mainly intended to be read by other researchers but they are also often read by managers and professionals, front-line service providers, policy analysts and other people interested in the topic. In general, journal articles tend to have a larger and more diverse audience than technical reports.

Usually a manuscript for a journal article is no more than 10–30 pages (double-spaced) in length. Double spacing is expected for paper copies, but some journals accept 1.5 or 1.3 spacing for electronic submission. Many journals have page or word limits for articles. Some journals specify a maximum word length (e.g., 5000 words) rather than a page length. Manuscripts for journals are usually submitted electronically to the journal's editor, although some journals still require paper copies to be sent by ordinary mail.

Theses and dissertations

A thesis or dissertation is typically written by a student as part of qualifying for a Masters, PhD, or other higher degree. The dissertation or thesis usually provides a detailed account of the design, methods and results of the student's research project. As well, it normally includes a comprehensive review of previous studies and other literature on the topic. Most theses and dissertations are written under the guidance of a university supervisor, with the finished work assessed by experts in the student's field of study. The expected length of dissertations or theses may be stipulated by the student's university or host institution. For example, there may be a guideline that PhD theses be about 50,000 words. Most dissertations and theses tend to be about 120–300 pages (double-spaced) long. In some institutions, dissertations are expected to be less detailed and shorter than theses. In other institutions, this distinction is not made.

A feature of theses and dissertations is that normally only a small number of printed and bound copies are produced. Some institutions also require electronic copies to be submitted on a compact disc (CD), to accompany the paper copy.

Other types of research report

There are other types of research report apart from the three discussed above. These include progress reports, non-technical reports, books, book chapters and spoken reports such as conference presentations. Non-technical reports are often written as a way of distributing or publicising research results to individuals and groups with no or very little existing knowledge of a research topic. As well, summaries at the beginning of technical reports (sometimes called 'executive summaries') and abstracts for journal articles are often deliberately written in non-technical language to increase their accessibility to a wide audience. For more detail on these and other options for reporting research results, see Chapter 11, Communicating Research Findings.

Preparing to write research reports

Start thinking about what to include in a research report, and how it will be written and presented, as early as possible in the research process. Even before the data collection and analysis phases of a project are completed, begin mapping out a broad preliminary outline of the report's structure. Start making notes on what information and ideas could be covered in different parts of the text. Expand and update this preliminary outline from time to time as new ideas come to mind about what to include in the report.

Once the writing of the research report starts in earnest, usually sometime during or after the project's data analysis phase, the preliminary outline can be used as a basis for preparing the first draft of the report.

Before sitting down to start writing the first draft, try to ensure you have all the information you need to write the report readily at hand. This includes not just the results of the data analysis but all other relevant project documentation, including research proposals, information sheets for research participants, survey questionnaires, interview guides, ethics applications, previous research literature and so on. Ideally, these should all be properly labelled and filed away on computer or in physical file folders so they can be retrieved easily without getting up from your desk. Periodically having to stop writing in mid-flow to track down vital information can be quite annoying and disruptive to the writing process.

When preparing the text for your first draft, do not forget to look at your research proposal. Check out how much of its text can be used in your research report. For example, with a small amount of adaptation, material from the research proposal might be able to be used in sections of your report describing how your study was designed and carried out, and why.

For further general suggestions on how to organise and prepare for writing research documents see Chapter 12, Writing for Research.

Writing a technical research report

This section outlines how to structure and present a technical report describing a research project and its findings. The information is designed to be applicable to a wide range of report writing circumstances in health and social science research. Many of the generic points made also apply to manuscripts for journals and student theses or dissertations.

When preparing to write a technical report, one of the most important first steps is to develop a structure for the report. Structure refers to the way the text of a report is organised sequentially under a series of headings. This includes chapter headings, and section and sub-section headings. Whatever report structure (format) you use, it should be logical, coherent and easy for readers to follow. Many people who start reading a report will not finish it if they find problems with its layout.

Box 13.1 outlines a structure and set of headings typically used as a basis for writing technical reports in health and social sciences. The information to include under these headings is described in more detail below.

Box 13.1   Common structure for a technical report

- Cover page with title and author(s) details
- Contents page
- Summary or abstract
- Acknowledgements
- Introduction
- Methods
- Results (or Findings)
- Discussion
- Conclusions
- References
- Appendices

Cover page and report title

The cover page should include the report's title, author name/s, the affiliation or address of the author/s and the date.

The report's title should be no longer than 12–15 words and in a larger font size (e.g. 16–20 point) than the rest of the text on the cover page. Make sure the title clearly conveys the main topic of the research. Many people will decide whether to read the report based on its title. Table 13.2 provides examples of good and poor titles for research reports. Avoid using abbreviations in a title or padding phrases such as 'An investigation of …'

In the title, try to include key words commonly used to describe your research topic. This will make it easier for people to find your report when searching the Internet for information on your topic.

TABLE 13.2 EXAMPLES OF GOOD AND POOR REPORT TITLES

Good titles	Poor titles
These titles are succinct and easy to understand[a]	*These titles tend to be too brief, too long or vague*[b]
Counter design influences the privacy of patients in health care	Community-based programming: Perceived levels of utility, practice, and encouragement among [...] Community College mid-level managers
Perceived occupational stress, affective, and physical well-being among telecommunication employees in Greece	Relationships among knowledge creation, diffusion and utilisation in the CRC process
Barriers and facilitators related to mammography use among lower educated Mexican women in the USA	Perceptions held by selected members of the [...] Community College Planning Council about their participation in the strategic planning process at [...] Community College
What policies and policy processes are needed to ensure that people with psychiatric disabilities have access to appropriate housing?	Place attachment and traditional place
Childhood mistreatment and adolescent and young adult depression	Supporting diagnostic decision making
Community inequality and smoking cessation in New Zealand, 1981–2006	That a shaky hand should rock the cradle

[a]These titles were selected from the journal *Social Science & Medicine*.
[b]These titles were selected from submitted university theses and dissertations.

Summary or abstract

A summary or abstract should concisely describe the key elements of a research project, particularly its findings. Summaries and abstracts should be able to be read in a few minutes. For relatively short technical reports, keep the length of the summary or abstract to one page or less. For longer or more complex reports, summaries could be several pages in length (e.g., 2–10 pages).

Summaries and abstracts should begin on a separate page. At the top of the page, put the title of the report (if it is not already in the page header). On the line directly below the report title put the heading 'Summary' or 'Abstract'.

Put plenty of effort into writing and revising your summary or abstract. Most people taking an initial look at your report will decide whether to read the rest of it based on what they read in the summary or abstract. It is therefore a potentially crucial entry point to your research report.

If you plan to circulate the summary or abstract as a separate document to a wide general audience, not just specialists in your research area, try to minimise the use of technical language and obscure terms.

Ideally, at least 50 per cent of the content of a summary or abstract should report the most important findings of your project. A common error is to fill up the summary or abstract with information about the research methods or project design and provide only a few lines on the *actual* findings. Another common error is to indicate that a project identified 'valuable lessons' or 'vital suggestions' but not to state what the lessons or suggestions were. Describe the actual research findings, do not just refer to them obliquely.

In a summary or abstract, always describe the project's sample size (where relevant) and the main data gathering techniques. When referring to relationships between variables, remember to state the *direction* of the relationship.

Introduction section

The introduction section outlines the aims and objectives of the research project, as well as its context and rationale (why the research was needed). Normally it also summarises findings of relevant previous research on the topic, especially if a separate literature review is not included elsewhere in the report.

Usually the section is headed 'Introduction', although other titles could be used as long as the purpose of the section remains clear.

When describing the aims, objectives or questions addressed by the research, set these out as outlined in Chapter 3, Developing Research Objectives and Questions. Specific objectives can be numbered and listed where appropriate.

For quantitative research projects, describe the hypotheses or specific models that were tested. If your research design involved testing support for an existing theory or model, you should describe the explicit hypothesis used to predict the expected research outcomes. Do not refer to *null hypotheses* (e.g., statements predicting no significant relationships between variables or differences between groups) as normally it is assumed a research hypothesis will predict some type of difference or change. If your project aimed to predict change resulting from an intervention, ensure the expected *direction* of the change is clearly stated (e.g., use an outcome like 'improved satisfaction' not 'changes in satisfaction levels').

Methods section

The methods section describes the types of information or data gathered for the project, where or from whom it was obtained, how it was collected and how it was analysed.

When reporting the methods used in a sample-based study, the usual convention is to discuss the following topics in the order shown:

- Sample (number in total sample, gender, ethnicity, how recruited)
- Data gathering methods (sometimes labelled 'measures', 'tools' or 'instruments')

- Data collection procedures (how the sample were contacted or recruited and given information about participation in the project)
- Data analysis
- More detailed demographic information about the sample (e.g., age, socio-economic status, health needs or experiences)

At the beginning of each sub-section of the methods section (e.g., Sample, Data gathering methods, etc.), summarise the key information to be covered in the sub-section.

For sample-based studies, the *sample size* that should be reported is the number of participants from whom usable information was obtained *and* who were included in the reported analyses, not the number of questionnaires distributed or people contacted and asked if they wished to participate.

When reporting focus group studies, the sample size is the *number of focus groups*. However, the total number of participants in each group can also be reported for the general information of readers.

Do not review literature in the methods section of a technical report, but do cite references for any data gathering or analysis techniques you used that were derived from previous studies.

Results or findings section

The findings (or results) section of a technical report describes the outcomes of the research project. (The terms 'findings' or 'results' are both suitable headings for this section.) Ideally, begin the section by providing a brief overview of the main results of the project. If your research project has been organised around a set of numbered research objectives, also note these in the overview.

When reporting findings in detail, a good technique is to report the findings in order of importance, starting with the most important findings. Alternatively, findings could be presented in the same order as the project's numbered research objectives. Use new paragraphs or sub-sections to report each new finding or set of results. A common error is to report findings in the order they appeared in the questionnaire or interview. Only do this if this order is the same as the order of importance.

In some technical reports, several sections or chapters may be needed to report all project findings. This may be especially necessary for projects covering a range of different research topics, questions or issues.

When describing results, move from an initial general description of trends to specific details. Report specific findings before reporting any interpretations you have made based on these findings.

If your project involved testing specified research hypotheses, results relevant to the hypotheses should be reported in the first part of the findings section. It should also be clearly stated whether the results support each hypothesis.

Make sure you describe your results precisely and accurately and state the direction of any relationships between variables. For example, the sentence 'male clients were disproportionately represented' is ambiguous. It should be either 'male clients were under-represented' or 'male clients were over-represented, compared to female clients'.

Try to avoid starting the findings section with a description of the socio-demographic characteristics (e.g., age, gender, ethnicity) of the study participants or sample – unless there is a good reason to do this, such as when reporting an RCT study or a similar study where the main focus is comparisons between treatment groups. In most social science research reports, socio-demographic characteristics of the study participants or sample are usually either described briefly in the sample sub-section of the methods section, or (if more details are needed) in a separate sub-section towards the end of the methods section. Another option is to include a more extended description of the characteristics of the sample in the report's appendices.

Quantitative results

Reporting quantitative data requires a good understanding of quantitative analysis and the knowledge to write clearly and concisely about numbers and outcomes assessed using statistical tests of significance. If you are not sufficiently familiar with how to do this, then you will need to get advice from others (e.g., Wilkinson & Task Force on Statistical Inference, 1999). The following specific points are intended to help readers avoid some of the more common errors people make when reporting numbers and statistical tests.

Reporting numbers and statistical tests in the text

When using numbers in the text, try to avoid starting a sentence with a numeral, such as a percentage. If you cannot, then write numerals in full at the beginning of sentences (e.g., 'Twenty-seven per cent of the 206 respondents favoured longer opening hours for the community centre'). Note that numbers under 10 are usually written as words and numbers 10 and higher as numerals (e.g., five children aged under 11).

If you are reporting outcomes of statistical tests, for most disciplines there is normally a standard format for reporting statistical findings (e.g., American Psychological Association, 2009). One of the most common errors beginning researchers make is to mention the significance level of a statistical test, but omit to mention which type of statistical test was used. For simple statistical tests such as chi-square, t-test and analysis of variance (ANOVA) the standard in-text reporting format is: value of test (degrees of freedom), significance level. Report these details immediately following the relevant text. Note that probability values (p values) are usually written without the leading zero before the decimal point. Report exact p values if available (e.g., $p = .002$) rather than levels (e.g., $p < .01$). Below are two examples of the correct way to report the results of statistical tests:

- Group A had significantly higher mean scores that Group B, $t(39) = 3.75, p < .001$.
- The three groups differed significantly, with Group C having the highest scores, $F(2,45) = 6.79, p = .005$.

Box 13.2   Reporting percentages

One of the most frequent errors when reporting numbers is incorrect use of percentages. If you are reporting percentages, report them as whole numbers (e.g., 22% not 21.7%) unless your sample is 100 or more. Percentages should only be used if your sample size is 30 or greater, otherwise they give a misleading impression of precision. If the sample size is less than 30, report the findings as frequencies without percentages. If you do wish to include percentages, put them in brackets after the frequency, e.g., 'Of the 27 respondents, 9 (33%) had visited the community centre.'

The general pattern for non-significant findings is to report these in the text without the full significance test details being included. Also, for commonly used statistical tests, do not include the formula or working for the statistical test in the text. It is assumed that a standard formula has been used, unless otherwise stated.

Tables and figures

Where possible, use figures and tables to highlight the project's major findings. This can enhance the overall effectiveness and attractiveness of research reports.

Tables are text-based lists arranged in rows and columns that contain only characters that can be produced from the keyboard in a word processor. Figures are diagrams, graphs or images such as photos. They contain non-text components such as lines, arrows, pictures or images.

Use the labels 'Table' or 'Figure' in a research report, not 'graph', 'diagram' or 'photo', which are not normally used as standard labels in research reports. Use tables or figures to highlight the *most important* findings or make certain results more accessible compared to a text description. Tables or figures are frequently misused to highlight trivial data. When used in this way they distract the reader from the main findings.

Tables and figures should be numbered sequentially in short reports (e.g., Table 1, Table 2) or sequentially within sections in longer reports (e.g., Figure 3.1, Figure 3.2 within section/ chapter 3).

Make sure you introduce all figures and tables in the preceding text. Never position a figure or table before the start of the text describing it, or without providing any explanatory text.

Other points to note when using tables or figures include:

- Do not use tables or graphs to present results for simple binary response categories (e.g., yes/no, male/female). Report the results for such categories only in the text (e.g., 'Of the 211 respondents 120 (57%) were women and 91 (43%) were men').
- If you are using statistical tests, do not use figures or tables to report only findings that are not statistically significant. However, it is appropriate to use a table to report a range of outcomes, including both significant and non-significant findings.
- Titles for tables should normally be placed immediately above the table where they are easier to read. Captions for figures are usually presented beneath the figure in manuscripts, although in some publications the caption or title is placed above the figure.
- Ensure the title of the table or figure accurately reflects its contents and is not too long. When reporting survey findings, one option is to use the question on which the results are based as the heading (e.g., *Table 5: How good or poor would you rate the service you received?*) If the question is too long to use as a heading, use just key words or phrases from the question (e.g., *How good or poor was the service?*).
- Always include the sample size in any table reporting percentages. The sample size can be put in brackets below the title (e.g., N = 57) or as a footnote at the bottom of the table. In tables, if percentages add up to more than 100 explain why (e.g., include a footnote stating, 'respondents could give more than one response' or 'percentages, do not add to 100 due to rounding error').

Where several categories or types of response are being reported in a table (e.g., items from a longer list) put them in order of frequency, with the highest frequency at the top. Omit items that have low frequencies (e.g. less than 10 per cent of sample). As a rule of thumb, report a maximum of seven or eight categories in a table. If you include categories like 'Other' or 'No response' put these at the bottom of the table. Do not include categories with no responses (0%) unless there is a good reason to (e.g., when it is a response option in a rating scale).

For rating scales, response categories (e.g., Very Good to Very Poor) should be reported in a table or figure in the order in which they were presented in the questionnaire or interview. Make sure you include clear labels for rating response categories, items or sub-headings in a table. (e.g., Quality of service: 1 = Very Poor, 2 = Poor, 3 = Unsure, 4 = Good, 5 = Very Good). Do not use numbers, letters or symbols on their own in a table or figure to represent response categories.

Tables 13.3 and 13.4 offer examples of a poorly formatted table and a well-formatted table. See how many errors you can find in the first table (Table 13.3). Then compare it with the corrected version shown in the second table (Table 13.4).

TABLE 13.3   EXAMPLE TABLE SHOWING POOR FORMATING: REASONS CLIENTS GAVE FOR DECIDING TO LEAVE THE PROGRAMME

Left the area, shifted to another location, moved out of town	52.37
On hold until later date	3.25
Service not required any more	20.1
Unhappy with staff assigned to client	5.3
Referred to another agency	13
Other reasons	7.2

TABLE 13.4   EXAMPLE TABLE SHOWING GOOD FORMATTING: REASONS FOR LEAVING THE PROGRAMME

Reasons for leaving (N = 96)	%
Left the area	52%
Service not required any more	20%
Referred to another agency	13%
Unhappy with staff assigned to client	5%
On hold until later date	3%
Other reasons	7%

When making a table, take some care with the layout of the numbers in columns to ensure they are easy to read. Numbers centred in columns are usually easiest to read. When reporting percentages, include the '%' symbol in the relevant locations in the table, as shown in the example in Table 13.4.

When creating figures, if you use shading to distinguish segments or bars, make sure the shades/patterns are easily distinguishable when printed in black and white. What shows up as clear, distinct colours on a computer screen can turn out to be indistinguishable in shades of grey. When inserting a *legend* or key within the figure, make sure the shading boxes and text in the legend are large enough to read easily. The default setting for legend text and shading in some software is too small to read when the figure is copied into the text of a report.

Qualitative results

The way qualitative findings are presented in a technical report will depend primarily on the type of qualitative methods and analysis used in the project. Different qualitative approaches, such as phenomenology, grounded theory, ethnography or discourse analysis, often require different formats for reporting findings (cf., Creswell, 2006). To learn more about these formats, as a first step look for articles in journals reporting the findings of research projects based on the particular qualitative tradition or approach you are using. Focus on articles that report the findings of just one research project in detail, rather than articles reviewing or commenting on the findings of many projects. There are also several books and articles available describing appropriate ways to write up qualitative research findings (e.g., Elliott, Fischer, & Rennie, 1999; Silverman, 2005).

When reporting categories or themes derived from an analysis of qualitative data, give each category a brief label followed by a description of what that category means. Here is an example taken from a study of nursing care:

Firm hand care

Technically competent, mediocre, or purely clinical care. Minimum level of nurse action to preserve integrity, adequate for patients who viewed themselves to be at low risk but not sufficient for high levels of vulnerability.

(Irurita, 1996, pp. 336–337)

In your report, include relevant quotations from the raw data to illustrate how specific text has been coded into the category described. When doing this, remember to remove all details from the quotes that could identify research participants or other people who have not consented to be identified.

For the 'firm hand care' theme noted above, Irurita included the following brief quotes to convey the meanings associated with the theme.

"perfectly adequate, technically", not demonstrating "feeling", "sensitivity", or "compassion", "probably a very good nurse ... just totally clinical", "putting in the hours", "only doing their job". (Irurita, 1996, p. 337)

If you are reporting findings from a qualitative study, such as a grounded theory study, where the analysis has produced a number of themes or categories, start by presenting a general overview of the categories or framework developed. Then describe each of the categories or themes in turn after this.

An example of how multiple levels of themes can be reported as a summary table at the beginning of the findings is shown in Table 13.5. The example is from a study of how family doctors diagnose and treat depression among Maori clients (Thomas, Arlidge, Arroll & Elder, 2009). Reporting themes in this way provides a useful overview that can help readers better grasp the project's main findings.

Discussion and conclusions sections

In some reports, discussion and conclusions are presented as separate sections. In other reports, they are combined into a single section. A third pattern is just to have a conclusions section with no separate discussion. The discussion section of a technical report usually covers topics such as:

TABLE 13.5   EXAMPLE TABLE SHOWING CATEGORIES: DIAGNOSING DEPRESSION AMONG MAORI CLIENTS

Primary categories	Specific categories	Descriptions
Identifying depression	Communication effectiveness	Good communication and a sense of trust between the GP and patient are important for identifying depression
	Recognising depression	Signs or indicators used by GPs to recognize depression
	Causes and risks for depression	GPs' views about causes of depression and risk factors
Treatment decisions	Treatment options and strategies	GP options relating to pharmaceutical (medication) and non-pharmaceutical treatments
	Patient expectations re: treatment	Patients' views about medication and other treatments
	Factors influencing treatment decisions	Patient factors affecting GP decisions about treatment including age, treatment preferences and availability of treatments
	Barriers to effective treatment	Barriers relating to medication and counselling treatments, and stereotyping of mental illness
Treatment outcomes	Patient compliance with treatment	Patient characteristics related to compliance and reasons for non-compliance
	Effectiveness of treatments	GP views about the effectiveness of treatments for depression
	Patient responses to treatment	GPs' reports about how patients responded to treatments

Source: Thomas et al. (2009)

- limitations or weaknesses of the research project
- implications of the research findings
- comparisons with findings from previous research
- practical applications of the research results
- prospects for further research.

In the conclusions section (which may be the last sub-section of the discussion or a separate section) specific conclusions or recommendations based on the project findings are presented. In this section, highlight the most important implications of the findings for potential users such as practitioners, service providers or policy makers.

When discussing project findings, avoid repeating in detail the findings already presented earlier in the report. Refer briefly to specific findings and then *discuss* them. It is also appropriate in the discussion section to describe limitations of the research. One way to help focus your thinking on this theme is to address the question 'how would you do your research project differently if you were to do the project again'?

References

Technical reports usually include a single reference list at the end showing all references cited in the text. See Chapter 7, Doing a Literature Review for information on standard formats for presenting a reference list.

Avoid using the heading 'bibliography' for the reference list (unless your discipline or department specifically requires it). In science writing, the term *bibliography* normally refers to a list of references compiled on a specific topic. The references in a bibliography are not necessarily expected to be cited in the document text. This is different from a reference list, where all the references in the list should be cited in the document text.

Writing a manuscript for a journal article

This section looks at how to organise and present a manuscript or paper for submission to a refereed research journal. Submission to a refereed journal typically involves a manuscript being reviewed by two or three (usually anonymous) referees. The editor of the research journal then decides whether the manuscript is suitable for publication.

For most researchers, especially beginning researchers, getting papers published in refereed journals can be a long and sometimes fruitless struggle. Many days or weeks can be spent writing articles that, in the end, after peer review and scrutiny by editors, are not accepted for publication. Some higher status journals have acceptance rates of lower than 20 per cent, which means by far the majority of manuscripts submitted to them will not be published.

However, the advantages of journal publication are also worth noting. For one thing, it usually means a lot more people will get the opportunity to read about a project's findings than if the findings were published only in a limited-distribution technical report or thesis. For another, being published in a reputable journal normally enhances a researcher's professional status and career prospects, especially if they are based in a university or specialist research centre.

Given the challenge of getting research results published in refereed journals, a critical factor in achieving success is making sure the formatting and general presentation of a manuscript submitted to a journal is polished and professional. This by itself will not guarantee publication, but without it the manuscript will almost certainly be rejected.

In contrast to technical reports, where considerable flexibility is often possible in the way a report is organised and presented, research journals usually have quite specific formatting and style requirements. To learn more about these, a first step is to go to the webpage of the journal to which you are planning to submit a manuscript. Copy or download the document or section called 'Instructions to authors' or another similar title. Read these instructions carefully prior to starting to write your manuscript, and again before you submit the manuscript for publication. Manuscripts written in ways that are inconsistent with a journal's required style are often rejected outright, without being sent to referees for review.

Most of the guidelines given previously in this chapter for writing technical reports (see above) also apply to the preparation of manuscripts for journals. However, there are some differences; for example, manuscripts submitted to journals do not have a contents page. Acknowledgements included in manuscripts are usually listed in an endnote before the reference list. Although published journal articles do not have a separate cover page.

manuscripts submitted for journal publication should have a cover page. Some journals also require specific headings to be used in the abstract and the main text.

A key point to consider is the overall length of the manuscript. Many journals have page or word limits. The limit may be expressed as a maximum number of typed, double-spaced pages (e.g., 20 pages) or as a maximum word length (e.g., 4000 words). If you plan to submit to a journal with strict word limits, it will be important to write concisely and trim any lengthy or redundant text.

Most journals do not allow appendices. However, a few do if there is a special reason to include them, such as to publish a new survey questionnaire developed during a project.

Writing an abstract for a journal manuscript

The quality of the abstract in a journal manuscript is especially critical. Online versions of journals often provide free access to tables of contents and abstracts of articles but require a subscription for full text access. This means many people will decide whether or not to get the full text of an article based primarily on how interesting and well written the abstract is. Box 13.3 shows specific suggestions to consider when writing abstracts for journal articles.

Box 13.3   Writing research abstracts for journal articles

Format

Abstracts summarise the main points of a research article. They are usually written with the same level of technical language as the article itself. Abstracts are typically between 150 and 400 words long and follow the pattern prescribed by the journal in which the article is to be published. Abbreviations and reference citations are not generally used in abstracts.

Common purposes and functions for abstracts

- Presents a summary of the main findings on a topic
- Provides an overview enabling readers to decide if they will read the entire article
- Supplies a framework which can help make reading the full report easier
- Provides key words and phrases for journal and database key word searches

Structure

The following is a common structure used when writing research abstracts.

Overview: indicate the purpose and scope of the research, including topics covered
Methods: indicate key elements of the research design, including sample size, types of participants, how data were gathered, methods of analysis.
Results: indicate the main, most important or most unexpected findings.
Conclusions: indicate the key implications of the findings (e.g., for future research or practice) as well as any major limitations of the research methods used or the findings.

Introduction section of a journal manuscript

This should start on a separate page after the abstract. For most journal manuscripts, this section will only need to be headed with the title of the article, not the word 'Introduction'.

Normally a literature review will be included in this first section, along with any other contextual information needed to help readers understand the research problem or topic being investigated. It is also good practice somewhere in the introductory section to provide a clear statement of the project's overall research aim and any specific research objectives, questions or hypothesis addressed by the project.

Methods section of a journal manuscript

The methods section is a brief statement indicating what the researcher did to collect research data or information for the project. Topics covered in the section often include: (a) sample size and demographic characteristics of research participants; (b) data gathering methods used (e.g., survey questionnaire, interview schedule or other instruments); (c) procedures used to recruit participants and administer data gathering methods; (d) how the data were analysed.

Sometimes an extra section will be included after the data analysis section giving more detail about features of the sample or research participants. At an appropriate point, the methods section should also state whether an ethical review of the project's research proposal was sought and, if so, the name of the committee or organisation that gave approval for the project to proceed.

Results section of a journal manuscript

The guidelines given earlier on how to organise and write the results (findings) section of a technical report (see above) are also relevant for writing the results section of a journal manuscript.

Be careful to use tables and figures sparingly when writing a manuscript intended for journal publication. A common error is to produce five or six tables when only two or three tables are really needed. Some journals still require that each table and figure is placed on a separate page following the list of references. However, with electronic submission of manuscripts, many journals now accept tables and figures located in the main text. If the journal to which you are submitting a manuscript requires tables and figures to be appended as separate pages, you should note in the text where each table or figure is to be inserted, using the format shown below:

Table 1 about here

Discussion and conclusions sections of a journal manuscript

The discussion and conclusions sections may be either a combined section or separate sections depending on the journal style. These sections have a similar style, format and content to that used for technical reports. However, generally they will be briefer. In each section, aim to cover your most important points first, followed by the less important ones. Note especially any potential limitations to your findings. A realistic assessment of the potential limits to the generalisability of your research findings is not a sign of weakness, rather it indicates the quality of your critical thinking skills.

Submission of journal article manuscripts

Manuscripts are normally submitted to journals either by sending a paper copy in the mail or submitting an electronic version via email or through the journal's website. If you are mailing a paper copy of your manuscript to the journal editor, make sure you include a covering letter and check how many copies are required for submission. The usual procedure is for the editor to send an acknowledgement letter or email to the first author (or the author nominated as the 'corresponding author') once the manuscript has been received by the journal. Following this, normally there will be a wait of several weeks or months before the author is notified about the outcome of the review process.

Multiple authors and authorship

Many journals now have specific requirements for the inclusion of people as authors on a manuscript submitted for journal publication (see Box 13.4). Especially in health and medical journals, it is quite common for manuscripts to be submitted with six or more people listed as authors. While in some cases this may reflect a genuine contribution from all the people listed, in other cases names of people may be included who have not made any specific contribution to the paper. This might include directors of research units where the research was carried out, members of the research team who did not contribute to writing the report (such as interviewers), or other people who have helped in some way during the project. The listing of multiple authors is also an effective strategy for increasing the number of overall publications among individuals in groups who collaborate in this way.

In general terms, most journals now expect the people listed as authors to have made a clear contribution to the manuscript being submitted for publication. That contribution would normally include: analysis of the data reported, contribution to the writing of the article and critical review of draft versions of the article (Annandale, 2007; Gordon, 2000).

Box 13.4   Eligibility for authorship

The *International Committee of Medical Journal Editors* has published detailed recommendations regarding who should be eligible for authorship in published papers. They state that:

- Authorship credit should be based on 1) substantial contributions to conception and design, acquisition of data, or analysis and interpretation of data; 2) drafting the article or revising it critically for important intellectual content; and 3) final approval of the version to be published. Authors should meet conditions 1, 2, and 3.
- When a large, multicenter group has conducted the work, the group should identify the individuals who accept direct responsibility for the manuscript. These individuals should fully meet the criteria for authorship/contributorship defined above and editors will ask these individuals to complete journal-specific author and conflict-of-interest disclosure forms. (International Committee of Medical Journal Editors, 2008, pp. 2–3)

Writing dissertations and theses

This section provides advice on the writing and presentation of dissertations and theses. For many researchers, the first complete research report they write will be a dissertation or thesis for a Masters or doctoral degree. While dissertations and theses in health and social sciences generally have quite similar formats and features to other types of research reports, such as technical reports (see above), there are some distinctive elements that are useful to know about. There are also some common errors people make when writing thesis or dissertations that are worth remembering and trying to avoid.

In this section, the term 'thesis' is used to refer to both dissertations and theses. Both these terms are commonly used in universities, colleges and other learning institutions, sometimes interchangeably. However, some institutions define a dissertation to be a shorter research report than a thesis. Remember to check your own institution's general requirements for dissertations and theses, along with any specific requirements for your subject area or discipline.

Table of contents

Like technical reports (but not journal articles), most theses provide a table of contents. When compiling the table of contents, be careful when you are setting the word processing software to compile the contents automatically. It is quite common for errors to develop in automatically compiled tables of contents and these may go unnoticed. Make sure you check for these errors and correct them before finalising your thesis. If you are compiling a table of contents manually, a good technique is to open the clipboard or paste editor and copy each heading in sequence from the actual text. Then go to the contents list and paste them back (usually in reverse sequence to that compiled on the clipboard).

Note that a table of contents should generally be no more than 2–3 pages long. Anything longer will be too hard for most readers to use effectively. If your list exceeds 2–3 pages, cut it down by listing only first- and second-order headings. Delete all orders of heading below that.

Literature review chapter

In contrast to most technical reports and journal manuscripts, theses are likely to have a separate chapter for a literature review. In many tertiary institutions it is a standard requirement that advanced level theses have a separate literature review chapter. Normally, the literature review will be positioned towards the start of thesis, before the research methods chapter and after the introductory chapter describing the aims and objectives of the thesis project. In the review, students are expected to show they have a good understanding of the findings of previous studies on their topic, and can critically evaluate them.

Review of methodology literature in a thesis

Theses are also often required to include a second literature review examining research design options and methodological issues relevant to the project. This review can be presented as:

- a separate section at the end of the thesis's main literature review chapter (often the second chapter in a thesis)
- in a chapter of its own
- in a separate section at the start of the methods chapter.

The first and second options are recommended, although the third would be acceptable. A common mistake, especially when using the third option, is to combine the text of the methodological review with text reporting the actual methods used in the research project.

Multiple chapters for reporting results in a thesis

For some theses it may be difficult to adequately report all the findings in a single results chapter. In this situation it may be appropriate to use two or three chapters to report the complete results of the project. If you decide to have more than one results chapter in your thesis, include an overview at the beginning of the first results chapter outlining what is covered in each of the chapters.

Order and number of chapters in a thesis

Be prepared to consider different ways to structure a thesis apart from the standard set of chapter headings shown earlier in Box 13.1. This may be especially important if you have extra information you want to include on some aspect of your study, or if the design of your research is complicated or unorthodox. For example, you may want to include additional chapters describing the context or setting of the research. Another possibility is that your research project consists of a series of two or three discrete studies that might be better reported as separate chapters, each with their own methods and findings sections.

In these and similar situations try out different chapter sequences until you find a structure that seems to suit your particular research project. Sometimes you may need to let the chapter sequence evolve over several weeks or months during the writing process, while you think about it and get feedback from others. The chapter order you finally settle on should seem logical and coherent to readers, not disjointed or confusing.

There are examples of completed PhD theses containing as many as 17 chapters. Although having this many chapters is not necessarily recommended, it can have the advantage of allowing you to write in some depth about topics directly relevant to your thesis but which would not sit well together in the same chapter. For example, in research involving different social service organisations in a particular area or district, separate chapters could be used to cover discrete topics such as the history of the development of the organisation, patterns of human or social services in the district, the specific needs of residents in the district, and so on. These chapters would provide a general context for the thesis topic and be based on information from a range of sources, including interviews conducted for the study. Ideally, the chapters should be positioned between the main literature review chapter and the methods chapter, as they are not considered part of the project's *research* findings *per se*.

Appendices in a thesis

Most theses include several appendices. Appendices may be placed either before or after the list of references. Types of documents commonly placed in appendices include:

- questionnaires used in the research project (although if a questionnaire has already been published elsewhere it may be sufficient to cite the appropriate reference in the main body of the thesis)
- letters from ethics review committees approving the research proposal
- letters from organisations confirming that the project's researchers are permitted to access information from the organisation or its clients
- information sheets and consent forms given to research participants
- tables or lists summarising socio-demographic features of research participants
- full lists of codes or categories developed when using qualitative analysis software.

An error some people make in theses is including too many documents in appendices. Avoid including raw project data, such as transcripts of interviews, or detailed information tracing the evolution of qualitative coding.

References cited in text and reference list

Ensure all references cited in the text of a thesis are listed in the reference list. One way to check this is to randomly select about 10–15 references from the thesis's introduction and literature review chapters. Then look to see if each one of these references is listed in the reference list. If you find one missing, you need to do a more systematic check. Examiners of theses usually do this check and it is often surprisingly easy to find references cited in the text that are not in the reference list.

Similarly, remove any references in the reference list not cited in the text. This problem often arises when references included in earlier drafts are deleted from the text, but not deleted from the reference list at the same time.

Checking and proofreading

Ask someone else to read through your thesis to check the general formatting and presentation. This can be very useful for picking up errors you have missed. If you have been closely involved for a long period in the writing of your thesis, usually it will be very difficult on your own to detect all the typing errors, misspellings and grammatical errors in it.

General tips on producing research reports

This final section presents general tips on report writing, formatting and presentation. These are applicable to the three types of research report discussed above as well as most other report types.

Box 13.5 highlights common errors that researchers should try to avoid when writing research reports. This list has been developed by the authors based on several years' experience of reviewing theses, technical reports and manuscripts submitted for journal publication. The text following the box adds further detail on some of the errors listed.

Box 13.5   Common writing and presentation errors in research reports

- Writing lacks clarity. Sentences not easily understood
- Key information not provided (e.g., sample sizes, context for the research project)
- Most important findings not highlighted
- Trivial information highlighted in tables and graphs
- Page numbers not inserted
- Information not presented in a clear, logical sequence
- No blank line or indented text used to mark new paragraphs
- Symbols and abbreviations used in the text are not explained
- Tables not self-explanatory
- Table and figure titles are too long or do not clearly describe what the table or figure contains
- Figures difficult to understand (e.g., too complex)
- Numerous spelling and grammatical errors
- Starting a new line for each sentence (i.e. using one-sentence paragraphs)
- References in text and reference list are incorrectly formatted

---

Heading and paragraph formatting

Use a consistent approach to formatting headings, sub-headings and paragraphs. When indenting sub-headings and the first line of a paragraph, use an indent of about five spaces (1.00 to 1.50 cm) only, not very large indents. If you are numbering headings, it is best not to use more than two levels of numbering (e.g., 3.6.1) otherwise the multiple numbering can become distracting.

Quotations in text

When using quotations, note that excerpts longer than two lines should be indented about five spaces as block quotes, *without* quotation marks. All quotations must include source details (author, year, page number). These details should be included at the end of the quote in the following form: (Jones, 1990, p. 10). It is good practice to italicise quotations to make them stand out from the text.

Numbering pages

For journal manuscripts and technical reports, all pages except the front cover should be numbered. The page following the front cover can be numbered as page 2. In some numbering systems, the opening pages of a report prior to the main text (e.g., table of contents, acknowledgements, abstract) are numbered with lower case Roman numerals (e.g., i, ii, iii, etc.). The first page of text in the introduction is then numbered as page 1.

Using abbreviations and acronyms

A common mistake made by new researchers is using too many technical acronyms and abbreviations. Although acronyms and abbreviations can help save time and a little bit of space while writing, used excessively they can make it very difficult for readers to follow the text and become a source of frustration for readers. Even some abbreviations commonly used in a specialist area, may not be understood by other researchers.

Abbreviations and acronyms are generally of four types:

- those that may be more widely used than the full written version (e.g. HIV/AIDS, SARS, pdf)
- those that are widely used in several disciplines but may not be understood by readers without a research background (e.g., SD for standard deviation, N for sample number, M for mean score)
- those that are usually only known by researchers working in a specific area (e.g., CVD for cardiovascular disease)
- abbreviations created by the researcher for terms frequently used in their own report but rarely used in other research writing.

Usually it is appropriate to use the first two types of abbreviations noted above. Check relevant journal articles to see which ones are in common use in your discipline or subject area.

Be careful about using abbreviations or acronyms that may be used only in a specialist area. If you do use these, always write the term or phrase out in full, followed by the abbreviation in brackets, the first time you use it in the text of your report, or the first time it is used in each chapter in a thesis. An example is 'coronary heart disease (CHD)'. Try to avoid using specialist abbreviations in your abstract, as this is often read as a stand-alone document separate from the full text of the report.

Avoid as much as the possible the temptation to use abbreviations or acronyms you have created yourself. By all means use your own acronyms to save time when drafting up initial versions of a report. However, when finalising the report, make sure you use the 'search and replace' function of your word processer to go through it completely and insert the full term or expression for all the non-standard abbreviations you have used.

Several websites are available for checking the common meanings of acronyms. Type 'acronyms' into your web browser to find relevant sites. Checking the meaning of an acronym you plan to use in a report can be revealing. For example, CHD shows up as both 'Coronary Heart Disease' and 'Congenital Heart Disease'. SARS shows most commonly as 'Severe Acute Respiratory Syndrome' but also as 'South African Revenue Service'.

Length of chapters and sections

After preparing an initial draft of your project findings, be prepared to trim ruthlessly to remove less relevant findings and details. This is likely to be especially important when preparing manuscripts for journals. Generally, when writing a technical report or a thesis try to avoid chapters longer than about 25–30 double-spaced pages.

Chapter and section overviews

In the first paragraph of relatively long sections or chapters in a report, it is a good idea to provide an overview of the content of the section or chapter. This gives the reader an indication of the main points covered and helps develop a frame of reference, hopefully making it easier for the reader to follow the remainder of the text.

Consistency in use of labels and key terms

Labels or key terms are often used in reports to refer to certain categories, themes, questionnaire scales or other attributes of a project's research methods or findings. When using labels or key terms, make sure you use the same ones consistently through-out a report. Develop a suitable label or key term and stick to it. Avoid using different labels to refer to the same attribute or category. This can be very confusing for readers. For example, if a report on complementary medicines uses terms such as 'herbal rem-edies', 'herbal medicines', 'herbal products' and 'medicinal herbs' – without making it clear whether these labels refer to the same group of items or different items – this can make it quite hard to interpret or apply the report's findings in any practical way.

Proofreading and checking writing style

Make sure you spend plenty of time during the writing of a report carefully reviewing and where necessary revising the report's general writing style, presentation and lay-out. If you are a sole author, before completing the final draft of the report get one or two other people to provide detailed oral or written feedback specifically on the report's formatting and ease of understanding. It can be very difficult picking up all the ambiguities and typing errors in reports you have written yourself.

Conclusion: Writing research reports

This chapter has outlined formatting and writing style features usually expected to be found in research-based technical reports, manuscripts for journals and student theses or dissertations. These features should be relevant to most research reports prepared in social science and health-related disciplines.

To get more ideas on how to write and present these different types of research report, find and study examples from your research topic area or discipline. Scrutinise each report in detail. Look closely at how the text and other information is arranged and formatted. Remember that some disciplines may have formatting requirements that differ in some respects from those outlined in this chapter. As well, specific formatting styles evolve and change over time (e.g., see APA Publications and Communications Board, 2008; International Committee of Medical Journal Editors, 2008). It is important to check relevant websites for your discipline, or relevant journal webpages, for details of current writing and formatting guidelines.

Exercises for writing a research report

1. Find and retrieve three journal articles on topics you are interested in from three differ-ent journals in your discipline or subject area. Construct a three-column table and write down the main section headings for each of the three articles, putting the headings for each article in one column. How similar or different are the section headings used?

2. For the three articles you located above, review the abstracts of these articles. How consistent is each of the abstracts with the outline shown in Box 13.3 'Writing research abstracts for journal articles'? About how many words were used in each abstract? What proportion of the abstract describes the findings of the research?

3. Locate and retrieve (e.g., as pdfs) two technical research reports from the Internet using the search procedures described in Chapter 7, Doing a Literature Review. Try to find reports between 50 and 150 pages long that describe in detail the findings of a single research project. Examine each report's table of contents and review how closely the report's structure follows that shown in Box 13.1. What headings are used that are not in the standard pattern for a research report? How effective are these headings and sections in conveying information about the research project?

References and further reading

American Psychological Association (2009). *Publication Manual of the American Psychological Association* (6th edn). Washington, DC: APA.

Annandale, E. (2007). Editorial. *Social Science & Medicine, 64*(1), 1–4.

APA Publications and Communications Board Working Group on Journal Article Reporting Standards (2008). Reporting standards for research in psychology: Why do we need them? What might they be? *American Psychologist, 63*(9), 839–851.

Caro, S. (2009). *How to Publish Your PhD.* London: Sage.

Creswell, J. W. (2006). *Qualitative Inquiry and Research Design: Choosing among Five Traditions* (2nd edn). Thousand Oaks, CA: Sage.

Elliott, R., Fischer, C., & Rennie, D. (1999). Evolving guidelines for publication of qualitative research studies in psychology and related fields. *British Journal of Clinical Psychology, 38*, 215–229.

Gordon, A. J. (2000). Guidelines for contributors to Social Science & Medicine. *Social Science & Medicine, 50*, 3–15.

International Committee of Medical Journal Editors (2008). *Uniform Requirements for Manuscripts Submitted to Biomedical Journals: Writing and Editing for Biomedical Publication* (Updated October 2008). Retrieved April 20, 2009, from: www.icmje.org/

Irurita, V. F. (1996). Hidden dimensions revealed: progressive grounded theory study of quality care in the hospital. *Qualitative Health Research, 6*(3), 331–349.

Matthews, J. R., Bowen, J. M., & Matthews, R. W. (1996). *Successful Scientific Writing: A Step-by-Step Guide for Biomedical Scientists.* Cambridge: Cambridge University Press.

Ono, H., Phillips, K. A., & Leneman, M. (1996). Content of an abstract: de jure and de facto. *American Psychologist, 51*(12), 1338–1340.

Pattow, D. & Wresch, W. (1998). *Communicating Technical Information: A Guide for the Electronic Age* (2nd edn). Upper Saddle River, NJ: Prentice-Hall.

Rudestam, K. E. & Newton, R. R. (2007). *Surviving Your Dissertation: A Comprehensive Guide to Content and Process* (3rd edn). Thousand Oaks, CA: Sage.

Silverman, D. (2005). *Doing Qualitative Research: A Practical Handbook* (2nd edn). London: Sage (see chapters in section on 'Writing up').

Thomas, D. R., Arlidge, B., Arroll, B. & Elder, H. (2009). General practitioners' views about diagnosing and treating depression in Māori and non-Māori patients. Unpublished research report. School of Population Health, University of Auckland, New Zealand.

Whimster, W. F. (1997). *Biomedical Research: How to Plan, Publish and Present It.* New York: Springer.

Wilkinson, L. & Task Force on Statistical Inference (1999). Statistical methods in psychology journals: guidelines and explanations. *American Psychologist, 54*(8), 594–604.

14   Careers in Research

This chapter provides some general advice on the types of career and work opportunities available to people interested in social and health research. Three main types of employment are considered:

- working as a university researcher
- working as a researcher in another kind of specialised research environment, such as a government agency or private sector research firm
- working as a self-employed, independent or freelance researcher.

The section looking at working as a self-employed or freelance researcher is the most detailed as this is a career option that has increased in popularity in recent years and therefore requires some special consideration here.

Planning for employment as a researcher

If you are currently studying at university, polytechnic or another type of advanced learning institution and thinking about a career or future work in social and health research, there are several things you can do to find out more about the employment options available and perhaps increase your chances of getting work.

As a first step, start looking at relevant websites (see Appendix 14.1 for examples) and read the blogs, comments and advice about getting jobs as a researcher. Talk or write to different people already working in research positions. Ask them about what degrees they completed, how they got started in their first job, what helped them establish their career in research and what advice they have for new or emerging researchers starting out in the job market. You might be surprised at the different routes people have taken to get to their current position and the diverse range of agencies and industries that employ social and health researchers.

When planning your university or polytechnic studies, consider taking courses or doing research projects on topics linked to future employment opportunities you are interested in. Many researchers, especially those working in non-academic settings, get their first job on the basis of knowledge and skills they developed at university while doing research on a topic, or using a research approach, that potential employers might be interested in (see Box 14.1). A useful strategy in such cases is to send a summary of your research findings to organisations who could be interested in the research.

Box 14.1   Getting a job from thesis research

As part of his Masters degree in community psychology, Grant developed and carried out a small community survey on resident needs in one district of the small city where he lived. He reported the survey findings in his thesis and sent a six-page summary of his thesis findings to the city council planning division. A few weeks later a manager from the council contacted Grant and offered him a three-month position to carry out a survey of residents' views about a proposed bypass road that would increase traffic on streets that at that time had low traffic density. He completed this survey successfully and submitted his report, which contained some useful suggestions on how to reduce the impacts of higher traffic density on the streets affected. Grant was subsequently offered a 12-month position in the planning division to carry out a series of surveys examining residents' views about changes planned for the city. He went on to develop a career as a research director working in local and regional government organisations.

While you are still studying, another way to perhaps improve your chances of developing a future career in research is to do paid or unpaid part-time work in employment settings that interest you. This can help develop work experience and build contacts that can open doors for you later. During an evaluation course taught by one of the authors (DRT), several students on the course were also working as front-line staff in human service organisations such as counselling agencies, church helping services, women's refuges and local government. Most of these students carried out the research project required for the course within the agency in which they were working. After completing their research projects, many of these students moved from providing front-line services to research, evaluation or planning roles within their organisation. The skills they had gained doing their evaluation research, such as proposal writing and data collection and analysis, proved valuable to the organisations in which they were working.

Conferences and networking

Attending conferences and research training workshops can be another way to build networks and learn about future work options in research. Many conferences provide information and meeting opportunities for junior researchers interested in employment. While a large conference may give the feeling of being just one person among several thousand conference-goers, smaller conferences can sometimes be useful for making contacts. Consider presenting a paper on your research, signing up for a workshop, or participating in other activities such as round-table discussions. Make sure you have a one-page summary of your research and a business card you can give to people who express an interest in your work. Look through the conference programme to see which papers or sessions are most relevant to your interests, noting the university departments or research organisations of the people presenting these sessions. Contact the presenters to get a copy of their paper and, if appropriate, comment on what you thought about their paper.

Another networking opportunity to consider is email discussion groups and blogs focused around research topics or disciplines in which you are interested. Do an Internet search to find discussion groups and email lists relevant to your research area or discipline. Sign up to get the emails sent through the lists you select. You can always sign off if the list turns out not to be useful. Look through the list archives to see what topics have been discussed recently.

Working as a university researcher

If you have completed or are about to complete a research degree, one option you may be considering is working as a researcher in a university or other type of academic institution. Most full-time teaching appointments in universities provide opportunities to carry out research, and much of the research in universities is done by full-time teaching staff. However, there are some university positions where the primary focus is carrying out research, with no or only a minimal teaching component. Examples of such positions are:

- research assistant working on an existing or forthcoming project for a limited time
- temporary employment to lead or run a specific research project
- a longer-term research position for 12 months or more where the person will be working on several research projects.

Research assistants are often employed for a limited time on specific projects to carry out tasks like interviewing, data entry and data analysis. If you have not done work like this before, it can provide valuable experience that can come in handy later. Even if you do not need to do interviews subsequently, knowing about the skills needed, and the challenges of interviewing, are important when supervising interviewers. If you get employment as a research assistant to do data entry or data analysis, find out as much as you can about the software and technical skills needed to set up the database systems being used. Ask questions and join in discussions so you have an understanding of the multiple tasks involved in running a project.

Researchers can also be employed in temporary university positions to lead or run a specific research project. This can include doctoral and post-doctoral fellowships, or funding to carry out a specific project that may be part of a larger university-based research programme. Such funding is often for a 12-month period but can be longer in some cases. The positions are often advertised in newspapers, specialist magazines or other sources. However, in some cases they may only be advertised on university or faculty email lists. Check university websites to see if they list these types of positions. If you do get employed as a researcher in this way, take full advantage of opportunities to learn new skills and publish in refereed journals. Sometimes these positions lead to opportunities to work on other, longer-term projects.

Some universities also occasionally advertise (in newspapers or on university websites) relatively long-term specialist research positions, which might last for 12–24 months or longer. These positions often involve carrying out specific research activities such as data analysis (quantitative or qualitative), maintaining a research database, organising and conducting surveys, or project management. Usually the positions will be located in larger university research units or centres and require a broader range of research skills and experience than the shorter-duration, temporary positions described earlier.

If you are aiming to work in a university research position, you can increase your chances of getting a position by developing a publication record, by publishing papers from your thesis research or other projects you have worked on. Where feasible, you should also seek joint project work, co-authorship or positions with experienced research-ers who are well-known in their field.

There are positive features about working in university research. As you advance, you are more likely to be able to choose your research topic or the design of your research project. There is also often a reasonable amount of flexibility in the working environment. The negative features are trying to make a living from 'soft money' or short-term funding. This often means that as one project nears completion, you are writing proposals seeking funding for your next project. Many of the proposals you write may be unsuccessful, so there is a lot of wasted effort. Many research positions (other than full-time teaching positions) are short-term contracts so you need to be able to live with the ongoing job insecurity this entails.

Working in a non-university research position

Some people may be interested in employment as researchers in non-university research organisations, such as not-for-profit social services organisations, government research units, commercial survey companies, or small commercial organisations that do contract research in specialised areas (see Box 14.2). More recently there has been a growth in organisations carrying out research related to conservation and the environment. Some of these organisations employ researchers with a health or social science background, often to carry out surveys or interviews with residents or users of recreational facilities.

Box 14.2   Examples of non-university organisations that may employ researchers

- National, central or federal government departments and ministries
- Regional and local government offices and councils
- Libraries and archives
- Museums
- News media organisations
- Television and film production companies
- Political parties
- Independent think-tanks
- Business sector councils and associations
- Lobby groups
- Trade unions
- Not-for-profit social services agencies
- Large charitable organisations
- Hospitals and health services
- Market research companies
- Pharmaceutical companies
- Food manufacturers

The strategies for improving your chances of getting employment in a non-university research organisation are very similar to those for getting a university research position. As a first step, check out job advertisements for researchers in newspapers, employment websites (see Appendix 14.1) and other sources to see what types of research positions are being advertised in your area. Identify advertised positions that interest you and make a note of the skills or attributes required or expected and the types of experience that would be desirable. In conjunction with this, identify companies or organisations engaged in specific types of research such as survey research, evaluation research or human services research. The webpages of these companies will often describe the types of research work they do, or projects they have recently completed.

Consider sending a copy of your CV to companies or organisations doing research in areas in which you are interested, to see if you can get an interview to discuss job possibilities. A critical factor will be to make sure your CV looks suitable for the type of positions you are seeking.

Working as an independent researcher

Recent decades have seen a proliferation of non-standard work arrangements for researchers trained in social science and health. These include part-time and casual positions, short-term contract work and commissioned projects. Integral to this has been the emergence of the independent researcher or freelancer. These are researchers who make their living by working on research projects for different organisations or clients on a contract basis (Provan, 2003).

This section offers advice for people thinking about setting themselves up as independent researchers. It is mainly intended for people with no previous experience of working in this way who are looking for some general guidance on how to go about it.

Is this really what you want to do?

Before committing to setting up as an independent or freelance researcher, take some time to carefully weigh up if working this way will suit you. Remember:

1. Compared to a permanent job, working as an independent or freelancer may be less financially secure. Your earnings will depend on how successful you are at finding project work and completing that work on time and to a good standard. Usually the bulk of the fee for a project contract is paid only once the project is finished. Depending on how many projects you are working on, and the stages you are at with them, at some times of the year you may have very little money coming in.
2. Contractors and freelancers, by definition, are normally expected to supply their own work tools and equipment. This means equipment usually vital to working as a researcher – computers, software, printers, scanners, photocopiers, mobile phones, audio or video recording equipment – must all be purchased by you.
3. Compared to more structured jobs, working as an independent researcher can require a fairly high degree of self-motivation and initiative. It is largely up to you to identify and prioritise tasks and get them done. There is no boss or senior manager organising your work for you.
4. Although working as an independent researcher does mean you will probably have more control over what tasks you do from day to day, and when you do them, there are still likely

to be quite a few pressure points in the year when you will have to work late into the evenings or during weekends to get projects finished.

5. Contract research usually involves investigating fairly concrete, practical problems, often to inform decisions related to services or policy. This may not suit people whose research to date has focused mainly on abstract or theoretical issues. Some adjustment in perspective and emphasis may be needed.

Box 14.3   Non-standard work

Non-standard work is any kind of work apart from permanent, full-time employment with a single organisation or employer. It includes contract work as well as part-time, temporary and casual jobs. For organisations that carry out research, these non-standard work options make it easier to hire in researchers with specialised skills at times when they are needed.

For some researchers, these non-standard work arrangements offer scope to better integrate work with other life priorities such as caring for family, further education, recreation, travel or hobbies. For others, they offer a stepping-stone into permanent work or new ways to earn a living in the face of redundancy or a shortage of full-time paid employment.

Numerous studies have reviewed the advantages and disadvantages of non-standard work arrangements (e.g. Fenwick, 2008; Gold & Fraser, 2002; Mirchandani, 2000; Osnowitz, 2005).

If your life circumstances, training or temperament are likely to make it difficult to accommodate one or more of the situations outlined above, perhaps working as an independent researcher may not be suitable for you, at least at the moment.

Any decisions you do make regarding setting yourself up as an independent researcher should not be rushed or made under pressure. If you are considering the option largely in response to external circumstances such as redundancy, a shrinking job market or a highly stressful existing job, this is perhaps not the best situation in which to coolly assess what is best for you.

Ideally, try to do your homework on the options for working as an independent researcher while you are in a fairly solid job with a steady income. That way you will have more opportunity to exert control over the pace and timing of your move to working as an independent researcher, should you decide to pursue the option.

Getting started

Once you have decided to become an independent researcher, spend some time thinking about how you want to market yourself and the professional identity you want to present to others. To some extent, becoming an independent researcher is a chance to reinvent your professional identity. You can shift the focus of your work away from research topics or approaches you find less interesting and towards approaches or topics you really enjoy or are particularly good at.

Develop a clear idea about the kinds of research skills and knowledge you intend to offer and the type of research work that you are most interested in doing. Do you want to offer a wide spectrum of different research services, or specialise in only one or two research techniques or topic areas? Promoting yourself as a person offering a fairly narrowly defined, specialised set of research skills may mean you have less competition for business. However, there may be fewer clients wanting these particular skills. A more generic approach, emphasising your familiarity with a wide variety of research techniques, may increase the number of projects for which you could potentially bid. However, it may also mean you will be bidding against many other researchers for this work, so perhaps lowering your chances of success.

Draw up a list of local agencies or people you would like to work with. Does the list have any common themes? Are you more inclined towards working for government or public sector organisations, or perhaps non-government community organisations or the voluntary sector? Or are you more interested in working for private businesses and corporations?

Think about the moral limits of your career and professional aspirations. Ethically and philosophically, are you prepared to work with any organisation or group? Or are there certain kinds of organisations you could never work for?

In the end, some trial and error may be required before you finally identify which of your research skills you want to publicise or highlight, and what types of clients you are most interested in working for. Test out the possibilities. Check out which research skills and approaches seem to be particularly in demand, or likely to be wanted in future, and by whom.

Establishing a base

Consider carefully where to set up your office. Some independent or freelance researchers prefer to work mainly on contracts where desk space is made available in the client's office building. Others prefer to use their own office, whether at home or downtown. Naturally, cost is a factor here. The cost of renting your own downtown office is likely to be much higher than if you work at home or simply arrange to use your client's office space.

However, there may be advantages to paying for your own dedicated office space, especially if working from home is not an option and you regularly need to meet with clients on a professional basis. Having your own office helps to show that you are taking your business seriously and that you are keen to be known and accessible to your clients.

Box 14.4   Equipment you may need

As an independent researcher, you will need to organise or supply your own work-related equipment. This will be especially important if you are intending to work in your own office, rather than in the offices of your clients. Research-related office equipment you may need to have access to, or to buy for yourself, includes:

- laptop and/or desktop computer and office work software
- Internet connection
- extra computer hard drives or pen drives for external storage and backup
- scanning, printing, photocopying and paper-shredding equipment
- ergonomic desk and chair
- tables and filing cabinets

(Continued)

> *(Continued)*
>
> - binding equipment for reports
> - mobile phone.
>
> Other specialist research equipment you might need to buy includes:
>
> - a still camera for photographs
> - audio and video recording equipment
> - transcribing equipment
> - statistical and/or qualitative analysis software.

Working from home: is it right for you?

Setting up a home office is a popular option for independent researchers, especially in the initial stages of developing their business. Potential benefits include:

- significant cost savings as you do not have to pay the rent for a separate office in town
- availability to contribute to housekeeping work or caregiving during the working day
- reduced need for work-related travel
- scope to work in a comparatively peaceful, private setting.

However, not everyone's circumstances will suit working from home. There may not be enough space in your home for a separate office area. There may also be too many other people at home with you while you are working, which you may find distracting.

Working from home is also potentially isolating professionally and socially, especially if you are living some distance from where former colleagues, other researchers or potential clients normally meet for coffee or lunch. If you are engaged in research projects that involve a lot of meetings with client representatives, or interviews with research participants, then you may find you are travelling to and from the city for meetings more often than you like.

If you do opt to work from home, try to set aside a part of the house as a dedicated workspace. Ideally it should be a space that you can close up and disengage from completely once the working day is over.

Getting known and finding work

A key to starting out as an independent researcher is making sure a suitable range of potential clients know you are available for work, the skills and services you offer, and how to contact you. This can be achieved in different ways, depending on your finances and the kind of professional image you want to build for yourself.

If you are a relatively seasoned researcher, with a recognised track-record of good quality research and an established network of contacts, then there may be little you have to do to publicise your availability for work. Potential clients, or people who could refer clients to you, will already know what kind of work you do, and the quality of it. Occasional informal communication with your network of contacts – a phone call, email or a coffee date – may be enough to ensure you are kept in touch with opportunities to bid for project contracts as they become available.

If you are a relative newcomer to research, with less of an employment history or a comparatively low professional profile, it will probably be necessary to publicise your availability for work more actively. Techniques could include circulating your CV or a small brochure outlining your skills and experience to representatives of the key agencies or groups you would like to work with. If possible, try also to arrange to meet briefly with these representatives personally so they can get to know you a little better.

Attending conferences, public seminars and other kinds of research-orientated gatherings can also be a useful way to get to know people and quietly signal your interest in future contract opportunities. Other ways of publicising your professional services, such as circulating business cards or developing your own website, may also have their value. However, to be most effective they usually will need to be backed up with some kind of face-to-face meeting or telephone contact between you and a prospective client.

As well as making efforts to get yourself known to potential clients, it will be important to keep your eyes peeled for contract opportunities publicly advertised in newspapers, on the Internet and in other media. Organisations often issue notices inviting tenders or expressions of interest for research projects. In particular, there are often policies or rules requiring relatively large, complex or costly research or evaluation projects to be put out for competitive public tender.

In some countries, dedicated websites provide centralised access to tenders and requests for research proposals issued by public sector agencies. Signing up for access to these websites can be a handy way to learn about potential project work and the different organisations that routinely fund and manage contract research.

Another potential source of project work is research grants from public sector agencies that fund researcher-initiated studies. An advantage of this approach is that you may be able to get funding for research projects that very closely match your interests and skills. However, in most cases you will probably need to collaborate with university or other institution-based researchers with a track-record of managing researcher-initiated projects to have a realistic chance of getting funding from these sources. Be aware that you may have to wait several months before you hear whether your application for researcher-initiated funding has been successful, which may not be ideal if you need work urgently.

When you do come across an interesting new project opportunity, take some time to carefully weigh up your chances of winning the contract. Try to get a feel through your networks for how many other people might be interested in the work. In many cases, responding to requests for proposals or submitting a competitive tender bid involves a lot of time and effort, without necessarily any guarantee of success. Ideally, aim to submit applications only for project contracts you believe you have a realistic chance of winning. Try to avoid a scatter-gun approach where you spend all your waking hours responding to every research request or contract opportunity that comes your way, no matter how unlikely you are to get the work.

Sorting out contracts

Once you do win a project contract, the organisation paying for your services will probably require you to sign a formal contract for services. This is a legal document detailing your obligations to the contracting organisation. Examine these contracts carefully and make sure you understand and feel comfortable with all the conditions you are being asked to meet. Get some legal advice if you are unsure about anything. Some contracts for services can be very one-sided in favour of the contracting organisation.

Good contracts spell out the obligations of the contracting organisation as well as the research contractor. For instance, it can be useful if a contract specifies timeframes within which your client should provide feedback on your draft research reports. The same goes for specifying how long the client should take to pay you after receiving your bills.

Handling the money

As an independent researcher or freelancer, you will probably be responsible for handling most of your business's day-to-day financial dealings. This includes bill payments, taxation, negotiating fees and invoicing clients for what they owe.

Before setting up your business, make sure you are up to speed with the latest tax requirements for small businesses. If in doubt, talk to someone reliable who should know, like an accountant or business adviser.

Box 14.5   Work-related services you may have to pay for

- Accountancy services
- Access to library resources
- Insurance for office, research equipment and vehicle
- Phone and Internet services
- Electricity
- Post office box/mail box
- Health, illness or injury insurance
- Income continuance insurance
- Repairs for computer and other office equipment

Working for yourself also means you have to put money aside to cover things such as holidays and sick leave. It can be hard scheduling holidays when there is no one to cover for you and clients are expecting you to be available at all times. Being sick can be difficult as usually you are the only person able to do your work. If you are particularly worried about the consequences of sickness while working as a contractor, consider taking out some form of income continuance insurance for sickness.

Setting fees and getting paid

Deciding what to charge for your work is always tricky. Many researchers with a commitment to social science and health issues are primarily motivated by a desire to make a positive difference to the lives of others. Making a good living financially is often only a secondary consideration. In this context, there is always the risk of undervaluing the work you do and not charging enough, especially when you are starting out and keen to attract work.

Remember that your hourly or daily charge-out rate should reflect not just the time you spend at the desk or out in the field, but all the other costs associated with running your business: equipment, travel, power, gas, phones, accountant fees, insurance, proposal writing, professional development and so on.

Before settling on a fee structure, ask around and try to find out what other independent researchers like you are charging. This will give some idea about what it might be realistic to charge, or at least a target to aim for during negotiations with prospective clients. You may also want to consider varying your hourly or daily rate, charging less for easy jobs and more for jobs that are complex or contain an element of uncertainty or risk.

Make sure your contract with clients includes a page showing when your fees will be paid, and how much. This is especially important for long-term projects involving several payments. If the fieldwork for a project involves considerable expenses, ask clients for up-front payments before the fieldwork starts so you can pay fieldwork personnel, travel expenses and so on.

Do not be surprised when projects end up requiring more work than you originally anticipated. The amount of time and resources needed for social science and health research projects is often difficult to predict, not least because no two projects are usually exactly the same. In particular, it is quite common to underestimate the time required to write final project reports by about half.

Coping with busy periods

A key feature of contract or freelance research is its unpredictability. Quiet periods, where you do not have any work, can be followed quickly by a flurry of enquiries from prospective clients desperate to have their research projects completed as soon as possible. While quiet times can provide a welcome opportunity to catch up on important background reading or other tasks, busy periods can be very demanding if you are the only person responsible for doing the work.

If you find you have suddenly got too much work to do in the time available, and you are starting to panic and worry, there are various things you can do to try to ease the load. One is to go back to your clients and tell them honestly about the difficulties you are facing. Sometimes the timetable and deadlines a client has set for a project may be reasonably flexible. Granting you an extra week or two to complete your work may not be a big issue for your client, yet it could improve your situation immensely.

Another strategy is to get someone to help you temporarily with your work. You may know another researcher who has some time free and is looking for part-time or casual work. Depending on their skills and experience, they could help out with tasks such as interviewing, data entry, data analysis or even report writing on certain projects. If you do bring in a temporary helper, remember to check with the project client to make sure they are happy with this arrangement. Some clients may get a bit uneasy if they hear somebody else is working on their project with you, especially if they hired you specifically with the understanding that you would do all the work.

Yet another technique to avoid or reduce pressure points is simply to say 'no' to some offers of work – as tactfully as possible of course. The risk here is that the client will not come back to you again if they need further work, although this is perhaps the lesser evil compared to not being able to do justice to existing commitments. If you do say 'no', try to refer the client to another researcher whose work you respect and who is likely to have time available.

To help prevent pressure periods from building up, try to encourage clients to let you know as early as possible if they have got projects coming up that you may be interested in bidding for. The quicker you know about any likely new work coming up, and when it needs to be done by, the better you will be able to plan your work programme to avoid bottlenecks and pressure points.

In the early stages of building up your research business, especially if you are a relative newcomer to the field, you may be reluctant to be too assertive in dealings with clients. You may not want to jeopardise your chances of getting further work in the future by appearing to rock the boat or giving the impression that you are difficult or pushy. This is normal and understandable. Once you have got a few successful projects under your belt and won the trust and respect of clients, there should be more scope to be assertive with clients about how and when you would prefer to do the work they are offering. In the ideal scenario, you will eventually develop such a good reputation as a contract researcher that clients will be quite willing to adjust their project timetables and work specifications to suit your requirements, if that is what it takes to guarantee access to your valued skills.

Looking after yourself

One of the advantages of working as an independent researcher, especially if you have a downtown or home office all to yourself, is the potential to do long uninterrupted periods of work, where you are able to really concentrate on what you are doing and be very productive. However, the downside of this is the possible increased risk of injuries or illness associated with sitting for long periods doing small repetitive movements. These risks are likely to be increased if you are working under pressure to a deadline or on a particularly difficult piece of work.

Look after your physical and mental well-being. Make the most of your comparatively flexible working hours and take plenty of short breaks from the office. Schedule recreational activities for times in the day that suit you best and do not skimp on taking regular holidays.

To reduce your risk of work-related discomfort or injury, make sure you get proper ergonomic office furniture (see Box 14.6). If you are working for long periods sitting in one position at the desk or computer, it is essential every hour or so to take a 5–10 minute break. Get up and walk around the office, do some filing or other tasks that get your body moving. While at your desk, take micro-breaks every 10 minutes or so and do some brief stretching exercises, especially for the neck, shoulders, arms and back.

Box 14.6   Armchair research

Richard is a 43-year-old self-employed researcher working from home. In his home office he has a conventional ergonomic computer workstation that includes an adjustable keyboard-tray and wrist-rest. His monitor is positioned at eye-level and he has a good ergonomic office chair with adjustable lumbar support. However, despite using this equipment and regularly taking breaks to stretch and relax, during periods of sustained computer use Richard finds he develops quite a lot of neck, back and arm pain. This pain is so uncomfortable at times that it is very difficult to work.

A visit to the doctor confirms that Richard's pain is very likely to be work-related rather than caused by any other kind of medical condition or problem. Richard starts to think he might have to give up being a researcher and look for new ways to earn a living. However, after talking with friends who have had similar problems, he begins to wonder if one factor contributing to his pain might be the way he tends to lean forward when using his

(Continued)

(Continued)

computer keyboard, especially when he is concentrating hard on his work. Perhaps this slightly bent-forward position is putting excessive strain on his neck and shoulders?

To test this idea, Richard tries a completely new workstation set-up. First he purchases a wireless mouse and keyboard for his computer and an extension cable for his computer monitor. Next, he moves his old two-person couch from the spare room into his home office, positioning it to within a metre of his desktop computer. After this, he gets a small, flat-topped mobile drawer unit from the local hardware store. He then puts his computer monitor on top of the drawer unit, positioning the drawer unit so that the monitor is at eye-level while he sits back comfortably on the couch. To operate his computer, Richard places the wireless keyboard on his lap and his wireless mouse on a mouse pad on the couch immediately beside his right leg.

After a few weeks of testing this new 'laid back' workstation set-up, Richard finds he no longer gets any significant pain when using his computer for long periods. He attributes this to the fact that he is now sitting back in a more relaxed position while working, with his back and arms firmly supported by the couch. Although this solution to the pain and discomfort associated with extended computer use may not be for everyone, Richard suggests people should at least give it a try to see if it helps.

Social and professional isolation can also be a problem, especially for researchers based at home. Try to maintain regular contact with like-minded independent researchers and other people working in your area of expertise – people who will have at least some understanding of the general nature of your work. Talking over your work experiences with these people can be a great source of support and inspiration. Joining professional associations can also provide similar benefits. As well, try to spend at least a few hours every month keeping up with the latest news and research publications relevant to your skill area and professional interests.

Conclusion

Making a career as a researcher is not usually easy; it has its challenges and disappointments. However, for people who like doing research it can also be intensely rewarding. Like other careers, there are multiple options available and status hierarchies to navigate. However, if you are willing to meet the challenges, research as a career does have advantages. Sometimes you get to work on projects in which you select the topic or have a personal interest. You can be among the first to find out what is really happening on a specific topic area. You may get to work with people who are experts in their field. Ultimately, you need to make your own decision as to whether a research career is suitable for you.

For those considering working as an independent researcher it can sometimes be fashionable to celebrate the freedom and flexibility of such working. However, it is important not to exaggerate these benefits. Most contract or freelance research of any significance involves working to quite tight deadlines for clients with high expectations. This can have a galvanising effect on the independent researcher, to the point where, if he or she is not careful, every waking hour can end up being spent either doing work or thinking about it. In short, while contract work offers some very real advantages, it also entails certain responsibilities and pressures not always obvious at the start.

Exercises for careers in research

1. Talk to someone you know who is an experienced university researcher. Find out how they got started. Ask them what they consider to be the advantages and disadvantages of working in a university position. Would they recommend it as a good option for you?
2. Scan the job advertisements in a suitable source (e.g., newspapers, employment-related webpages) and identify all the advertised positions that interest you. Make a note of the skills or attributes required or expected and the types of work experience that would be desirable. Then draft (or redraft) your CV so it is more consistent with the profile you identified from the job advertisements.
3. Find a source, such as webpages or telephone lists, which list the companies in your area. Identify companies engaged in research-related activities (e.g., survey research, evaluation, human services research). Go to the webpages of the companies that you would consider working in and take notes about the types of research work they do, or projects they have recently completed. Write a draft letter (about one page) you could send to these companies, enquiring about employment opportunities and summarising your skills and areas of experience that are most relevant to the research carried out by these companies
4. Imagine setting up your own home-based office (if you do not already have one). Which area of your home, if any, would be suitable to use? How much space do you think you will need? Would it be a dedicated office space or would the space be used for other activities as well? How would you organise an Internet connection? Would you need a wireless Internet connection so you can work anywhere in the house? Where would you store all your equipment, files and papers? Would you need to improve the security of your home, such as adding a monitored security alarm or better locks on external or internal doors? Would you have a special lounge or reception area for clients? Estimate the likely financial costs of setting up your home office.
5. Design an imaginary webpage publicising your new independent research business. Think of a catchy name for the business and a motto – something that sums up your attitude to working as a professional researcher.

References and further reading

Baxter, L., Hughes, C. & Tight, M. (2001). *The Academic Career Handbook.* Buckingham: Open University Press.

Fenwick, T. (2008). Women's learning in contract work: practicing contradictions in boundaryless conditions. *Vocations and Learning, 1,* 11–26.

Gold, M. & Fraser, J. (2002). Managing self-management: successful transitions to portfolio careers. *Work, Employment and Society, 16*(4), 579–598.

Johnson, A. M. (2009). *Charting a Course for a Successful Research Career.* Amsterdam: Elsevier B.V. (available from http://www.info.funding.scival.com/).

Mirchandani, K. (2000). 'The best of both worlds' and 'cutting my own throat': contradictory images of home-based work. *Qualitative Sociology, 23*(2), 159–182.

Osnowitz, D. (2005). Managing time in domestic space: home-based contractors and household work. *Gender and Society, 19,* 83–103.

Provan, L. (2003). The UK Freelance Network. *Applied Clinical Trials,* June, 80–84.

APPENDIX 14.1

Websites with information about academic and other research positions

(Tip: Try a browser search using 'academic research jobs' or 'research jobs'.)

Academic & Research Job Board (US) – focuses on jobs in education, psychology and management.
http://jobs.infoagepub.com

Academic Jobs EU – website facilitating recruitment and providing career-related services to European academic institutions.
www.academicjobseu.com

Academic Research Jobs (Australia) – academic research jobs and careers in education, childcare and training industries.
www.careerone.com.au/education-childcare-training-jobs/academic-research

CanadianResearch.org – provides recruitment services for the Canadian research community, offering advertising (both print and online) and website design, production and hosting.
www.canadianresearch.org

Career.edu – job board for the international research and academic community. Used by scientists at over 600 institutions in 38 countries. The service focuses on universities and government research agencies.
www.career.edu

jobs.ac.uk – a website for careers in academic, research, science and related professions in the United Kingdom.
www.jobs.ac.uk

Research is Cool – a UK and international research recruitment and social networking site. Includes social networking features (R-Net), research vacancies and career advice.
www.researchiscool.com

Times Higher Education (UK) – website with information about academic jobs. Includes advice and blogs about getting academic work.
www.timeshighereducation.co.uk

UniJobs – Higher Education and University jobs, both academic and non-academic, in New Zealand.
http://unijobs.co.nz

Concluding Ideas: Research Projects and Research Careers

At its heart, a research project is an exercise aimed at uncovering truth and developing understanding. It is an attempt to make better sense of the sometimes messy, confusing or difficult stuff of existence. By concentrating attention on certain issues or problems, cordoning them off from the seamless web of totality, collecting pieces of evidence in different ways from different sources, then thinking about the connections or relationships between these pieces of evidence, looking at them from different angles, the hope is that we can come to know or understand aspects of the world, life or people better than we did before.

Unfortunately, there are many ways in which research projects can go wrong. Sometimes they never get started. Some are poorly conceptualised or planned and never get funded. Others get started but dissipate as their research design proves unworkable or unrealistic. Other projects are completed but end up yielding less than useful research results, or producing research reports that are hard to follow or vague.

This book hopefully has provided a framework and set of resources to help people successfully navigate through the potential hazards of designing and managing a research project from start to finish. Foremost among the core principles and skills identified here are those aimed at ensuring that research projects:

- start with clearly conceptualised and well-defined research objectives or research questions
- are informed by a good understanding of the methods and results of relevant previous studies
- are based on a well-thought-out, properly organised and feasible research proposal
- have the necessary financial support from grant making agencies or sponsors
- are recognised to be ethically appropriate and as safe as possible for all participants
- are managed effectively, including record keeping, relationships with colleagues and supervisors, data storage and data analysis
- communicate their findings, and how they were reached, to the people that matter – accurately, fairly and clearly.

Many of the readers of this book are likely to be relative newcomers to research. Some will be students doing their first major undergraduate research project or postgraduate dissertation or thesis. Others may be just starting out in a research position in a government agency, private company or community organisation, or as an independent or freelance researcher. For some of you, completing your first major research project will be the beginning of a life-long career in research, perhaps as a university academic or teacher, or as a researcher or analyst in government or business. For others, it will open doors to research jobs or contracts in a range of agencies or organisations, after which you may move on to careers in other areas.

Irrespective of the career path you end up following, the experience of doing your first significant research project is likely to be a formative period of learning. From it you will acquire an important set of skills that should prove useful in numerous future areas of work. This is because planning and carrying out a research project is a great test of all-round thinking ability and real-world project management skills.

Research is inspired and driven largely by the desire to solve or answer some kind of question or problem. Curiosity, the wish to know more, a reluctance to accept conventional explanations, a hunch that there could be more to something or someone than meets the eye, all these can be a stimulus or starting point for research. For this reason, the core principles and skills highlighted in this book are likely to have applicability not just for career researchers, but for virtually anyone engaged in problem solving or investigative tasks in the health and social sciences.

Appendix 1

Example of a Completed Research Proposal

This section contains an example of a completed research proposal. The proposal is divided into seven parts:

- Introduction
- Aims and objectives
- Research design and methods
- Ethical issues
- Relevance to health
- Timeline
- Dissemination of results

Beginning researchers often want to see examples of completed research proposals, so they can use them as a guide for writing their own proposals. However, for professional and privacy reasons, it is quite uncommon for copies of actual research proposals to be published or made freely available. Given this lack of access, we decided to write an example of a research proposal specifically for inclusion in this book.

To prepare the proposal, we first selected a research report published in the *New Zealand Medical Journal*[1]. This paper was chosen because it had a clear, well-defined topic and was not too complex. Using the details of the study described in the research report, we then imagined what a research proposal for the study might look like. The result is shown below.

We wish to emphasise that this proposal is entirely our own creation. The author of the published paper is not responsible for content of the proposal, except as acknowledged.

---

[1]Cunningham, W. (2000). The effect on medical practice of disciplinary complaints: potentially negative for patient care. *New Zealand Medical Journal, 113* (10 Nov), 464–467.

Proposal to investigate the impact of disciplinary complaints on general practitioners

Prepared by
A. Researcher
Department of Primary Health Care
University of Higher Learning
Private Bag 12345, Brownsville
Email: a.researcher@network.edu

Prepared for:
Dr M. Supervisor
Department of Primary Health Care
University of Higher Learning
Private Bag 12345, Brownsville
Email: m.supervisor@universityhl.edu

February 2010

Proposal to investigate the impact of disciplinary complaints on general practitioners

The Medical Practitioners Disciplinary Committee (MPDC) is responsible for receiving and investigating complaints about the conduct and competence of doctors. Between 1992 and June 1996, the Committee received 1672 complaints across all medical disciplines (Cunningham, 2000, p. 464). Approximately 70 per cent of these complaints were either resolved informally through negotiation between the agents of the doctor and the complainant, or dismissed after the Chairman of the MPDC found there were no grounds for the complaint. Of the complaints proceeding to inquiry in 1992, 67 per cent were upheld. This decreased to 35 per cent in 1996 (Cunningham, 2000).

It is generally assumed health care services are improved by having systems in place, such as the MPDC, for receiving reports of care perceived to be inadequate. However, to date little attention has been given to evaluating the possible effects of medical disciplinary complaints on the quality of care provided by doctors in this country.

Research in the United States suggests medical practitioners who receive a complaint against them experience significant immediate personal reactions. These include feelings of being stunned and misunderstood, as well as in some cases intense feelings of anger and rage indicative of an assault on one's sense of self and personal integrity (Charles et al., 1984; Charles et al., 1985; Cunningham, 2000). In these situations doctors may have difficulty coping. They can experience depression and adjustment disorders and increased tension which aggravate existing conditions, such as hypertension and heart disease. Subsequent effects are likely to include changes in practice behaviour, such as becoming phobic about certain patients, situations or procedures, and a loss of the joy of practice (Cunningham, 2000).

In other countries, such as Canada, Britain and Europe, studies indicate that the threat of litigation leads to medical practitioners reducing 'high-risk' activities such as obstetrics and anaesthesia and focusing on defensive medicine (Cunningham, 2000; Rosser, 1994; Veldhuis, 1994).

Aim and objectives

This proposed study aims to investigate the personal and professional impact on general practitioners of having a complaint made against them to the Medical Practitioners Disciplinary Committee (MPDC), where the complaint was subsequently dismissed by the Committee without a formal hearing.

The key objectives of the study are:

1. to investigate general practitioner (GP) perceptions of the effect of having a complaint made against them, and
2. to find out the impact of the complaints on doctor–patient relationships and how GPs practise medicine.

As no previous studies were found in the research literature examining these issues from the perspective of GPs in this country, the project is exploratory and aims to identify the main issues and themes GPs regard as significant.

Research design and methods

Qualitative research methods are especially useful for exploratory studies, since they enable a large amount of detailed information to be gathered from a few individuals about their experiences related to particular issues or events.

For this project, in-depth interviews will be completed with approximately 15 general practitioners who have had a complaint made against them to the MPDC, but where the complaint did not proceed to a formal hearing.

Sample

It is planned to interview at least 15 GPs with a maximum of 18 GP interviews. The MPDC has been consulted about the project and indicates that it is willing to assist with the recruitment of study participants. Using the MPDC's complaints database, the secretary of the MPDC will randomly select 30 GPs who have had a complaint made against them in the last five years that did not proceed to an inquiry. The secretary will then send each GP a letter outlining the study and inviting them to take part. The letter will contain a card for GPs to sign and return if they agree to take part in the study. It is anticipated that at least 15 GPs will agree to take part in the study (50 per cent acceptance rate).

Data gathering methods

Telephone interviews, rather than face-to-face interviews, will be used as the main data collection method for the study. This is essentially for reasons of convenience and cost. GPs are experienced at relaying detailed and sensitive information by telephone and it is anticipated the quality of the information obtained in this way will be similar to that from face-to-face interviews.

The interviews will be semi-structured depth interviews lasting approximately 30–60 minutes (Britten, 1995). All interviews will be conducted by the principal investigator (A Researcher). An interview guide will be developed listing possible topics to be covered in discussions. This will provide a basic structure for the interviews. However, considerable scope will be available within this framework for GPs to identify and comment in detail on issues they consider most relevant and meaningful to their experience of having a complaint made against them. The following topics will be included in the interview:

- Circumstances of most recent complaint
- Circumstances of any other complaints
- GP views about reasons for complaint(s)
- Immediate responses to complaint and coping strategies
- Comments about involvement of other people or organisations in complaint process
- Longer-term effects of complaint(s)
- Effects of complaint(s) on providing general practitioner services
- Reflections on the experience of having a complaint.

Data collection procedures

The principal investigator will pilot test and, where necessary, revise the interview format prior to the start of the interviews. This will include conducting three trial telephone interviews with GP volunteers from a number of Dunedin practices.

GPs who agree to be interviewed will indicate this by returning a signed reply form to the MPDC secretary. This will include a section granting permission for the doctor's name and telephone number to be passed on to the research team in confidence. No other identifying material will be passed on to the research team.

Each GP who returns a signed acceptance card will be telephoned by the project's principal investigator and given an opportunity to ask questions about the study. If the GP confirms their willingness to take part in the study, a suitable time will be arranged for the principal investigator to phone back and conduct the interview.

All interviews will be recorded on audio-tape cassette using a special microphone attached to the interviewer's telephone handset. A second backup tape recorder will be kept in reserve in case the first tape recorder malfunctions for any reason.

Audio-tapes will be fully transcribed by an experienced dictaphone typist contracted specifically for the project. Members of the research team will check the quality of the transcripts by reviewing three randomly selected transcripts while playing back the taped interviews.

Analysis of data

Interview transcripts will be analysed using the grounded theory inductive approach described by Strauss & Corbin (1990). This technique enables the systematic identification, categorising and sorting of key themes and sub-themes evident in the text segments of the transcripts. The themes and sub-themes identified will provide a foundation for developing a theoretical model regarding the effects on medical practice of a complaint that did not proceed to a hearing.

At the end of the telephone interviews, each GP will be asked if they wish to receive a summary of the main themes and sub-themes emerging from the study. If they do, a mailed summary will be sent to the postal address they provide. GPs will be asked to forward comments on this material to the research team, either in writing or by telephone. This feedback will be used in the final stages of data analysis and theory-building.

Ethical issues

Ethical approval for the study will be obtained from the University Ethics Committee prior to commencing the selection and recruitment of GPs. All documentation relating to the study, including transcripts, will be stored in locked filing cabinets in the offices of the Department of Primary Health Care, University of Higher Learning, when not in use.

The principal investigator will not seek personal information from GPs participating in the study, other than details needed to contact them for the interview. If, during interviews, or on other occasions, GPs do for any reason disclose other information that could lead to them being identified, this information will be kept confidential by the research team and not revealed to others. All information from the study released by the research team (e.g., journal articles, reports, conference papers) will be presented in such a way that the identities of participating GPs, as well as people involved in complaints made against them, cannot be determined. If any of the GPs participating in the study appear to need help to overcome personal or professional issues they are still dealing with as a result of a complaint, they will be supplied with contact details of appropriate support people and organisations in their area.

Relevance to health

The current patient-centred model of medical care is founded on the notion that it is not possible to remove the person of the doctor from his or her interaction with the patient (Weston & Brown, 1995). What doctors, as human beings, bring to a consultation inevitably affects the nature of their interactions with patients and, potentially, the outcome of the consultation. Overseas studies suggest that a medical practitioner may experience a profound emotional response when they have a complaint made against them. This may reduce their ability to function effectively in practice, make them more defensive and highly sensitised to the possibility of complaint, and make them less willing to offer potentially 'high-risk' services. Such responses have significant implications for the delivery of primary medical care in this country. Patients may not be receiving optimum care because of the adverse impact of unfounded complaints on their doctor's confidence and sense of self. If this is the case, then possible remedies may need to be explored. These could include providing better professional and personal support services for GPs at times when complaints are made against them.

Timeline

It is proposed to start the project in June 2010 and complete the data collection and analyses by January 2011. It is intended to prepare a report for publication by May 2011. The timeline for the main tasks in the project is shown in Table A.1.

Dissemination of results

The results will be disseminated using presentations and written reports as outlined below.

Presentations

Preliminary findings from the study will be presented at one of the monthly research workshops held in the Department of Primary Health Care. It is planned to present a paper on the main findings at the forthcoming annual conference of the College of General Practitioners in September. Presentations assessing the implications of the study will also be made to representatives of the Medical Practitioners Disciplinary Committee, medical defence societies and other organisations with an interest in medical complaints, including the Health and Disability Commission and the Ministry of Health.

TABLE A.1   TIMELINE

Time period	Main tasks
Jun–Sep 2010	**Phase 1: Planning and development** Prepare draft letter and consent forms for GPs Develop and pilot interview guide Prepare ethics committee application
Aug–Sep 2010	Obtain ethical approval Finalise letter and interview guide
Sep–Oct 2010	**Phase 2: Recruiting research participants** MPDC selects 30 GPs MPDC posts letter and consent forms to GPs GPs return agreement to participate
Nov 2010 – Jan 2011	**Phase 3: Data collection and analysis** Undertake telephone interviews Transcribe interview tapes Audit transcripts Review transcripts to identify emerging themes Theory building Send transcript and summary of themes to GPs
Feb – May 2011	**Phase 4: Report writing and dissemination** Initial draft of departmental research report Presentation at departmental seminar Presentation at primary health care conference Presentation to MPDC and Ministry of Health Finalise departmental research report Publicise departmental research report Prepare journal article for publication

Reports and papers

A full description of the study and its results will be written up and published in an edition of the Department of Primary Health Care *Occasional Research Reports in Primary Care*, electronic copies of which can be downloaded free from the Department's website. A flyer publicising the report will be posted to each of the more than 300 individuals and organisations on the Department's mailing list. A hardcopy of the full report will be sent to the Medical Practitioners Disciplinary Committee. A paper summarising the study's main findings, suitable for publication in a peer-reviewed scientific journal, will be prepared and submitted to a primary health care journal.

References

Britten, N. (1995). Qualitative research: qualitative interviews in medical practice. *British Medical Journal, 311*, 251–254.

Charles, S. C., Wilbert, J. R. & Franke, K. J. (1985). Sued and non-sued physicians self reported reactions to malpractice litigation. *American Journal of Psychiatry, 142*, 437–440.

Charles, S. C., Wilbert, J. R. & Kennedy, E. C. (1984). Physicians' self reports of reactions to malpractice litigation. *American Journal of Psychiatry, 141*, 563-565.

Cunningham, W. (2000). The effect on medical practice of disciplinary complaints: potentially negative for patient care. *New Zealand Medical Journal, 113* (10 Nov), 464–467.

Rosser, W. W. (1994). Threat of litigation. How does it affect family practice? *Canadian Family Physician, 40,* 645–648.

Strauss, A. L. & Corbin, J. (1990). *Basics of Qualitative Research: Grounded Theory Procedures and Techniques.* Newbury Park, CA: Sage.

Veldhuis, M. (1994). Defensive behaviour of Dutch family physicians: widening the concept. *Family Medicine, 226,* 27–29.

Weston, W. W. & Brown, J. B. (1995). Overview of the patient centred clinical method. In: M. A. Stewart, J. B. Brown, W. W. Weston, et al. (Eds.), *Patient Centred Medicine: Transforming the Clinical Method.* Thousand Oaks, CA: Sage.

Index